**Spyros Karagiannis** is a Greek entrepreneur with more than 15 years of experience in sales and has trained more than 500 people in Dubai, Bahrain, Cyprus and Greece. Certified by the IBMI Institute of Berlin for "Leadership and Team Development" and by John Maxwell's Leadership Academy for Leadership and Change, Spyros uses his ability to connect with people on a personal level through the power of his "Who I Am" philosophy. This connection is the key ingredient that makes people to get the inspiration they need to go to the next level of their personal lives and careers.

Spyros Karagiannis is not a theoretical motivational speaker or something similar. Each one of his philosophy's principles comes along with real stories that happened in his 15-year career. These real stories have shaped him into the person he is now and are educating others' mindsets.

You can find more information at **www.whoiamphilosophy.com**

To my dad, mom and brother,
who instilled in me the belief to grow with every breath I take,
no matter the cost.

I love you guys!

Grou!


وأودّ أيضًا أن أشكر إمارة دبي ومملكة البحرين اللّذَين تبنّياني كطفل لهما، وساعداني على النموّ لأصبح الشخص الذي أنا عليه اليوم.

Spyros Karagiannis

## WHO I AM – THE BLACK BOOK OF CHANGE

AUSTIN MACAULEY PUBLISHERS
LONDON * CAMBRIDGE * NEW YORK * SHARJAH

Copyright © Spyros Karagiannis 2024

The right of Spyros Karagiannis to be identified as author of this work has been asserted by the author in accordance with Federal Law No. (7) of UAE, Year 2002, Concerning Copyrights and Neighboring Rights.

All rights reserved. No part of this publication may be reproduced, stored in a retrieval system, or transmitted in any form or by any means, electronic, mechanical, photocopying, recording, or otherwise, without the prior permission of the publishers.

Any person who commits any unauthorized act in relation to this publication may be liable to legal prosecution and civil claims for damages.

ISBN - 9789948750635 - (Paperback)
ISBN - 9789948750628 - (E-Book)

Application Number: MC-10-01-0565001
Age Classification: E

The age group that matches the content of the books has been classified according to the age classification system issued by the UAE Media Council.

Printer Name: iPrint Global Ltd
Printer Address: Witchford, England

First Published 2024
AUSTIN MACAULEY PUBLISHERS FZE
Sharjah Publishing City
P.O Box [519201]
Sharjah, UAE
www.austinmacauley.ae
+971 655 95 202

# Chapter 0
# I Am Spyros

Hey there. My name is Spyros Karagiannis and I am currently the CEO of a sales and marketing company in Bahrain. Bahrain is an island surrounded by the Arabian Gulf and is connected to Saudi Arabia by a bridge. If you look at a map, on the left, you will see the country of oil, on the south is Qatar and even southern on the east, there are Abu Dhabi and Dubai.

OK, so now that I have shown you around, geography class is over.

I want to make clear that this book is not my autobiography, it is my truth. *Who I Am. The Black Book of Change* is my philosophy about leadership and sales, the reason why I left my home country when I was 35 years old, moved to Dubai and became the best sales manager in the brokerage firm I was working in 2018 and 2019. It is the reason why I started as a salesperson and got where I am today within 4.5 years.

This book will require time, patience and faith. You will not find the meaning of life, the solution to your problem – personal or professional – or the "magical" and "secret" recipe of success in these pages. If you are looking for a recipe, I can always give you one for scrambled eggs, salmon and cream cheese that will blow your mind away.

I am sure though that if you "get the meaning" of the book, you will start taking charge of your life. You will see that *only you* have the power to choose, affect and create. If you fully understand this and see that our brain is the most powerful muscle we have and that if it had not been for it, we would still be in the Ice Age eating seaweed, you will also understand that there are no limits for someone who has the *willpower*. There are no limits for someone who *needs* something.

No more excuses. There is only room for results from now on.

However, I must admit that this book is not easy to understand and absorb for everyone. You must get rid of your ego and any kind of limiting beliefs. You will need to let go of everything you have learned so far about how to "succeed" and focus on the meaning this book conveys. The meaning of this book can be found in stories about personal experiences and conclusions drawn from various situations. It is not just random ideas or something that I happened to read in another book. Everything you are about to read is my truth based on results, presented through specific actions and examples.

So consider carefully everything you are about to read. You might as well identify with some of the examples. I am sure you will and this is where you will realize that it is not so hard to succeed in life no matter what your goal is. It is not hard as long as you understand a couple of things. Once you do understand them, accept them and take them in, you will see that the way up to your idea of "success" might be easier than you thought it would be. It is not as bad as you believe.

I have been thinking about writing this book for a long time, for more than four years. But, I kept postponing it. I am not a procrastinator. I was simply too tired or used to thinking that I was not "there" yet. I have found all kinds of excuses such as "the moment is not right, there is a game on tonight" or "this is not the right way, I will do it when I find a better one." The more I postponed it, the more reasons I found to convince myself that the right time and peacefulness were necessary if I wanted it to be right. This is something hard to achieve though. I could not even make it at the weekend when I wanted to unwind after a long working week. This is how I turned 40 and I had not written the book yet.

But I am not a procrastinator.

I swear.

Life is structured in a way that makes it impossible for us to find the right time and circumstances to create anything. All you have to do is to dive in. All you have to do is to make up your mind and just go for it. As Tony Robbins quotes, "It is in your moments of decision that your destiny is shaped." This is a great quote from a great teacher who will be brought up more than once in this book and, hopefully, will stick in your mind. I will also share a secret with you. It is something that you might find on Instagram as well but you never come to apply because:

*Theory is for everyone. Action is for the few.*

So, I finally took action too and I regret that it took me so long.

## Who I Am

I was born in Athens, in August 1981. My father was an electrician and my mother was a hospital waitress. I also have one brother who is three years older than me. Since we were kids, our father used to bring us along to the construction sites where he worked. We were a bit grumpy, but he used to explain to us that even if we did not like it at the time, we would see the benefits of it in the future. Over the years, we caught the bug for the job.

You read right. The bug. I did not find many things in life and my future career that made me feel as satisfied as I felt after the completion of a construction project. Take an office under construction for example. We started from scratch, wearing overalls and muddy boots. The place was full of rubble from walls demolished by the workers. Soon after that, our main work began. We ran the electrical wires through the walls, installed and mounted the electrical panel, installed the power switches and sockets, and hung the lights from the ceilings. And in the end:

"Power it up!"

"Power what up?"

"Your brain circuits! Man! Wake up! Power up the electrical switch. The 10 Amperes fuse."

That was my cousin Markos, contentious but always with a sharp sense of humor, which happens to be my favorite type of person. Now I know whom I took after. Talking about role models.

"Give me a break, Markos! Just tell me which is the right fuse."

"Let's try the first one and we'll see. We first need to find which one is which. Come on, I want to watch the football game afterward."

"Hurry up," my brother agreed. "It's 9 o'clock in the evening!"

I could not disagree. There were hundreds of days when we finished work late at night.

"Take your hands off. I am powering it up!"

And that was it. Let there be light!

We turned the lights on and everything was so bright. No matter how tired you might be, nothing can beat this feeling. Even irritation goes away to be replaced by smiles of satisfaction. I believe that few people can understand the sense that you get when you create something that bright!

This same bug was also the reason why I decided to study electrical engineering when I was 18 years old. Six years later, when I graduated, I tried to get into the National Technical University of Athens, but since I did not make it, I decided to do my military service instead. After completing my service in 2007, I started working in various sectors of the construction industry. I worked as a foreman on construction sites, I did feasibility studies for construction projects and I also worked as a salesperson. In 2015, I was the project manager at a big construction company with strict rules. The CEO was quite tough. As he mentioned in the interviews, he hired me because my experience in construction sites was "hard to find" and because I had "a professional attitude and a strong character." I stayed at that company for one year, that guy was too weird for my taste.

At the same time, in 2011, I became a member of a US multi-level marketing company, which gave me the chance to attend a lot of self-improvement and sales conferences held by well-established coaches in Italy, France, Germany, Hungary, Slovenia, Cyprus and Greece, having paid more than 15.000$. Just to be there. My communication skills were also further developed at the time as I was trying to build my team. Some of the benefits I got from this were that I discovered many different aspects of myself and I met people who had higher standards from mine. I loved it! My social circle was broadened and a window to new ideas and experiences was now open. This experience was one of the biggest investments I have ever made in myself.

During that time, my passion for books grew. I was already 30 years old when I read my first self-improvement book *How to Win Friends and Influence People* by Dale Carnegie. This book is taught in many universities in the US. It made me realize that human beings are by nature quite simple. We tend to believe that we are complicated due to the constant conflict between logic and emotion, and this is where it gets confusing. But human beings are simple.

Since then, I have read so many books that I have lost track. Writers such as Napoleon Hill, Spencer Johnson, Jordan Belfort, T. Harv Eker, Grand Cardone and Tony Robbins are only some of the writers who blew my mind. They helped me break my old habits by building new ones and made me see the world through their eyes. I have to admit that I am not an easygoing person, I am tough, strict and stubborn. It is not easy for someone to get access to my mind, but these guys found their way in and this is why I like them.

From 2010 to 2019, the construction industry was hugely affected by the situation in Greece which almost led to bankruptcy. After reviewing my CV, many companies told me that I was "overqualified" for the job and could not fit within their budget. This is how I decided to set off for somewhere new. I decided to get into a different industry and get into investment banking, in the hope of a better future.

As weird as it may sound, I got a job in a marketing and sales company. What other options did I have? I made phone calls from 9 in the morning to 6 in the evening. I was already 35 years old. However, I enjoyed my new occupation, so I quickly saw the results and started earning a decent income from the sales commission. Not too long after that, I got promoted and I became the manager of the existing customers of the brokerage firm we were working with. A year later, I was the sales manager of the after-sales department, managing the team that was responsible for the investment portfolio of the parent company. A year after that, I became the senior sales manager and my duties and scope of responsibilities were at the highest level. In the meantime, I was licensed the brokerage license by the Cyprus Securities and Exchange Commission as, due to the strict regulation, it was of paramount importance that I have it.

During these four years, I had the chance to work with and train a lot of young people with no formal education and no previous knowledge of finances. Before working with us, most of them worked as waiters, storekeepers, or plumbers. They had jobs on the clock. However, they had a trait that was hard to find: the strength and the desire to achieve great things. They had not had the chance to pursue their dreams in Greece or with their previous managers. Greece had always been way too small for them, but people who are intended for great things, sooner or later, find their way.

I already knew that success was not easy to attain, but it was made even clearer to me after working with them. By training and mentoring them, I understood that thorns, mines and nuclear bombs were inevitable on the way up to a successful career. Disappointments, insults, doubts, distress, irritability, stomach problems caused by stress, arguments, ego, bone-crushing ego and bones literally crushed after punching the wall. I have been there.

After all that, it is time for victory at last. This means high wages, luxuries and a great career. For some of us, this has been part of the goal. It was our definition of success and the recognition that came after the, seemingly endless, conflicts with ourselves. We have proved that what matters is not your degree, your relationship status, how much money you or your family used to have, what is on TV, or who won that reality show. What matters is who you *are* and *what you are made of*. Under these circumstances, you come to understand who you really *are*.

That brings us to today when I am the CEO of a marketing and sales company in Bahrain. My office is in one of the tallest and most luxurious buildings over here, overlooking the most beautiful side of the island. My goal is to provide every single person with the best possible training and guidance about "who" they need to be first and then about "what" they need to do. By introducing them to the "Who I Am" leadership philosophy, the same philosophy you will read about in the following pages, they are motivated to bring the results that we both desire. In this way, I help them achieve their goal. My personal development and progress were also based on the same philosophy.

I have always thought of myself as someone who would achieve great things. From an early age, I had the desire to "conquer the world." I could not understand though how all these people who had achieved their goals had managed to get there. To be honest, I do not expect anyone to understand what it takes for someone like me to start as a salesperson and become the CEO of a company in 4.5 years. I could write a million books and still not be able to describe it.

Having many years of experience in Greece, Cyprus, Dubai and Bahrain and taking into consideration my, proven to work and personal development, I have concluded to one fact which happens to be the main principle of the "Who I Am" leadership philosophy:

*The only thing that separates failure from success is you.*
*Who you truly are.*

And not what you do.

## Who I Am – The Black Book of Change

The meaning of *Who I Am – The Black Book of Change* shows the difficulty that comes with any kind of change we pursue. It might sound simple or you might think that you can change, but the truth is that it is way too difficult. It is also extremely painful and hard to handle. Gandhi might have said, "Be the change you want to see in the world," but the truth is that it is easier said than done.

The problem is that no one fully understands the real meaning of change or what it takes for anyone to become the person they need to be on their way up to success. No one understands the number of sacrifices needed. It is hard to see that your psychology and your attitude must be changed. It is also hard to undergo the process of getting rid of numerous well-established bad habits and limiting beliefs.

This is why people do not change. They do not find the courage to do so. They talk about change and they embrace it, but they do not act on it. Not only do they not know what they need to do, but even if they do, they give up when the first obstacle comes up and go back to the safety of everything familiar. They come up with hundreds of stupid excuses or, simpler than that, they are in denial. They tend to react, defend themselves or feel offended when they confront change. They find it threatening. It goes without saying that they take no action whatsoever.

Later on, you will understand that what is most important when it comes to change is the reason (or the purpose) why you started seeking it in the first place. You will understand the reason why most people choose an "easier present" over a "better future." To make the long story short, you will understand that:

*People make decisions based on the way they feel today.*
*Not on how they'll build their tomorrow.*

I strongly believe that the universe always finds a way to put you in the same situation over and over again, throwing you curve balls until you understand that your mindset is wrong. The more you keep having the same mindset, the more the universe persists in the effort to wake you up. As long as you do not change, the universe seems to be trying twice as hard. As long as you do not get the hint, the effort becomes even greater. Whoever created the universe has such an amazing sense of humor that makes Ricky Gervais, my favorite comedian, look like Ancient Greek drama.

This is the main reason why I wanted to write *Who I Am – The Black Book of Change* in the first place. From my experience, people do not understand that change is the key to success. And even if they do understand it, they do not know what the next step should be or they refuse to take action.

At the same time, you will understand that the "Who I Am" leadership philosophy is based on change and you will learn about the main leadership skills you need to have to achieve your goal. This philosophy has been developed during my journey so far. Based on this philosophy, I achieved everything I have achieved so far and I have been using it ever since. Change and transformation of any kind is the key to everything, no matter what your goal is.

## Setting Things Straight

I have never seen chapter 0 in a book. If there is such a book, I have not read it. But chapter 0 has a specific meaning for me. If I do not make some things clear beforehand, then this book will not have as great an effect on you as I want it to and it will be a waste of your time. It will be one of those books that we happened to read but never managed to get the meaning of it. I do not want the *Who I Am – The Black Book of Change* to be one of those books.

So let me make something clear before moving on. I do not claim to have found the meaning of life nor am I trying to share it with everyone. It's nothing like that. I never aimed at changing the world. This book is nothing but my truth. The truth of an ordinary man like everyone else. A person with a typical personality who decided to change. The stories and the quotes you are about to read have derived solely from my personal experience. What you are about to read in the following pages is my journey from being a simple salesman to the CEO of a company in 4.5 years.

It is not the greatest success story and it is not meant to be compared with anyone else's story. But I wish I had had the chance when I was younger to read the story of an ordinary man, get inspired and find the courage to believe that I too can make it.

I had never read such a book. Every single book on that topic was written by millionaires having decades of experience. The gap between me and them was huge and everything they had to say was not even close to my reality. I believed their stories, of course, but I found it too hard to believe that their story could also become mine.

This is why I wrote this book. I wanted it to be the link between you and someone close to you and your standards. The distance between me and you is next to nothing. Perhaps, you have already accomplished more than I have and it does not matter. What is important is that my accomplishments are the result of the leadership philosophy that I have developed, the philosophy I have been using to train others and the one that I am going to share with you in this book.

The way you will choose to use the book afterward is only up to you.

For me, this book is a personal bet. I see it as a mission to pass on the knowledge that got me here to help others break out of their reality and reach further than they have ever imagined.

Are you up for a challenge?

*Don't be afraid of the challenges.*
*You'll either win, or you'll have a nice story to tell.*

Have a great journey!

# Chapter 1
# Not Just a Theory

When I was younger, I could not understand how some people managed to achieve so much. They are only humans after all. Take the moon for example. How was it possible that someone's dream to set foot on another planet came true? How was it possible that a huge airplane – a spaceship as I would find out later – managed to take off the earth, pass through the clouds and the sky to go into space? What happened next? How did those people land on the moon? How did they know what was the right place and the right speed to land? Where did that astronaut – Neil Armstrong as they told me – find the courage to set foot somewhere that no one had a clue about what it would be like? I was not even born in 1969, but as a kid, I always considered this great achievement a modern-day miracle.

In 1991, when I was ten years old, I learned about the Apollo 11 journey, about Armstrong and his famous quote, *"That's one small step for man, one giant leap for mankind."* We did not have the Internet back then, so it was difficult to find information on a topic you were interested in. You had to learn from what you were taught or even worse, from what was in the school curriculum. Most stuff was just boring. I was lucky though as I learned a lot from my family.

**Fanis**

My uncle, Fanis, who lived with my aunt Charoula and my cousin Teresa on the ground floor of a two-story family house in Kifisia, Athens, used to tell me about Muhammad Ali's achievements. He was probably the greatest boxer of all time. He became the heavyweight champion in 1964 and 19 times after that. His real name was Cassius Marcellus Clay, but he changed it to Muhammad Ali for religious reasons and that was what everyone called him. My uncle used to tell me mainly about Ali's resilience and the fact that although he grew up poor, he had the *will*, the *ego* and the *persistence* to overcome all the difficulties and he found the courage to fight all these boxers. He used to win the matches in three rounds and no one could beat him as he was "The Greatest."

"The guy was a God! He could have even beaten the legendary Hercules," my uncle used to say fascinated as he spread his arms wide to show me how big Muhammad Ali was. I used to look at him amazed. I was speechless. My uncle knew how to make a story sound interesting as he was always passionate when he spoke. He has always had a moving way to tell stories, something that makes him a modern-day storyteller.

"Is he a real person, uncle?"

"Yeah, of course he is! That guy can achieve great things, my boy. He can even beat God. It's all up to him. He is the proof that it doesn't matter where you come from. The only thing that matters is what you want, where you're heading, and if you are who you must *be* to make it happen. You need to *be* more than enough to achieve this. You must *be* brilliant and unique."

*Wow, you must be more than enough to achieve this. You must be brilliant and unique. Great words,* I used to think. That was Ali and that was my uncle who passed on his knowledge to me when I was a child. The only thing that matters is who you *are*. You can achieve anything as long as you have ego and persistence.

### Charoula

On the other hand, Fani's wife, my aunt Charoula, was passionate about politics. I remember sitting with Teresa, her daughter, around the kitchen table when my aunt helped us with our math exercises. She used to be good at math and had her way to make us understand how simple it is. Because of her strong character and her temperament, she could not stand whining, misery and injustice. She also hated being submissive. You might say she was a revolutionary. She also had a trait that no one else I have come across until now has. She talked about Mahatma Gandhi and Martin Luther King, who both fought for man's freedom, as passionately as she did about Julius Caesar and Adolf Hitler, who were known for their expansionist policies and the brutal way they treated people. I still remember asking her:

"Aunt, how is it possible for you to think that all these people have something in common?"

"Listen to me. It's one thing to be able to identify the traits of good leaders, the ones that help them achieve their goals and another the goal itself. Gandhi was a politician and a leader who fought for Indian independence in the 1940s and was the inspiration for numerous civil rights movements around the world. His personality was great. We will watch the movie "Gandhi" and you will understand what I mean. Martin Luther King was also inspired by Gandhi's vigor. He fought against slavery in the United States in 1955 and advocated for the civil rights of African Americans who lived in slavery. On the other hand, Caesar was a great leader, but his purpose was really bad. So was Hitler. But we are still talking about leadership and the traits of effective leadership are always the same regardless of the purpose. If your purpose is good, you can learn from all the leaders and that's the hard thing to do."

The truth is that even today, every time I read about people who have achieved important things, either good or bad, I always try to spot the traits that made them achieve their goals. I have always tried to figure out the psychology, the thoughts, the decisions and the reasons behind these decisions as well as the personal lives of those people. How people decide to use their leadership skills is a different story and I do not want to go there.

**Vasilis**

My dad did not always agree with my aunt Charoula on all that. He used to think that she was too progressive. Every time they disagreed during Sunday lunch, my uncle Fanis made fun of them as he thought they took everything way more seriously than needed. In fact, whenever he wanted to prove that the situation was not that serious, he used to pull my brother's ear and tell him, "Put the potato down." My brother used to complain as he was usually eating some cheese or bread at that moment and my mother used to fill the glasses with more wine as most of them were empty. We used to have fun. Good times.

"Come on, Chariklia" – that is what my father used to call my aunt – "I like your stories about Gandhi and everyone else. They fought for all these things or, regardless of what they stood for, they did their best. They achieved their goals and people remember them either as heroes or as tyrants. So far so good. But I don't hear any stories about you and me and ordinary people in general. Don't you think that we too are "leaders"? We work all day long to be able to afford a few things and make sure that our kids are healthy. I wake up at six o'clock every single day, I have a cup of coffee, I go to work and I forget to come back. And it's not that I spend the day sitting in an office, I spend the day in construction sites. I stay there until four o'clock and then I do odd jobs here and there to gain some extra money. If I come home earlier than eight o'clock, I can't help but think that I wasted my day."

"Vasilis, that's not what I said. The people I mentioned happened to become widely known. It doesn't mean that there aren't many more people who have the traits of a good leader. Many other people, just like you, can also be called leaders. People who want to provide the best possible for their families and overcome any obstacle or difficulty that might be in the way. This is how you were raised and this is what your parents taught you. This is who you are and these are your values. I do not doubt that even if you lose your job tomorrow, you would find another one the next day. You *were* born a leader, just like them, and you will never be out of work.

"You too *are* a great example of what I said before."

That was true. My father worked really hard, until the day he retired. It was not that he had no other choice because he did. It is just that this is what he knew, what his parents had taught him and what he kept doing. In fact, during his career, he was a highly respected electrician. Many shops around Athens and even more contractors wanted to work with him. He loved his job and he wanted the best for his family and himself. He was strong, decisive, fair and honest, and he did not try to make excuses. He completed his work on time and the result was always great.

"*There is no such thing as "I can't". If you want, you can do anything,*" he used to tell me whenever we worked together on the construction sites and tried to convince him that I was not able to do something. I always managed to do it, whatever it was, in the end though. For whatever magical reason, I always succeeded because he kept telling me that I could do it.

I was always confused by my aunt and my father as a kid. They had unlimited love and respect for each other, but every time they discussed topics like this, I could not help but admire their vigor. They were so passionate that no one could change their minds. As long as they remained reasonable and fair, such small political or cultural differences meant nothing at all. I have to admit that those two, through everyday situations, were the people who first taught me the traits of a good leader. They taught me that:

*It's not important what you do,*
*but who you are while you do it.*

It does not work the other way around.

Many people have gone down in history and even today, many people make a difference. Who is not familiar with Nelson Mandela, who in the mid-90s fought against the so-called "Apartheid," the political and social dominance of the country's white minority? Or Fidel Castro, the leader of the Cuban Revolution, and Napoleon, the leader of the French Revolution? George Washington who fought for American Independence? Marie Curie, who discovered radium? Let's talk about smaller-scale successes as well. Let's remember Arnold Schwarzenegger, who started his career as a simple bodybuilder and with his determination and perseverance, he became one of the most famous and richest Hollywood actors with over 60 films to his credit. He even became the governor of California. Michael Jordan, an NBA player who played for the Chicago Bulls, started out in a college in South Carolina and at first, he was the third pick in the draft. But he was destined to become the greatest NBA player of all time. Let's talk about Bono, the singer of the widely popular band U2 who have been together since 1976. For more than forty years, he has been the leader of the band that wrote the famous "One" and "With or Without You" songs. There must have been some disagreements or fatigue after all these concerts, but Bono is now a 61-year-old man who cannot imagine his life off the stage.

All of these people and hundreds of others have shared particular traits. If you read books about leadership or books about the stories of particular people who have made a difference, you will find certain traits that lead people to great achievements. You will find a specific analysis of what these people did, what they said, how they reacted and the reason behind all that. You might understand that some of the key traits that a leader has are an extraordinary *vision*, a strong *desire* and the *resilience* to overcome any difficult situation.

## Worth wondering

If you think about it though, more probably than not, Mandela, Caesar, or Gandhi had not read any leadership books. It is a bit hard to believe that when Jordan won all those trophies with the Bulls, he had the time to read "The Traits of a Good Leader," if there was such a book.

So, what is the difference between those who have no idea about leadership but still achieve great things and those who do know what leadership is, but it takes a lot of research and effort on their side to achieve their goal if they do at all?

How come Jordan never said "I quit" but there are millions of people who started creating something only to stop on the way?

How come there are so many people who do whatever possible to achieve their goals but they remain unnoticed?

How come it is so unfair at times?

There is only one answer to that and the "Who I Am" leadership philosophy has been developed based on that.

*It's not important what you do,*
*but who you are while you do it.*

We are the result of our past influences. We have learned things from our parents, from school, etc. We have been programmed. Everything we hear, see, smell and feel is deeply integrated into our subconscious. This is how our character is formed and every single stimulus shapes it. This is what we are made of.

Imagine a glass of water, clear, transparent spring water right there for you to drink it. But somewhere along the way, you drop a drop of blue color and then, a drop of white. Right after that, you will see that the water in the glass will turn blue. If you add some vinegar, a little salt, a few drops of red color and some soil, we can all agree that the water will be quite different from the water we had in the glass in the beginning. It has now become a mix of colors, tastes, textures and smells. This is exactly what happens when our character is formed. Our character stores every piece of information it receives and, even if you do not see the effects right away, they will be obvious at some point sooner or later.

In fact, the job of a psychotherapist is to find all these materials that have fallen into the glass of water at different times of your life and analyze how they have "damaged" you.

Human beings, by nature, absorb information from anything that happens around us. The younger we are, the less we filter what is going to be stored in our brains. We are like a quite absorbent sponge. In fact, according to psychology, during the first three years of our lives, our character is formed. This is why it is so important for a child to grow up in a healthy family environment. It is really easy to affect a young kid if you fight at home with your spouse, even if some parents do not seem to understand it.

As we grow older, we develop mechanisms to filter the information received and it is harder to be influenced. Water has already gotten dirty and has its own color, smell and taste, so it is difficult to replace. This is why it is so hard to change your stubborn father's mind or why it becomes harder to compromise in a relationship as you become older.

It must become clear that those who provide us with our first stimuli, who are of course the members of our family – mam, dad, grandma, grandpa – should be extremely careful. Considering that until the age of fifteen, we spend most of our time at home, other than school, it is easy to understand that our family is the source of the traits that are deeply ingrained in our personality. Our home is the place where our beliefs, habits and our character, in general, are developed. This is where our self is shaped.

Taking all the above into consideration, we can tell that humans are destined to achieve great things but sometimes, things get stuck along the way. This is because of things that influence us daily. There are a lot of families that seem to be healthy, but in reality, the situation is quite bad. Some parents teach their children how to swear or how to hit other children, claiming that violence is the best solution. On the other hand, some parents teach their children core values, such as respect, solidarity, modesty, strength, determination and so on. Some parents encourage their children to read books from an early age and not to spend endless hours watching TV, etc.

That is where the greatest difference among people lies: in the way they have been formed and, as a result, in the way they perceive different situations. Let's take Messi for example, who, at some point in his life, was influenced by something or someone that made him believe that he could become the number one football player. From that moment on, the belief that he could make it was so deeply ingrained in his mind that every single thing he did was only to bring him one step closer to his goal. This is why he has had all these long training sessions, why he has such a strong temperament and all these disagreements with his teammates and his coach. He only had one thing in mind, to become the number one football player.

What would have happened though if Messi had been influenced by an idea supporting racism? Or if, while watching "American History X" with his father, the latter started cheering when Edward Norton killed that guy on the sidewalk? What would Messi think, especially if his father was a role model for him? Let's admit that there is a chance that he would not have become the great athlete we all admire.

Our genuine identity is shaped by beliefs. Who we are and what we do is based on our identity.

There are a million ways to influence someone's mind and as I have already mentioned, the younger a person is, the easier it is to be influenced. So if you are lazy, grumpy, over-analytical, phobic, anxious, strong, chill, sexist, fearless, respectful, if you love books or animals, or if you do not love animals (you bastard) and so on, it is because, at some point, you received the respective stimulus. That stimulus was developed in your subconscious and formed a belief or a habit.

**Where do you belong?**

For millions of reasons, the members of a family should be conscious of the stimuli they provide their children with. Maybe you too are in a toxic environment, or even worse, you create it. Have you ever thought about it? Have you ever thought that every single argument with your spouse has a huge effect on your children? Have you ever thought that every time you call people names, every time you honk your horn at traffic lights, every time you whine, you fight about football, you give wrong advice or deny admitting any given reality, you greatly affect your child or everyone around you in toxic ways?

This is the truth though about anything you do. Even if you believe that your child did not see something, did not hear, or did not understand it, there is no doubt that you are wrong. Children understand much more than you think they do. Words and opinions, which will later become a way of life, are stored in their subconscious based on every single reaction of yours. All these will be part of their experiences and will affect their attitude toward life, their habits and their decisions. Over the years, any of these habits can be the source of many possible problematic situations and, depending on the importance of the habit, it might be easier or harder to get rid of it.

If you want to set the grounds for a nice future for your children, begin the process from the first time you see them in the maternity hospital. Keep the following in mind: you are a hundred percent responsible for the way that your children grow up. The responsibility is solely yours.

I have met and worked with people who are afraid to come out of their shells. I have trained young people who lack even the slightest sense of self-confidence. I have also worked with people who lack basic communication skills. People who are afraid to step out of their comfort zone and people who believe that if you become wealthy, you will turn into a bad person. People for whom any rejection is a reason to quit. People who, no matter how much I have trained and mentored them, will never succeed. I have worked with people over 35 years old who finally quit because their mothers could not live without them, which is sad.

On the other hand, I have met vigorous and persistent people who can see opportunities and do everything to succeed. I have worked with people who would not leave the office until they were done with their work, no matter what time it was. I have worked with people whose discipline was an example to others. The position they were in and their goals were clear to them and they would follow the steps of the ones who had already achieved such goals as they knew that this was their only chance to find the way to get what they wanted. I have also worked with people who did their best to belong to a group, grow and focus on the life they had created for their family and themselves, overcoming any possible difficulty, without complaining. I have worked with people who started crying after I pushed them hard for results, but despite that, the next day they were on time, stronger than before, because they knew what they were after. This is what I call *determination.*

I am pretty sure that every parent around the world is struggling because they understand the size of the responsibility towards their children.

At this point, let's praise all those parents who have taught their children to work from a young age, making them understand that if they want something, they have to fight for it.

Let's praise all those parents who have taught their children that it takes hard work, respect, modesty, persistence and patience to earn money.

Let's praise all those parents who have taught their children that if they try for something but still do not get it, it is not a failure, but a valuable lesson.

Let's praise all those parents who think before they speak, who control their reactions and who teach their children that the answer to any question can be found in a good book. The parents who let their children know that their personality can be shaped by a good book and that a good book can broaden their minds.

Let's praise all those parents who choose divorce over a bad marriage because that is the best for their children.

Let's praise all those parents who make their children see how special and unique they are and teach them that they can build empires and islands if they want to.

Let's praise all those parents who can tell the difference between education and building character, between knowledge and belief.

Finally, let's praise all those parents who fight to create a better future for their children and who help their children become a better and stronger version of themselves.

That is the starting point of all the main beliefs. However, even if our parents or we ourselves went wrong, it's normal. It happens. The silver lining is that there is always a way to turn things around. In the following chapters, you will find out more about the "Who I Am" leadership philosophy and how much it can help you to get to success, either professionally or personally. As you might know, "The way you do anything is the way you do everything," and in the following pages, you will understand not only who you are, but also how to shape your character and your habits.

So hold on tight.

P.S.1: At this point, I want you to open the Notes app on your phone. Once in a while, I will be asking you to write down a few things. Please do not ask why, just do it. You will understand how important it is along the way. Keep in mind though that you will never be asked to share your notes with me or anything like that. It is something we are going to create together, but it will belong only to you. What you need to do, is to take part in it and just do it.

P.S.2: Write down the following question:

1) What was the most positive influence in my life as a kid? It can be a family member or a friend. Does it still affect me?

P.S.3: Answer the above question.

# Chapter 2
# Leaders of Today Who Prove It

**The first leader I ever had**

My dad used to take me to work with him ever since I was little. I started going with him at the weekends when I was 15 years old. My brother and I helped my father when he ran wires through the walls of newly built houses and we helped him carry his tools and give him his cigarettes. As years went by, I went to work with my dad more and more often. I had more responsibilities and my experience developed. By the time I was 25 years old and got my degree in electrical engineering, I had had my fair share of construction sites. My father knew what he was doing from the very beginning. He was pushing me and my brother from a young age because he wanted us to become independent, to keep going no matter what and to achieve our goals through hard work and determination.

It might sound like something easy to do when reading about what a kid used to do from 15 to 25 years old, but the truth is that my brother and I missed a lot to build these *habits*. Now that I think about it, missing a bike ride with our friends on a Saturday morning was not such a big deal. We were still friends in any case, but back then, it seemed like a truly hard blow. We endured it though and it turned out to be good for us. Our father laid the foundation for us to thrive in our lives, he programmed us.

My father's influence and the habits I built because of him made me believe, over the years, that I was a little different from everyone else. I was more optimistic, outgoing and more of a dreamer than most of the people I knew. I was not afraid to try new things and I used to take situations less seriously than the other kids my age. I always wanted more: more experiences and more risks. I knew that I was destined for something greater than a monthly paycheck or an ordinary everyday life. I was not afraid of anything. I was alert and talked about new ideas. I thought about where I wanted to go and afterward, I tried to figure out ways to get there. I wanted to change the world, at least my world.

## Mr. Apple

When I got my degree in Electrical Engineering, I was 25 years old. A year later, I had also completed my military service. I came across Steve Jobs' famous quote, "People who are crazy enough to think they can change the world are the ones who do," and that was when I decided to do something crazy. It was the wildest and scariest leap I have ever taken as it was the first time I stood exposed without the protection of those who cared about me. I was scared, but I also felt completely free and lighthearted. As it turned out, this decision would completely change the course of my life.

I quit my father's job.

That was by far the most critical decision of my life as I chose insecurity over security. I chose something difficult over something easy, something challenging over something settled, something extraordinary over something ordinary and something crazy over something rational. That is when I started following Steve Jobs' journey. I always found him inspiring not necessarily because of what he had achieved, but because he seemed to be different than everyone else. He stood out from the crowds. People would point the finger at him, but he ignored them. I felt the exact same way about all the crazy ideas I had from time to time. I felt that I was more than just different,

I felt unique. I thought to myself, *Since he built an empire out of his crazy idea, I can too. Let's see where it takes us. In the worst-case scenario, I will learn a valuable lesson. In the best-case scenario, I will achieve great things. Is it a dream, extraordinary optimism, or madness? I have no idea. We'll see.*

However, it is hard to absorb that a man who, with his partner Steve Wozniak, founded in a garage the company that would become one of the top five companies worldwide might be wrong. Let me repeat that: in a garage. If you think about it and realize how passionately they wanted to achieve something great, you will see that it was more than a moment of madness. Steve Jobs' famous quote is based on the truth.

"Can you imagine it? Can you imagine investing all your money to create in a garage something that doesn't exist and none had thought about it before? Can you imagine the hours of work, the vigor and the patience it takes to isolate yourself from friends and family and not care at all about what is happening out of your garage? Would you go through a process like that and give up everything else to achieve your greatest goal and your vision? How badly would someone want something to all this through?"

"That's nonsense, Spyros. Don't believe everything you hear. If the situation is as ideal as presented, how come there aren't five more people with similar stories? They spice up their stories to set an example for everyone else and make people take action. They try to sell copies of their biography and tickets. That's their job. They try to fool you. We know all about it. Also, the Personal Development seminar you took me to seemed too good to be true. Moving as all these might sound, this isn't how the world works. Even if I isolate myself in a garage, it won't make any difference. So, I'll keep going to my simple everyday job as it is the safest thing to do and when I get my chance, I will make sure that I won't miss it. But I'll do so if there is someone who can tell me what I should do next."

"But, Giannis, what Mat was talking about in the first couple of hours was that "What your mind focuses on, is where your body will go." So, I will choose to listen either to you who, no offense, has spent the past nine years in the same job or to Mat and follow Jobs' example. The guy spent his time having one crazy goal in mind: to found the number one company worldwide. The strangest thing is that both Mat and Jobs are exactly at the point they had ever wanted to be. If you want to learn from someone who "has made it" but, in the meantime, you ignore someone who is trying to show you the way, sorry man, but you have no clue whatsoever."

"That's fine, you can believe whatever you want. These guys will rip you off by selling dreams and ambitions. Don't say I didn't warn you. As for me, when I see my chance, I'll take it."

"You won't as long as you don't open your eyes, dude."

I had this conversation with Giannis, a friend of mine, who I had brought along to a conference organized by a multi-level marketing company in June of 2011. The conversation did not lead us anywhere. He never listened to me because he probably never wanted to. After all these years, we are still really close.

He is about to get married to Aggcliki and every time I come home from Dubai, I always find a couple of hours to see him. He is one of the smartest and most positive people I have ever met. But he never listened to me. It is too bad though because he still is in the exact same job, with the exact same salary, and every time I speak to him, he keeps mentioning how he would like to quit his job, try something different and move forward. He never took the leap though.

Some people are happy when they take things easy and they prefer to avoid big responsibilities. They are not willing to take the risk. Not everything is for everyone. As a co-worker of mine put it one Sunday in April of 2018, "Spyros, thank God for those people who avoid responsibilities. This opens room for us to achieve great things." These are not the exact words he used, but let's keep things low-profile, at least for now. Up to this day, that guy, Manolis, keeps achieving great things.

So, was Jobs crazy? As crazy as his words implied, he was. Crazy enough to have the desire to change the world. A landmark day for him was the day when he launched Apple 2 in 1997. It was the first mass-produced computer. That was when he became one of the greatest people. This was followed by the first Macintosh in 1984, which was considered to be a great invention at the time.

In 1985, he got fired. As simple as that. He got fired from his own company nine years after the foundation of Apple. I would not like to be in his shoes when he went to his office to pack his stuff. How disappointed he must have been and how much he must have hated everything and everyone. How easy is it to let go of everything and just leave? That was a betrayal and betrayal is hard to tolerate. Your ego falls apart and so does your self-esteem. Your feelings fall apart as well. What else is left? The easiest thing to do is to quit and this is what everyone does. It is the easiest way because it *protects* you from the disappointment you feel when you quit. It is a vicious cycle. That is exactly what most people do. They quit because it is easy.

But if someone *is* "crazy," they remain "crazy" no matter what. Even if you tried, you could not change them. This is something that no one has ever been able to do. When people have an ultimate purpose in mind, when they *are* "crazy" about it, no one has the power to stop them. Jobs ignored the disappointment and the rejection and took matters into his own hands. He knew he could make a difference. He *was* the difference. All he had to do now was to prove it, once again.

He founded NEXT, a company specializing in entrepreneurial activities. Right after that, he founded PIXAR, probably the biggest animated film production company, the first film of which was the famous Toy Story. Eleven years after being kicked out, he became once again the CEO of Apple. There is information that reveals that, at the time, Apple was in the middle of a financial crisis that would lead to a collapse. Steve Jobs saved the company. His *vision* to make Apple the greatest company had not faded away and he was still shaped by the same vigor. He remained the same "crazy" guy he had always been because that was the only way that could lead him to success.

At that point, the upward course of the company began and it was about to be one of the five greatest companies worldwide. In 2007, the famous iPhone was released. The game for all the other companies in the industry was over. Ever since we have all been amazed by an iPad, a pair of Air Pods, or an iWatch. The technology that Apple makes use of, its expertise, its advertising campaigns and its diversity were some of the elements that made Jobs' vision a reality. He proved it at every opportunity.

As ideal as Jobs' story might sound, it is not far from the truth. The question is if you want to see the truth and accept it. No one else can choose for you. Jobs could have stopped trying as you and I have done at times. He was meant to be like this. He was meant to fight. He was selfish, bold and "crazy." No one taught him to be like that because that would be the "recipe for success." That is who he was. All he had to do was to be himself.

Jobs has taught me that:

*No limit can stop the urge of a man with a purpose.*

You are going to read the above quote several times in this book because it is part of my truth. No one can stop a man with a strong goal in mind. Because this goal means the world to this man. It is the reason to be alive. Even your wildest vision can become your own truth, so do not be scared. No matter how much time it will take and how many sacrifices you will need to make, keep being excited and focused on that goal. Be unique.

*Stay Hungry. Stay Foolish – Steve Jobs*

## I am Zlatan

Of course, leaders are not only those who have people following them. You do not need to build an empire to be considered an important leader. There are also people who are independent and have great leadership skills. My favorite example is Zlatan Ibrahimović. When I was 35 years old, I found out that we were the same age. I am exactly two months older than him, not a single day more than that.

Ibrahimović is one of the most remarkable football players in modern history. He started his career in 1999 at the age of 18 and two years later, he signed with Ajax, which is the number one team in the Netherlands. Since then, he has won numerous awards and has played in great teams such as Juventus, Milan, Barcelona, Manchester United, etc., and has always been a high-level player. What is remarkable about Ibrahimović is not the fact that he is a well-known athlete, he is known to be quite cranky.

For several reasons, I have identified myself with Ibrahimović. He was growing up and I was growing up too. He was trying to face the "beasts," by literally fighting with the opponents in their penalty area to score a goal. I was struggling to find the path in my career in Greece during the crisis that would make me feel confident about my future while the country was in debt, or to be more precise, to the brink of economic disaster. There was no way out for the Greek people. Everyone was full of insecurity and doubts and everyone was left in the dark about the future. We were trapped in a country that could not move forward or even take a step back. By taking a step back, I would at least feel that there is some kind of change. But not even that happened.

In 2016, I was at a place in life when I needed to believe in something or someone. This is why I followed Ibrahimović consistently. He dared to show his teeth at every opportunity, mocked those who dared to question him and always showed up to prove that he was the best. Years went by and while the global retirement age for a football player is 34–36, he was unstoppable. He was the first to arrive at the training and the last to leave. He rushed first during the game, he seemed to be the most passionate and persistent player, he gave everything he had and scored the best goals. Strength, vigor, questioning and recognition over and over again. He kept going as if he were 25 years old. He seemed to be a superhuman.

Some people though thought he was a bastard. A selfish man who only cared about his image and wanted to challenge the football players and the football fans. However, none of them achieved what Ibrahimović did. As much as a "bastard" he was considered to be, to me he has always been a man of extraordinary strength and persistence who keeps going when everyone else would just quit.

That was also a period in my life when I had had enough of all those people who find a problem to every solution. People who deny moving forward. People who, while sitting on their couch, complain about everything that the government, which they too have voted for years, did not do and who refuse to spend ten extra minutes at work without getting paid for overtime. People who complain at the first chance and boast about things they have not achieved. In the summer of 2016, I felt disgusted by the world around me. I wanted results and values that could teach me how to move forward. I did not want to sink into despair. In the summer of 2016, I desperately wanted a change.

The self-centered and "modest" Swedish football player once said the great quote, "I think I am like wine. The older I get, the better I get." In July of 2016, he left the French Paris Saint-Germain having scored 38 goals during the past season, being the top scorer in the French League and he signed with Manchester United. He was 35 years old.

That summer I decided that, since I had not managed to find professional and financial fulfillment in the construction industry in the past almost twenty years, maybe it was time for me as well to move on to the next chapter. Actually, not "maybe", I had to. It was a *decision* I had to make and I had to make it fast before it was way too late. So I decided to go for it.

I became a salesperson in a marketing company, which had nothing to do with what I had done so far. Since Ibrahimović found the strength to keep going and even level up at the age of 35, why should I consider myself too old for a change? I did not know where this new path would take me. I thought it might lead me to the career that I had always wanted and, as it turned out, it did. I would probably meet people who shared the same vision as me: to reach high and confront titans and fail until they become strong enough to win. People who would not take defeat as a failure but rather as an opportunity to grow. Successful people who cannot remember when was the last time they watched TV and who read books about personal or professional development instead, and focus on their future and the future of their family. People who do not keep checking their watch to see if it is time to take a break or if the shift is over. People who care only about the outcome. The result.

What I did know was what would change if I kept my job as an electrician: nothing at all.

Ibrahimović's story taught me that there is no such thing as the right circumstances, the right age, or anything like that. It taught me to move forward, break the limits, throw myself into what I want and get it at any cost. Did he fight to get what he wanted? So did I. Was he strong? So was I. Was he bold? So was I.

He taught me that:

*If I don't choose to be different,
I choose to be the same.*

So choose correct and do so now. People who are close to you, friends and family, will question you. They will try to convince you that you "should not do it" to protect you. Some co-workers will judge you for your attitude. They will claim they find it funny but the truth is they are just jealous of you. There will be obstacles that will make you think that you are on the wrong way. However, you need to keep going no matter what. You need to speed up. People are familiar with feeling comfortable and with having few responsibilities. You need to move forward and not stop for any reason. Do not stop until you get exactly where you want to be. As you keep going and achieve small goals, you will find the strength to go even further.

If you worry about what people tell you, keep in mind that those who support you and celebrate your achievements with you are the only ones you should care about. A lot of people will show up when you are sad, but only a few will be there for you to share your happiness with. Most people believe it works the other way around, but this is only because people are needy for attention and want others to feel sorry for them, so ignore them. They want to have a shoulder to cry on, while leaders want to be surrounded by people as they move forward and celebrate each and every success.

To all those who will not be there to celebrate with you, just send a picture of your palm with your three middle fingers up and tell them to read between the lines.

They will get the message.

**Nothing Else Matters**

That's all good, so far so good. Everyone is happy, etc.

But there is a black spot in leadership: coexistence with other leaders. Creating greatness when you are not alone but share the vision and dream with someone else and are called to build it with them. What happens in this case?

Overwhelmingly, the efforts of those who tried to cooperate with someone else and reach their "common" peak, fell from the 21st floor with their heads leaving behind a mess. And why is this happening? It is simple. Because simply the way of thinking about how this "common" peak will be conquered differs between two minds. When two people are different, or at least their basic habits or beliefs do not coincide, then things are challenging in the beginning, complicated as time goes by and really tough when they get serious. And let's not go too far, even a simple goal to put two people together, if they are not "compatible" the situation can create extreme situations. An example from everyday life?

It's all yours, bro!

- My love, what time does the plane leave for Zurich tomorrow?
- At 10, my love!
- Oh, I'm so glad, my love! Honeymoon in Switzerland!! Hooray! We need to be at the airport at least 3 hours earlier so that we can have a check-in and then sit and drink a coffee calmly, waiting to leave!
- 3 hours? 3 hours is too much, my love. One, one and a half hours is enough.
- Well, not an hour and a half, Dimitris! I don't want to get stuck waiting in line for hours!
- Eugenia we're not gonna get stuck. I will not leave the house 4 hours before the flight to be there 3 hours earlier and wait like… You know…
- Of course there will be a line! Don't be such a prick! Every time we get there and we're running to reach the counter on time? You know I HATE that! It's sometimes like you don't want us to go!
- There won't be a line, we'll do the check-in online and that's that. Don't start again. I am tired!
- I'll start and finish and I'll continue and I'll stop whenever I FEEL like it!
- Could you FOR ONCE in your life be more relaxed and let's go on our little trip in peace without having to do that? Without all this controlling attitude of yours? Because I'm sick of it!
- YOU ARE SICK of it? YOU? It's not my fault you're such a shithead that you think that I'm going to waste ALL of my honeymoon with you waiting in

line when I could go earlier and sit down and put a cup of calm coffee in my mouth?

- Let's not talk about what your mouth can do!
- You are an ASSHOLE!

You know how these things go. The implementation of a plan by two people is, many times, more than a «mission impossible. It is suicide. Constant and conscious retreats, discussion, explanation of feelings, and efforts to understand one another are required. And if the thing goes too far, you can choose — either a handful of Valiums or a shotgun.

But just as there are stories that prove the rule, there are also few that defy it entirely. And these stories are the ones that have the strongest taste and smell. Which make your skin shiver and makes you wonder if these stories are from this planet or from a fantasy world like that of Peter Pan from Neverland or the world of Pandora in the movie Avatar. How exciting! And for me, the greatest story of mutual respect and cooperation between two leaders is that of the creators of Metallica. The lead singer and guitarist James Hetfield and their drummer Lars Ulrich.

Who hasn't heard the "Nothing Else Matters", the "Unforgiven", the "Turn The Page" and the "One"? Whose hair didn't stand on end when they first heard the "Until It Sleeps" (crap! That happened to me just by typing that…) and who hasn't hummed the "Enter Sandman" prayer? And there are still so many emotions that these two gentlemen have given us with their musicians. All with the energy and passion that defines their music, the atmosphere of mainstream musical appetites and the aggressive tone of the drums. These are some of the characteristics that made them one of the "Big Four" music bands of thrash metal, next to giants like Megadeth, Anthrax and Slayer.

Since their formation in 1981, they have released 11 studio albums, won 10 Grammy Awards and have performed over 40 tours around the world, selling (by simple calculations) billions of tickets. And as if all that wasn't enough, Metallica founded the "All Within My Hands Foundation", where in collaboration with other charities, they aim to support workforce education and put a stone in the fight against hunger. At the same time, they help students learn new trade skills and donated significant funds to those affected by the war in Ukraine. All this through the income from their concerts and record sales. Today, Metallica is not just a music band. It is a corporation. A large business, operating globally and employing a large number of people, while also managing its wealth and investments.

The two joined when the drummer, Ulrich, posted an ad for musicians back in 1981. Since then they both shared the same passion and vision. Great music and creating a band that would differ from the rest of the world. Their goal sounds ideal, but the important thing was - and still is - that both of them knew that it could be workable and achievable, only if they kept their relationship in excellent (well, you can call "excellent" an exaggeration) condition. In their case, the phrase "two minds are better than one" is not enough. It requires two strong personalities with real faith and will, with a low index of egoism and an increased index of patience and understanding.

That makes "Misson Impossible #18" a doll for Zoe, my beautiful niece, to play with.

It's vital to who they are because that's what has defined Metallica's course over the years. What if they are excellent musicians and have been playing guitar or the drums since they were 5? What if they have an eighty-four-piece drum set? What if even today the album "Black (1991)" is in the Top 5 of the best music albums in my collection or if "Master Of Puppets (1986)" is the #2 best metal music album in history, based on rollingstone.com? Without these two personalities, all this would be useless and meaningless, and Metallica would be one more music band that would lost in the friction and egos of their members. There are countless examples of bands that played great music but didn't survive. Why? Simply because their members were not built internally, like personalities, so that they could bear this burden.

Hetfield and Ulrich, fortunately, understood this. That as long as there is a shared vision and trust in the abilities and character of the other, each of us is called to do and retreat in order to succeed. Without being who we are supposed to be, failure is a given. A difficult task, that is indisputable, but not impossible. Because ego, as you will read below, is a ruthless bastard. That if it gets inside you, it is extremely difficult to get out. I've seen it. Many times. And most of the cases are incurable.

Even I have fallen into this trap. But luckily I always had someone who looked after me. And fortunately, I have always had the strength to banish selfishness from within me. And it hurts. A lot...

Of course, let me make a parenthesis here. There is also a limit to retreat during your relationship with your partner and this is the point of not canceling yourself and your needs. Just because you need to back off, doesn't mean you have to fall into the void. This is a line you should never cross. Because if you cross it, you become a target of other people's "appetites". Absolute castration begins. And a true leader gets castrated, tomorrow gets castrated as well. Hope, creation, freedom, wealth, the new and the different are castrated.

Have you ever seen a castrated man? It's the saddest thing I've ever seen in my professional life. A man without guts and courage. Cut off from the root due to a bad family climate or the limited beliefs that he grew up with. Let's not take it too far because it's really sad. But surely the responsibility of a castrated man rests on him and him alone.

But the creators of Metallica found their way and their chemistry. I am sure that many times they disagreed, fought, broke up but found each other again. But they remained true to their goal and their relationship. And they went up on stage once more and created a panic in the crowd. And they wrote another album that skyrocketed their sales. And we heard another track that played in our headphones for weeks and even today we still haven't grown tired of it.

I once read a research about intra-company disputes and how they develop the organization if there is a proper management of them. In fact, the research brought the example of Metallica and more specifically said that Hetfield has competed with Ulrich since the first day of their creation. That's what made Metallica what they are. This is what pushed the band forward.

"We didn't just want to be better than every other band. We wanted to be better than each other."

Thus, selfish self-interest has helped Metallica's progress. This was and is an exhausting journey, but it brought and still brings results. In practice, Hetfield usually develops most of the songs' riffs (basic melody and identity of the song) and Ulrich composes them as songs. Throughout their creative process, Hetfield always speaks his mind and Ulrich always provides a counter-opinion—or vice versa. They say that this is not done on purpose, but the view on the same thing is different. So whatever Metallica produce, just talking about music, plus everything else that makes up their organization, it's all a constant tug of war.

As the years went by the band's fame and financial earnings grew exponentially. Along with their ego. Especially after the album "Black", which was very different from the music of the previous albums, the members of

Metallica reached a great level of dispute. But along the way and in order to preserve their achievements and continue their course, they found a way to express their feelings and thus find a middle solution that satisfied each other. In fact, Ulrich once stated:

"20 years of hate sold 100 million records... Look at us (and this shit of psychiatry)"

If you are one of those who have a similar problem with a partner/friend in your professional field, or something you started with someone, while it seemed ideal at first, then went bad, remember that you are not alone. These things could happen to the best of the best. The only thing I would advise you to do is to ask for help. An advisor, a mentor. Someone anyhow to provide you with directions different from what you have tried so far. To bring to the table ideas on the one hand to not break up with your colleague and on the other hand to maintain together what you were originally inspired to create together. There are solutions for everything except stupidity. Even a lobotomy doesn't make it go away.

The example of Metallica proves that what matters in life and success are not material goods. Fame comes and goes. The same goes for money. The things that matter most are your destination, the unnegotiable love of what you do, the choice of people you have by your side who push you higher and further, and most importantly, having the fortitude and character to lift all that weight.

Be who you should be.

To survive through time, nothing else matters.

No questions asked: I want you to take your phone in your hand, read the following question and write down the answer to the file you opened in the previous chapter.

2) Who do I think is a great leader and why?

**TIPS**: Be careful. It is quite important to give a detailed answer. Try to write at least 50–80 words. Mention the name of the leader first, then write about their achievements and finally, write about any positive outcomes. Feel free to describe your admiration or any other feeling you might have. You can use the Internet to get an idea if you want to.

HEY! Don't cheat! I asked to "write it down" Not to think about it.

You'll understand further down that it is not enough just to think about it. It is important that you write it down in detail. At some point, you will understand why you need to write things down on your phone. Trust me and just do it. Your effort will pay off in the end.

# Chapter 3
# Let's Go Deeper. Shall We?

This theory might be a bit hard to swallow for now but the truth is that some people have achieved great things regardless of if they were recognized as leaders or not. They all had one thing in common. They had it, as we say, within them.

We encounter this theory in our daily lives very often, even though it cannot be perceived by the "naked" eye. If you think about it, there are cases of people who, even though did not have to put in a lot of effort, managed to make a difference. In every class in every school there was a kid who studied little, but somehow always managed to have better grades than someone who studied for multiple hours. In every company, there is someone who, for no reason, brings better results than someone else. In every group of friends, there is a man or woman who is better at dealing with the opposite sex than the rest. In some cases, this can even get to the point of being annoying. I have seen many examples of a beautiful lady being accompanied by a man as ugly as an orangutan, badly dressed, or with the intelligence of a small child. He is to be hidden so nobody can ever find him.

It is very strange, isn't it?

Our daily lives are full of stories and examples that prove that who you are is much more important than what you say or do. Let me give you some examples. Have you ever seen a salesman wear a nice suit that many people would be jealous of, but for some reason, he does not convince you? Have you ever tried to convince somebody over something, but you always end up arguing, no matter how many times you try to explain it to them? And you ask yourself "But why don't they understand?". Have you got any friends who, for some weird reason, always have a good pick-up line to say to someone they meet at a bar or a party?

As if they had the words ready to use. As if it was a setup. Like a well-set-up game of football. Have you ever wondered why this is happening?

For real, has it ever happened to you?

## Konstantinos the Romantic

It has happened to me. It happened one night in a bar in Gazi, in Athens. We were out with some friends from the Toastmasters Association, a club that aimed at developing public speaking skills and other virtues of leadership. To be exact, it is a worldwide association and if you want to learn and practice the skill of speaking in front of people, this club is what you need. It helped me with more than just my career.

One of my friends was Konstantinos. A very friendly, extroverted and cheerful guy who, for some magical reason, drew all the attention to him when he spoke. He had a way to make it impossible for you not to listen to him. He was grounded, confident and bold. At the time, I failed to understand how he did what you are going to read at the bar without us getting beat up, but years later, I did.

At one point during the evening, he asked my opinion about a girl who was sitting opposite us with her boyfriend. I guess he was her boyfriend, but I could not tell for sure from the way they were sitting. Just then, the girl's friend stood up and went to the restroom. Konstantinos thought that the door was open and the dog…well, in the restroom. Determined and with great confidence he stood up, approached her, and said something to her, that I was not able to hear. That was it. She smiled as if they had gone way back. And while he was talking to her, she was looking at him in the eyes as if she was waiting for his every next word to come out of his mouth. She did not speak. She only looked at him and she liked him. I saw her. I understood her. She was charmed by what Konstantinos was saying to her and when he came back to us, she stood gazing at him. What he had said must have been special, I thought.

We all asked Konstantinos what he had told her.

"I'm not gonna tell you," he said with a smile full of confidence.

"What do you mean? You're going to leave us hanging like this?" I asked him.

"Okay, I'll tell you, but you have to be very delicate because if something goes wrong, you might get slapped."

"Tell us already!"

"I told her, 'You're very beautiful and it's a pity that your boyfriend is losing even a few minutes of his time with you to go to the restroom.'"

We were shocked!

"Come on, dude! You're pulling our leg," I told him. "There's no way you used this pick-up line. Such lines were used in movies in the 1980s. There's no way it worked."

"I'm telling you…"

"And what should the guy have done? Pee on himself? That's not very charming, I have to say," said Vaso.

No one believed him. Konstantinos looked certain though. His eyes were full of confidence. And despite we made a joke out of it, I truly wondered how that line could have worked with that girl. There must be some hidden secret behind all this. I thought it is impossible to say something like this to an unknown woman who is being accompanied and not send you to hell immediately. And to make things more perplexing, it seemed that the girl did not say anything to her boyfriend. As if nothing had happened. Konstantinos had affected her so much in such a short time. It is inconceivable to make someone do what you want without even touching them, without imposing it, without even telling them.

*It's not important what you say, but how you say it* and more specifically, *who you are when you say it*. This would be the right way, to sum up, what I am trying to say. Konstantinos proved that whatever he would have said to her, she would probably have had the same reaction: she would look at him speechless. And this is because it was not his words that impressed her, but the way he was looking at her, his body posture, the erotic vibe of his words, and the general vibe he was giving off. This is something that cannot be learned. You either have it or you don't. You either are or you are not. Konstantinos fully came off exactly as he was in reality. Everything he said to that girl *was* just himself. In fact, I doubt that he thought long about his words. He did not need to.

Let's assume I had said the exact same words. What would be the outcome? I believe that in the best-case scenario, she would laugh at me and in the worst-case scenario, I would get beat up by her boyfriend. Because the way I would say these words would be completely different than how he did, simply because

I am not him. Despite how much I would want to reproduce Konstantinos' words to win over this girl, my failure is assured.

*You act based on who you really are,*
*not on who you wanna be.*

Except if you want to change.

Remember that...

In the end, what is important is that it becomes clear that each one of us acts based on who we are. Based on our upbringing, the education we received from our parents and our social circle, our experiences, and everything that has influenced us. All that has been incorporated into our internal DNA, as I like to call it, consists of our views and habits. All of us act, talk and express ourselves, based on what we have learned in our life up to this point.

Konstantinos had been influenced by different things and had different experiences from me. Through these, he learned to handle situations very differently. This is what separates me from him and this is always the difference between two people. Even if our actions are the same, the manner is always different.

### Amar's Transformation

The most typical example I use to analyze the "Who I Am" leadership philosophy can be found in sales companies. It does not matter which company, the kind of product, which country and which culture. In a company, everyone sells the same product, in the same work environment, with the same methods of closing a deal but in the end, some succeed and some do not. Even when it is something that they want very much. Why does this happen? Why do two people, even though they are given the same opportunities and have the same outlook, get different results?

In January 2021, I took on the management of a marketing and sales company located in Bahrain. By promoting an investment company, the sellers get in contact with a large number of potential investors and present them the opportunities. For example, if there are official predictions from analysts that Apple's stock will grow by 15%, the sellers would invite a large number of people and present the offer and if they choose so, the clients would invest a sum of their choice in Apple.

Despite how easy it might sound, only a small percentage, always compared to the total amount of people who are hired, manages to close deals with investors. The others, for some reason which you will understand later, do not make it. The same goes for a real estate company or a car dealership or a telecommunications company or even a bank that promotes credit cards. There are hundreds of sales companies out there. As long as someone produces something, there is always someone who has to sell it.

In my company, there was Amar. A 24-year-old young man from Bahrain. Before he came to us, he had worked at a supermarket for a while and later started his own business and had a restaurant with a friend of his, a bit before the coronavirus outbreak. The restaurant, just like many others, closed a few months after that. Amar seemed very clever from the beginning. I was astounded by how quickly he grasped brokerage terminology and his exceptional perception.

But when he was required to communicate with some potential clients, Amar had difficulties even making them listen to him. As the days went by, I understood that it was getting worse. He started getting disappointed. Because not only was he getting constantly rejected from the other end of the line before even opening his mouth, but he was also seeing the others who had entered the company at the same time as him having better results.

I left him without further instruction because I wanted to understand who he *was*. According to my philosophy, only when I understand who someone *is* will I be able to "help" them. I also wanted to see if Amar would give it all until the first waves pass or if he would drown. If somebody wants something but after a few efforts gives up, they either do not really want it or they are a coward. I detest phrases like "I want to, but maybe this is just not for me." If I hear it from someone, it assures me that they are a coward and that they have found an excellent excuse to give up.

The days went by and Amar showed no signs of improvement, so I had to take matters into my own hands. I went to him one morning while he was talking on the phone and I looked at him. He immediately hung up and looked at me in desperation.

"What's up? How come you get such low numbers?"

"Mr. Spyros, I don't know and I'm getting disappointed. I can tell that the others are doing so much better than me and I'm still struggling only to keep the client on the phone. All the clients just tell me, 'I'm not interested.'"

"Why are they not interested?"

"I don't know."

I looked at him with apathy.

"Why are they not interested?" I repeated.

"Some say they are in a meeting, others say they don't have time and sometimes they just say that they are not interested."

"So is it their fault? And what do they say to your coworkers? You were trained in the same way, you use the same database and got taught the same approach methods. What is the difference between you and them?"

He looked at me perplexed. I leaned a bit closer and showed that I wanted to say something specific that he had not yet understood, but at the same time, I wanted him to discover it on his own. I repeated, "What's the difference between you and Mohammed?"

No answer.

"You have exactly the same resources as Mohammed. Same training, same approach methods, same telephones, same database, only your clothes and your weight differ. So what exactly is the difference, Amar?"

No reaction. *Exactly as I expected,* I thought.

"Amar? Are you with us? What's the single difference between you two?"

"Me?" he asked puzzled.

"There you go! It's not that you are doing something different from Mohammad, it's the way you are doing it. It's HOW you're doing it. And HOW you're doing it is based 100% on WHO you are. Do you agree up to now?"

"I do, Mr. Spyros."

He had not understood yet. He agreed with me because he did not know what else to say. A typical malfunction. A minor short circuit in an abandoned house in the middle of the desert that caused the power shutdown of the entire Saudi Arabia.

Poor Ammar…

"Amar, let's take things from the beginning. When you call potential new clients, what kind of people are they, typically? Think carefully before you answer. Who they are, will help you understand what they need."

"They are business owners, probably twice my age, with greater experience, and they have been rejected a lot in their lives. They manage a number of people, work many hours and have talked to hundreds of people like me."

"Congratulations, Amar, you are getting there."

"So, he doesn't want to hear anyone else like me, a *seller* who struggles to close a deal?"

"Amar, I knew you were brilliant. Now you're using your talents. Excellent."

I put my hand on his shoulder and sat on the chair next to him. He was looking at me with a look between confusion and discovery. At that moment, I felt that his mind was working at maximum capacity trying to fully understand my words.

"Amar, Jordan Belfort, in his book *The Way of the Wolf,* wrote that the first 4 seconds of a call are the most important because that is the amount of time that the human brain requires to realize to whom it is talking. We are beings perfectly trained in the usage of phones. In the last 140 years, from the time Graham Bell invented the first telephone, we have talked millions of hours while having listened to even more hours of conversations. With such training, we can understand much more than we think by talking on the phone. As a result, the fact that people don't want to talk to you is because subconsciously, you *aren't* a person they would like to talk to. Trust me, they aren't trying to insult you. It's how things are. They understand what kind of person you are from your first words. That's why they hang up immediately."

"What am I supposed to do?"

"Amar, why did you come here in the first place?"

"To make money."

"How much money?"

Time stopped flowing. The earth stopped moving…

"Amar, wake up! How much money?"

"A lot?"

"Amar, if you want to make a lot of money stop acting like a little child who is asking for permission. Wake up, take a deep breath and listen to me carefully. Stop being defeatist and weak. Stop being comfortable with nothing and celebrating mediocrity. Start demanding from the world because otherwise, the world won't give you anything. The world won't let you get away with anything. If you want to win, you'll have to become a fighter first. If you want to conquer, you'll need to be a winner first. If you want to make money, you should know that you deserve it and get out there and get it. No begging hand will get more than what the others decide to give to it. The following three things will save you: First, when you talk, raise your chest and body. When you are hunched or you have your head lowered you give off the impression of someone defeated.

People always notice that. Secondly, speak up and be decisive. Nobody wants to be associated with someone who doesn't have the confidence to back up his words with a strong spirit. And third, don't let them hang up. Fight. Raise the tone of your voice, stop feeling small and inadequate, stand your ground, and don't accept anything other than victory. In my company, I don't want losers. Either you stay here and fight or you'll find an office where things are easier and you'll be feeling more comfortable."

*If you're not programmed to win,
you're doomed to fail.*

Harsh? Indeed. But of course, I knew what I was doing. He had shown me that he wanted to stay and that he had the potential to evolve himself. He wanted to be a fighter and he wanted to have high self-esteem but he did not know how to do it or what his limits were. He did not know how to fight and what to fight for.

When I showed him the exit door (and *not* a way out), I made him understand that if he chose to consider himself a fighter who deserves everything he wants to achieve, then he had to find a way to express it and *become what he wants* to represent. In this way, I "made him" choose between acknowledging and becoming who he wanted to be or getting fired.

In this harsh way, I pushed him into the position I wanted. He felt he might lose something he took for granted. He felt the threat. His "ego" shattered and made him want to save whatever could be still saved. The moment this thought crossed his mind, I had already won. I knew what his next choice would be.

He chose the hard path. The path of change. He backed his belief that he really wanted to keep the position and that he could become a key player in my company. He kept trying more determined than ever. And he got rewarded for this decision.

He immediately started utilizing the things I had told him. Every 10 minutes, I went next to him, raised his chest and showed him my throat, reminding him of the importance of the tone of his voice. Other times, I took things further and yelled at him, "Nobody is going to believe you if you don't show your teeth. If you don't show that you're a salesman and that you are harder than a rock. Try harder. Where is your strength? Why should they listen to you? Make them listen, force them to listen." and he would put in even more effort and more passion. Amar's change had begun.

On that same day, he brought the best numbers in the whole office. He had understood.

Amar started to change his "internal DNA." He is a sensitive child, even-tempered and kind. But when he has to face people tougher and more confident than him, he is called upon to change who he *is* if he wants to get the desired results. If he had not changed who he was, all the approach methods and all the hours of training would have meant nothing. He would waste his time, energy and his mental wellness. Every attempt would come down crashing. And so would he.

The script itself is never important and it will never be.

*It's not important what you do,*
*but who you are while you do it*

### The "Who I Am" Philosophy

Amar's story is one of the hundred stories I have come across in my time as a sales manager in the stock market and as a CEO here in Bahrain. Some of these stories have kept me awake at night because I could not accept that two different people, while they have been trained in the exact same way, might produce different results. I refuse to accept that even when the answer is right in front of some salesmen, they refuse to change.

"But how can I make them understand?" was what I was trying to figure out.

So I developed the "Who I Am" leadership philosophy. I was fully confident that "It's not important how you say something, but how you say it," I knew that two people cannot have the same results, no matter how similar their situation is. Because of this, I developed a strong urge to help people change who they are so that they can get closer to what they want to achieve. As a hardcore salesman, I wanted to be able to compare myself to the strongest and cover the distance between me and those who were considered to be the best. Additionally, I wanted everyone who was on my team to be at the top. If they were not, I would show them how to do that.

This was the stimulus that made me develop the philosophy I have built and which you are about to read below. Using this philosophy, I managed to become the No1 sales manager of 2018 and 2019 in the investment company, a place that "grows" through healthy competition between its members but is at the same time rough, abrupt, and very challenging. Besides my personal growth and success, the two best members of my team were always the 2 best representatives on the company rankings. I had never been prouder. Seeing both of them getting awarded were moments I will never forget. Moments that indicated that my system, besides for myself, worked for others too.

Let's go back to Amar. If Amar had the idiosyncrasy, character, habits and beliefs that Steve Jobs had, who tells me that he could not have created a counterpart like Orange, or something similar? If Martin Luther King was not born in the United States but in North Africa, who tells me that he would not have become one of the greatest leaders in history? If a great painter was not stuck on thoughts like "that's impossible," "that cannot happen" or "don't bother" and grabbed every chance that was presented to him, who tells me that he could not become the next Walt Disney instead of painting for himself and his friends and family?

Exactly. Nobody can tell me that, but I am sure that everybody would agree with me that by changing one's views and habits, you can change their course. By changing what he or she believes in, and in turn, changing *who they are*, you can change the course of their life.

Through the transmission of this knowledge and philosophy, and with the condition that you will accept and apply it to the letter, with consistency, discipline and patience you can do miracles! You will be able to build bridges when at first you were afraid of heights. You can become No. 1 where you would finish last. You can have sex when before you were afraid of talking to her or him. It can change your life course and make the "unreasonable" seem "reasonable." With all this knowledge, YOU have nothing to hold you back.

We must, at last, come to a point in life when we have to "open our eyes." The same goes for you. Freeze time and look around you. What is happening? Where are you, who are you with and where do you really want to go? If you are stuck in a job you do not like, find the strength to quit. If you are in a toxic relationship, break up. If you still live at your parents' house, leave. To sum it up, if you are unhappy with your daily life, change it.

As you will realize below, few are willing to carry this burden. Few choose to change because they lose their balance. When everything seems like it is under control, the slightest change can make things get out of hand within seconds.

That is when excuses, withdrawals and weakness occur. People quit when the first challenge comes up because they do not have the necessary strength to carry on.

I know very well that all of us have distinct personalities. We have our own way of talking, acting and thinking. Even if many people believe that "people do not change," the "Who I Am" leadership philosophy which you will read below is backed up with stories that prove the exact opposite. We can change our internal DNA. It is simple, though not easy.

However, there is no doubt, that you can turn black into white.

# Chapter 4
# Success Begins with a Purpose

Ah! "Success."

One word, a thousand interpretations, a million opinions and few examples. A term we come across on every corner of the street, in every book. A term analyzed by thousands of people throughout the world. It is given a different meaning by each one of us and is communicated in different ways. Some seminars help you achieve "success," develop the right way of thinking, the right habits and so on. Do you want to talk about books? There are thousands of authors in the world, some are experienced and some are swindlers.

All of them are right in a way. Some people disagree and others agree with whatever has ever been written. It is, of course, very important who you *are* when you are listening, reading, or conversing. Because in most cases, the meaning you give to the word "success" depends on who you *are* the moment you hear about it and what *you want* it to be. Because let's face it, we all hear what we want to hear and we interpret things in a way that works for us.

Did I confuse you? It is okay. Hold on to that thought and let's carry on.

I believe that we can all agree on the fact that "success" is something personal. Something completely yours. Nobody can define it for you and nobody can disagree with you on this. It is like staring at an abstract painting. Someone might look at it and see a window with raindrops falling on it and you might see a cow that has just grazed the whole meadow. Nobody is right and nobody is wrong. It is what you choose it to be.

As for those who are not chasing after it, it is not like they do not want success. It is just that they can live without it. They are content with a simple life, without worries. They prefer the easy way over the difficult one. They choose the present over the future. They choose the certain over the uncertain.

And it is completely fine! Often, it might even be healthier. They have fewer troubles and problems. So let's not judge them. It is their own personal matter.

So what is success?

## SO WHAT IS SUCCESS?

Out of all the interpretations I have read or heard, I got attached to the one Jim Rohn once gave: "Success is something you attract by the person you become." I heard this phrase somewhere in 2011 in a multi-level marketing training event I attended and back then – yes, I admit it – did not understand it. It took me a while until I "got it." While the idea of the book you are reading was spinning in my head, I came across this phrase. Then everything became clearer. The concept of success, theoretically and practically, is defined by who you *are* at every moment that you perceive it. Your needs, as an entity, change according to who you are at every moment. The same goes for success.

I respect those who have defined it and are chasing after it or those who can live without it but support the ones who need it.

## INSTRUCTIONS MANUAL

The only certain thing is that there are no "shortcuts" to success. Even if we want to "shorten" the distance, it is not possible. Even if we want to make it easier, it is not possible. There is no recipe nor an "instructions manual." If there ever existed one, then maybe – and I am only guessing here – we would be better prepared to face the difficulties coming our way. It would be easier. But maybe, on the other hand, having seen and understood the potential difficulties, we would not even bother trying to attain success. We might falter before even trying.

Humans are complex beings. We have to admit it.

It would be fun though if a manual like that existed, don't you think so?

If I had it in front of me, I imagine it would be something like this:

## INSTRUCTIONS TO ACHIEVE SUCCESS

1. BE AMBITIOUS
2. YOUR FRIENDS WILL MAKE FUN OF YOU AFTERWARDS
3. IT'S UNLIKELY THAT YOU WILL FIND A PARTNER THIS DECATE
4. AT LEAST YOU HAVE YOUR DREAMS
5. YOU ALSO HAVE DAD'S MAGAZINES THAT YOU FOUND STASHED AWAY
6. ACTION
7. FAILURE
8. YOUR FRIENDS ARE MAKING FUN OF YOU AGAIN
9. REJECTION
10. MAYBE YOUR PARENTS WILL HAVE ANOTHER CHILD MORE NORMAL THAN YOU
11. ACTION!
12. EMOTIONAL ROLLERCOASTER No1
13. DON'T DOUBT YOURSELF, KEEP GOING AND BELIEVE!
14. ACTION!
15. TOTAL FAILURE
16. EMOTIONAL ROLLERCOASTER No2
17. IGNORE THE OTHERS AND CONTINUE!
18. ACTION!
19. EMOTIONAL ROLLERCOASTER No3, 4, 5, 6, 7, 8
20. FIGHT MORE!
21. DOES IT HURT? IT DOESN'T MATTER! KEEP GOING
22. BANKRUPTCY
23. REALLY? YOU THOUGHT IT WOULD BE EASY? YOU IDIOT!
24. EMOTIONAL ROLLERCOASTER No9, 10, 11, 12, 13, 14
25. LET ME REPEAT: ACTIOOON!
26. FAILURE
27. WHAT? IT SHOULDN'T BE LIKE THIS? YOU'RE FUNNY
28. WHAT? DO YOU WANT TO GIVE UP? YOU'RE FUNNY ONCE AGAIN! QUITER!
29. ACTIOOON!
30. FAILURE

31. EMOTIONAL ROLLERCOASTER No15, 16, 17, 18, 19, 20
32. YES, YOU NEED TO FIGHT MORE
33. YES, MORE!
34. MORE!
35. ACTION!
36. EMOTIONAL ROLLERCOASTER No21, 22, 23, 24, 25
37. TOOT TOOT… THE ROLLERCOASTER HAS SWEPT YOU OFF YOUR FEET
38. YOU FOUND THAT FUNNY? NICE!
39. FAILURE!
40. NO! HERE IS ANOTHER REJECTION. I HOPE IT DIDN'T BOTHER YOU
41. EMOTIONAL ROLLERCOASTER No26, 27, 29, 29, 30, 31
42. LET ME REPEAT ONCE AGAIN: ACTIONNN!

This is how I imagine the instructions manual for success. If the numbering tired you out, then you can easily compare it with the success story of Rocky Balboa, the character Sylvester Stallone created. He got punched hard in the ring but despite that, he had the power to stand up and continue fighting. The poor guy got beat up a lot.

That is why many yearn for it, but few pursue it and even fewer achieve it. Because very few stand up again after getting beat up this bad.

I experienced this when I first went to Dubai in 2017 before I had even clearly defined what success was for me. I was working roughly 12–14 hours a day, in a place where nobody spoke English and a manager who was completely incapable but had outlandish demands. Every morning, I woke up with pain in my chest because of the stress, and in the office, everyone called me a grandpa because of the age difference I had with my coworkers. Pimples started appearing on my hands and feet because of the stress and I almost cried one evening because of the pressure.

In the process, I understood that this was only 5% of the effort people have to make to succeed since it has not yet stopped. It never does. Not for me, not for you nor for anyone else pursuing success. It requires constant strength, patience, tenacity, nerves of steel and dedication. This is why no one among those who were there when I started managed to get very far. Their excuses and their ego were bigger than their ambitions.

Everything else is just meaningless words that the experts use to sell wisdom and self-improvement while having no scars from hardships or battles, not a single result or similar experiences. They have nothing that can back up their words. There is no degree that can even come close to reaching the importance of experience. That is why you need to be careful who you believe and listen to. But we will talk about this later on.

## YOU DO NOT TAKE IT, EVEN IF THEY GIVE IT TO YOU

One sunny day in Dubai, sometime in 2020, a partner of mine from Greece sent me a message to let me know that he would send me a new employee for the after-sales department.

"I found someone great to send to you. His name is M. He is a very strong guy, very kind and determined, and needs a lot of money since he has a wife and a child. He has struggled a lot here in Greece and has fought tooth and nail to make ends meet. He wants something more stable with bigger returns. He is a perfect fit for your team and he almost "begged" me to come to your team to work there."

"Fine. Send him. How old is he?"

"36. When should I send him?"

"How should I know? Tell him to kiss his wife and child goodbye, tell them that they will meet again at Christmas, and put him on the next plane to Dubai. Now that I am still here. Because if I leave once again, he will not be able to find me. If things are as you describe them to be, he will not bother with the last-minute notification. He should have his suitcase ready within ten minutes. He should be aware of the magnitude of the opportunity that is being offered to him here. Otherwise, he will not endure all of this. You know it."

"He will. He really needs this."

"I am telling you this because *a lot of people want to eat, but few are willing to hunt*, says the wise lion. Let's hope his family is his priority and that he will be able to endure the burden of our work."

"He's got it. The man wants to earn money. Do whatever is in your power to help him."

Three days later, M. landed in Dubai. He was a 36-year-old man, very kind, fit and serious. A perfect choice for our line of work. In the first days, he talked to me about his family and explained that the reason he had come was to work for a certain period of time to make enough money to bring his family too. They would find a nice apartment in the country where, as he said, "The sun never sets." He had already started imagining his and his family's future in Dubai. He was very proud of that.

I liked his attitude a lot. M. had an end goal. A definite purpose: his children and his wife. I truly believed that he could become great and make as much money as he wanted and make them happy. What I had not understood though was how badly he wanted it.

He stayed for a month. He did not last longer. He went back to Greece and started searching for work elsewhere.

In my reality, there is no such thing as "I can't," there is only "I don't want to." That is what I was taught when I was young. If I want something a lot, I do everything in my power to gain it. Even if I have to work hours on end, even if I have to be deprived of something, to change, to crumble up, to fall, to rise and then fall again. If it is for a special and powerful reason, I am willing to do everything. Especially for my family. Nothing has ever stopped me and will never do. I am saying this while being humble and with zero elitism and egoism. I am saying this truthfully. Nothing and no one can stop me.

But not everyone is like this. People who have undergone a similar experience will say, "So what, it was not meant for him. It is not for everybody." I agree up to a point, but not completely. Because if I were to agree, then I would have to assume that success is only found in an environment that you perceive as ideal, in any daily life you want to have. As you may easily figure out, I do not believe this. There are times when you will be able to choose your surroundings and your environment, but things will never be exactly as you want them to be. Never.

If you prefer to be comfortable over accomplishing your mission, then success is not for you. And that is exactly why it is not for everyone.

Which is the correct choice when somebody has to feed their child while at the same time, there is a game on TV? If they feed the child, they will miss the match and if they watch the match, the child will be hungry. If you say, "Of course the important thing is that the child eats," that means that what is important is the result of an action and not the action itself. What is important is that the child eats. Even if it means skipping the match or cooking for hours. Period.

The same goes for success. There will never be a suitable environment, you will always be lacking something. And the only thing that matters is the outcome. Period (No2).

As for the example of M., I know the reason why he left Dubai but I will not mention it as it does not matter. To me, every reason that makes you put the needs of a child aside in order for you to feel secure and free of troubles is insignificant, maybe even cowardice. Everything is about your choices and about who you *are*. If he chose to abandon a good future for his family to feel better about himself, then this is worthy of criticism because he will do it again. He has probably done it before. That is who he is. Has learned to back down.

No excuse can be the reason to back down.

*If you can still see the light at the end of the tunnel,*
*going anywhere else but forward makes you a coward.*

Despite how many times you try to explain that people like M. will deny it of course.

I understand, naturally, that sometimes things fold out in a way where you get stuck. Daily life can bring you to a point where you forget who you are and what you can do and you get stuck. Day in, day out. You are just alive, with the rhythm that you have gotten used to, with your habits, with the way you do things. You sleep the same way, you wake up the same way, you drink your coffee the same way, you go to work until you are done and at the end of the day, you go to sleep the same way. It is the same circle, over and over again. Like a mouse who runs inside a wheel and believes it will reach somewhere.

"What a stupid animal," someone would say.

Ironic though, isn't it?

On the other hand, I can understand. All of us can understand, I imagine because it is human. We have all found ourselves in this position.

How many people in the world do not dare to find a better job, because they are afraid to lose what they already have? Others, like M., find a great job, but it proves to be too difficult or outside of their capabilities and choose to quit, and go without work again, no matter how big of a salary they would have gotten. Hundreds of examples prove that:

*People choose not to lose what they have
over pursuing what they want.*

Do you want to talk about personal life? Let's do it.

How many times have you met individuals who, although know that their relationship is a dead end, are unable to break up with their partner, because they "cannot," as they claim? Others come up with all kinds of excuses to explain their partner's abusive behavior. Whether it is mental or physical. "It's okay, he didn't mean it," "he got carried away in the heat of the moment." Many examples prove that people will not search for something better because they are afraid of losing what they already have and think that they will not find something better. This is the case regardless of how small, cheap and meaningless what they have is or how much greater and better what they do not have is.

Honestly, what do people believe will lose if they pursue what they want? Why do they give up? Why do they throw in the towel? Why do they come up with excuses? What are they doing when, although they know what is out there, remain with the plain, the small, the usual? What are they doing when, although they realize that they are the mouse inside the wheel and that it leads to nowhere, they refuse to open the cage and get out?

Cage! I just hit the bull's eye! Not literally of course. I mean I found the right word.

From my personal experience, after having trained many people in the last years, I have come to understand that people act primarily based on who they *are* based on their habits. So in turn, every new action that is outside of their comfort zone and their beliefs shakes their internal DNA. They realize that everything outside of their own reality is outlandish. They subconsciously reject its nature and thus try to automatically comply with it. They refuse to do anything out of character, anything else than what they have learned all these years.

People, by nature, choose the version of reality that is closest to them and support it till their last breath. Remember that. For this reason, every single opinion of a person is his or her reality.

Yes, we all live in a cage. A cage made of habits, values, insecurities and fears. A cage that was constructed during our childhood and has remained the same until today, since we have adopted these values as our reality. This is a reality that we have constructed on our own, a perfect world that gives us security and seems as if it smiles at us, prompting us to stay there.

There is no such thing as an absolute free will. It's an utopia.

We prefer to spin the wheel, inside our cage, because that is how we learned to live. Every other reality outside of this, every beauty of success, can come within our grasp and we will reject it as something unattainable. In fact, when people manage to escape and step out of the wheel they were supposed to be spinning, we wonder. Instead of looking at how we ourselves can escape too, we keep spinning the wheel because "This is what we were taught," "This is just how society is," and "This is what is acceptable." As if we have chains tied to our feet. We are in denial.

*"The chains of habit are too light to be felt until they are too heavy to be broken,"* said the great Warren Buffett once and that phrase perfectly encapsulates what I want to highlight at this point. You also understand that any change is much harder than you think so you choose to leave things as they are. You choose to do absolutely nothing. Because it is more comfortable like this. There is no danger and no fear, just tranquility.

Going back to the example, let me highlight that whatever M. felt while working with us, whether it was caused by an inside or outside factor, he saw it as "pressure." Something that tried to change his internal DNA and change who he *was*. Automatically, without having bad intentions, he believed subconsciously that any condition, besides the one he was used to, was abnormal, unnatural and uncomfortable. At the same time, returning to his old habits and to his safe environment seemed the only thing that made sense. Regardless of the purpose that this condition served. So he quit.

Even if somebody were to explain to him what was at stake behind his decision to quit, it would not change his mind. His truth formed his choices. This is the case for all of us. This is who we are.

And as certain as I am that this has happened several times in his life, I am even more certain that this has happened to nearly all of us. We all have found ourselves in situations that made us feel uncomfortable, but if we persisted a bit more, it would become the future that we had dreamed of. And as utopian as it might sound, that is the truth. Because only those who keep going, defying the odds, are those who manage to make it.

Steve Jobs named them *"crazy"* because this is what common people view them as because they are different.

The moral of this brief story is that many people desire success but in the face of any obstacle, be it big or small – the size is completely subjective, I mean the size of the obstacle, do not let me be misunderstood -, most people back down. Not because the problem was big, but because its nature was foreign. In fact, in our attempt to solve it, the problem acts upon our habits and reshapes them. It aims at changing their substance and redefining them. That is why M. quit. Without realizing it, he did not want to change his habits.

Success is easy to talk about but hard to achieve. The attempt to achieve a goal or the process of becoming who you ought to be will challenge you. It will tear down your theories and make you doubt and rethink. It will make you argue and break up. It will make you pay the price, an expensive and constant price.

Let's make something clear now while it is still early. I do not intend to change those who do not want to change. I am not your father or your partner. Those who understand the concept of change and its necessity, understand it. Those who want to build a great future for themselves and the people they love will do so. Those who want to understand the point of this book and push themselves to become what they should be will do so. It is exhausting to try to convince somebody to become something that he or she does not want to be.

M. tripped over his own two feet. He and he alone is responsible for his actions. Like all of us are.

He left one morning and he did not even say "goodbye."

Situations like these catch me off guard. I cannot accept that there are people out there who are so weak. People who dare to say that they desire success but are not able to endure even the smallest changes. If they had to deliver food on rainy December days on a motorcycle or put down tiles at 40 degrees Celsius, what would they do? Would they start crying and calling for their mother? How difficult is it to work at a company in an 8-hour job, in an office with coffee, water and tea?

That is why when I find myself in conversations regarding success and hear phrases like "oh, I can't do that, it's not for me," about things that need to get done, I get frustrated. Because this means that they want to succeed but they also want to remain the same. It is all showing off and posing (what a word, by the way). It is like wanting to learn English but not taking classes. It is like wanting to learn to sing but not taking vocal lessons. It is like wanting to find a girlfriend but not leaving your house. It is like wanting to eat spaghetti with meatballs and being a vegetarian.

How can some people even believe that something like that can happen?

Well, it cannot, so eat lettuce instead.

The road to any kind of success depends 100% on you. It depends on what your habits are, what your views are, the stimulus you had, how you grew up, how you live your life at this very moment and what your circle is like. It depends on how your family, your friends and the neighbors' gossip affect you. It depends on how many hardships you can endure, how many problems you can solve, and how many emotional ups and downs you can escape from. Success depends solely on which materials you are made of. It depends on who you *are*.

This is where the "Who I Am" philosophy is based on.

I am almost certain that even if people had a way to learn what is required to achieve their goals, few would choose to go down that road. Even if people were given a list, few would take advantage of it. Because nobody likes change.

But those who choose to follow that road are aware of the fact that they first choose difficulty and then the outcome. They first choose to feel uncomfortable and then succeed. They choose to struggle first and then come out unscathed. Those who like pursuing success do not have an escape plan. The bigger the challenges they face, the more certain they become that they will manage to succeed.

No one can guarantee your success. Do you know why? Because, simply, no one knows your limits, your character, the level of your persistence and how much you want it. Nobody, besides you, knows if you grasp who you are in comparison to who you should be, if you accept any change in order to succeed, if you give up somewhere halfway, if you keep blaming others for your own failures or if you will simply say "it was not meant for me" and leave. That is why it is not guaranteed. Simply because you yourself cannot guarantee it.

## EVERYTHING STARTS WITH THE PURPOSE

And the questions start coming in:

- In what way do those who ignore the obstacles and keep going differ from those who stop? What is the secret ingredient that makes someone able to face problems, hardships and obstacles, and so on?

- At last, I want someone to share this secret that everyone keeps sealed tight and is not revealed to the rest of us as if there is a danger that it will be stolen or, as it might disappear because it will be overused.
- What the hell do I have to do to make it? It cannot be that hard!

## *A purpose is a necessity.*

Has it ever happened to you that your mind is going around a thought so specific, that you are unable to make it stop? A thought so specific and so well drawn out, that its shape is unquestionable? A thought so emotionally powerful that even if you try to put it aside for a while, you fail? Or when you try to focus on something else, that thought comes back with such a force, that it shatters any other thought you might have?

Has a thought ever stuck in your head that was so perfect that you wanted, no matter the cost, to make it a reality?

Have you ever had an obsession?

When something like this happens to us, our brain unconsciously focuses there, because it draws us. It is an explosion of feelings that if you have not felt, you cannot understand. When this occurs, we ignore fears and dangers and the only thing we want is to get there.

Have you ever broken up with your partner and even if time has passed, the only thing you could think about was him or her? Have you ever wanted to bring someone close to you again so much that you would cross mountains to hold them one last time?

Have you ever thought that you do not care what will happen when you see them, what they will tell you, if your friends will make fun of you, if you will be crying your eyes out, if you will manage to make them want to come back again? Have you ever been in a place where nothing else matters? Absolutely nothing.

Has it ever happened to you? Have you ever reached such levels of emotional outbursts?

The greatest secret to any kind of success is the purpose and the need to achieve this purpose. It is a secret that everyone knows, but few utilize. It is a secret that is so self-evident that is not even considered a secret. So people, instead of focusing there, focus on anything else except their purpose. Because the "secret" is simply too obvious and stupid for them.

But this is it.

# SUCCESS BEGINS WITH A PURPOSE

*Your action defines how much you want it!*

Let me explain. When you have an ultimate goal, it means that you are possessed by a need that must be satisfied. It should be satisfied regardless of the obstacles, you are called upon to overcome, the hardships you have to face, the disappointments you have to ignore and the rejections you have to come to terms with.

A need is called a "need" because of its power to lead those who have it in a certain direction. Necessity, subconsciously, shows the way. It is what activates the mind to work. The greater the need, the greater the will to realize it, the greater the belief in it, our passion and so on.

Naturally, you have your own needs too, big or small, important or unimportant. From getting up in the morning and drinking a glass of water to the need to sleep at night. You need to maintain personal relationships with some people or stay alone a bit to find peace. You need to go to work and not miss out on the daily pay or loaf around and stay in bed until the evening. We have a million needs and based on these we plan ahead and make our decisions on how we will act.

The decisions that you will have to make for a need of yours will determine the magnitude of your need. For example, if you need to buy a car, then you will have to decide if you will be saving up for a while, if you will borrow from a friend, or if you will be working overtime. Sometimes your need is so big that you have to go for all the suggested options at once.

*Our actions define the magnitude of our needs.*

To sum up, how much you want something can be defined *only* by the extent and the passion of your actions.

The key is your purpose itself. The extent of your need to achieve your goal is the answer to all questions regarding success. How badly you want to succeed in something is the key that opens up the door to "success" and holds it open for as long as necessary.

Personally, I ignored this aspect of success for many years. Whenever I read about the "purpose" in books or heard about it, in seminars about growth and leadership I attended in many cities in Europe, I ignored them with discretion. I said, "The author is right. Everything starts with the purpose. I'll find it. I'll sit down one of these days when I have time and think about it and I'll find it. But now tell me what I have to do." Every time, I had the answer served on a silver platter but I searched for the answer I wanted to hear. That was my reality, a blind and naive reality.

Over the years, I kept doing the same thing, while reading the books of Napoleon Hill, Dale Carnegie, or anyone else. It made no difference at all. All of them mentioned the "purpose" and I was still looking for what I really wanted to do. I wonder how a hand did not suddenly come out of one of those books back then to slap me in the face and make me pull myself together. The truth is that would have saved me a lot of time and gray matter.

When I finally caught up to it halfway through 2017, I sat my ass down and dedicated myself to what I wanted to achieve. I spent two weeks of thinking and analyzing in order to find out exactly what I wanted. I convinced myself that what I wanted to achieve must not only shake up me. It should shake up the whole world. And I found it. From there on out, I found a goal that until today, while it might slightly shift, is based on the same principle.

My search proved also to be my biggest challenge at the time. I simply stopped focusing on *what* I was doing and started focusing on *why* I was doing it. In the process – you will understand later on – I focused on *how* to do it and on who I had to *be* to do it correctly. *What* I had to do, as you saw in Amar's case earlier, was never a priority.

The purpose is your ultimate need. A need that is so powerful that all your actions aim at its satisfaction. A need so powerful that every thought will reinforce your belief in the realization of this goal and every breath you take serves to keep this one thing alive. Your goal will become your walk and your smile. It will be your influences, your views and your fanaticism. Your goal will become your relationship with your friends, your reactions to your partner and the extent of your respect towards your fellow human beings. Your goal will become the way you drink coffee. It will become the way you flirt, the way you hold a cigarette and your taste in whiskey.

The purpose is whatever you have dreamed of as a child and believed you would be able to do. It is your passion and everything that you love. You would abandon everything and everyone to achieve your goal. For your goal, you would go through the fire, you would become a rug to be stepped upon, you would turn the earth upside down to make it a reality and you would sacrifice everything.

Your purpose is your co-worker. It will grow from your actions and you will grow after every small or big victory. With your objective stuck in your mind, the slightest chance that you will make will be enough fuel to push through even the toughest of obstacles. Your impatience will be your food and the reason why you will solve every problem. Every issue will be resolved. Every emotional up and down will be under control, every trace of egoism will disappear and every unfortunate incident will be a great lesson. Your objective is your superpower.

Your purpose is the start of every decision you will have to take. It will affect your behavior and shape your desires. It will give you a sense of direction and the meaning of life. It will help you find out who you will become and what you are destined for. You will find yourself.

You will become your purpose. And you will be unique.

Think about it: do you believe that if you had to rescue your one-year-old child from a burning house, you would chicken out? Do you believe that there is anyone in the world who would be able to stop you? I do not think so. You would go through the fire in the hopes of holding your child in your hands and hugging him or her. You would go in with force, boldness and determination, and you would not dare leave without the child. You would prefer to be burned alive rather than live even one day knowing you did not do everything you could to save the child.

Now tell me if you would act the same if instead of your child, you had to save your mother-in-law…

Remember:

*No limit can stop the urge of a man with a purpose.*

Nothing can stop someone who has a clear goal and more so when the goal is so vital and powerful. Nothing at all. Keep that in mind, whatever happens in your life. When you are searching and wondering, "Why do others make it and I don't?" It is because they have such a powerful purpose that they disregard everything else but its realization. Their need is greater than any obstacle or insecurity. Their need is so powerful that they cannot live without their purpose.

And this was the greatest lesson I did not get until I was 36.

If you know people who do not get offended easily, who leave their pride aside, who do not bother with the current trends, who do not watch reality shows or play PlayStation hours on end, it is because they are busy making their goal a reality. If you see people who are more energetic in their personal and work life, it is because they have such a vital goal that they need to give it flesh and bones.

## WHAT ABOUT YOU? DO YOU HAVE A GOAL?

That is why if you do not have a goal, the first thing you need to do is to find one. Sit down, take your time and find one. Being fully aware of your capabilities and without fantasizing, you will understand that you have found it when it will be the first thought that comes to your mind when you wake up in the morning and the last before going to sleep at night.

For some people, this purpose is inseparably linked with their workplace and their professional success. For others, it is the responsibility they feel toward their family and friends. Others find meaning in spirituality and religious practices. Some people find meaning in some of the above examples and others in all of them.

What about you? What makes you feel successful? Most people, like me, associate success with a healthy financial state and independence. If you are one of them, how would you like to manage that? By doing what? By founding your own company? Of what kind? Maybe climb up the ranks in your current company and get the best possible position on the floor? Maybe you want to get involved in real estate, either as a representative or as an investor? Maybe it is founding a huge team in the multi-level marketing company you work for and being rewarded for your leadership skills and the results of the meeting? Maybe it is to be a successful singer or an athlete? To go to the moon? To write a book? To open up an art gallery as a successful painter or a sculptor?

Maybe you are one of those people who do not associate success with their career or money but simply want to be happy. Maybe you want to travel the whole world and take pictures of cultures and places that few people have been to? To create a healthy family with two children running up and down the corridor and being at peace? To come to terms with yourself? To get rid of any unnecessary and annoying person in your life and only focus on those who really matter? Maybe you want to open up a restaurant by the sea and fish all day long with music, drinks and good company?

So what is that one thing that you desire and when you achieve it, you will say, "I did it!" ? What is that one thing that, after wandering in your mind for so long, you will finally say, "Yes, this is what I want, this is exactly what I want to do"? What is that one thing that if it came true, you would call all your friends and family to share your joy? What is that one thing you would post on Instagram a hundred times a day so that the whole world learns about it? What is that one thing for which you would turn the world upside down to achieve? What is that one thing that makes you feel free? What makes you proud and unique? What is that one thing for which you would jump into the fire to make a reality?

Whatever it is, if you are pursuing success but you have not defined it in your mind or on a piece of paper – even better – you will not go anywhere. There is no point in reading books about success or attending seminars if you do not know what success is for you. It is impossible to learn how to shoot if you do not have a clear goal in mind. There is no point in learning how to drive if you do not know where you are going.

So, start from there, from the purpose. Sit, read, search and find what you really want. When you find it, define it. Take your phone in your hands and write it down. Give shape to it. Analyze it, imagine it and describe it. In every detail. Do not get cheap on the ink. The more you write, the better. Take as much time as you want. Do not rush. Take as long as long as you need, until you find it.

## A FIRST IDEA

Let me be clear, once again, at this point that I am neither your father nor your partner. I will not explain to you how you will find your purpose because it is something that only you can do. It is personal.

Although, I am quite sure that if I do not give you one or two pointers, you will probably continue to the next chapter without having defined with certainty what your purpose is. You will continue to search for the meaning of life or ways to succeed and it will lead nowhere. Years will go by and you will be a part of the goals and aims of others. They will have the power to decide over your present and future. I will not allow that. I will do anything in my power to prevent this from happening.

In the previous chapters, I asked you to create a file on your phone and answer a few questions. I want you to continue doing it and you will understand later on why I am asking you to write things down.

Grab your phone and answer the following question:

3) Do I have a goal or is it all in vain?

**TIP 1**: If you do not have a goal, start by answering the following questions:
a) When was the last time you made time stop and stood still somewhere to wonder if your path is the one you want it to be? If your relationship
b) or your job are as you want them to be?
c) What makes you feel complete as a human? What is your passion? What is that one "thing" in which you know, deep inside, you could become No1 if the circumstances were right?
d) Who are the people in your life that you consider important and for what reason? Would you turn your goal into a reality for them or for someone else? Imagine that person and describe him or her.
e) What would you be willing to do NOW for yourself, if you were not afraid and if the obstacles you face did not exist?
f) Is there an obstacle that you cannot overcome?

**TIP 2**: It is extremely important to provide a detailed answer. Try to analyze it in at least 50–80 words.

Even here, I need you to be disciplined. The process of writing leaves marks on the course of all of us. On many occasions, you will find yourself not being able to recognize the thoughts you have written down. When I discovered the power of writing, my whole world changed. This is why I ask you to trust the process again. You will understand more later on.

For now, I want you to answer these questions, because your journey has just begun. Make sure you have everything packed up.

# Chapter 5
# Leadership Is a Matter of Attitude

I want you to pay attention to the following. When you have a purpose, it is as if you have a mission to accomplish. As if you have made a promise and you must keep it no matter what. As if you have a close-guarded secret. Once found, your purpose is the damn greatest thing in your heart and your mind. It is something that must be carried "out" and for that to happen, YOU are the one who must come "out" ahead.

What do I mean? To accomplish any purpose, goal, or whatever our perception of "success" is, first you need to change and become the kind of person who has everything it takes to make it. After that, you will make it indeed. That is where most people go wrong and that is the basis of the "Who I Am" philosophy.

*The goal you have set*
*will make you the leader you need to be.*

The importance and the necessity to achieve your goal will create the demand, from your own self, to become the person you need to be before you even become that person. Your goal and your journey up to it, the journey that will take you from nothing to everything will turn you into the person you want to be or the person you must be. The experience, the difficulties and the insecurities will turn you into the great leader you must become to achieve your goal. Your persistence, your patience, your discipline and your authority are some of the values that you will manage to develop along the way.

Your purpose itself will require you to become who you need to be in order to succeed, not the other way around. Your purpose will be the one in control. It will pick you up from the floor when you are tired, it will become your therapist when you are afraid, it will hug you and tell you to hang in there when you are disappointed and it will pull you out when you feel like you are drowning.

This is exactly the reason why difficulties are welcome on our way up to success. They are the ones that will give life to the leader within you. It will feel like riding a psychological roller coaster of horror and this is what will make you stronger and will toughen you up. This is what will help you develop your unique temperament, your self-confidence and your momentum. Difficulties will turn you into a great leader.

So do not be afraid of challenges. Accept them and keep that in mind.

*Don't be afraid of the challenges.*
*You'll either win, or you'll have a nice story to tell.*

You will not be considered a leader because you have people to follow you, but because you, yourself, follow your purpose no matter what. Because you lead yourself first in your effort to make a difference and then you lead everyone else. Because you demand to see the change in yourself first and then in everyone else. Because you refuse to go back and you refuse to negotiate. Because you do not look around and you stick to your goal no matter what, even when no one is watching.

Keep that in mind, because you are not a leader only when you are at work or only when there are people around you. If you want to be a leader, you must build habits with which you will be consistent even when you are alone and at ease.

If you have a clear purpose in mind and faith in it, you can create cities, change regimes or bring down governments. You can build a future for yourself and your family and get to "success," whatever that means to you. Your purpose itself has the power to turn you into the kind of person you need to be to make it. It can turn you into a leader.

With no purpose in mind, I regret to tell you that you will be someone temporary and meaningless.

### The "Who I Am" Philosophy

Having read all these books, from John Maxwell to Dale Carnegie, from the story of Mac Donald's to Elon Musk's, from the manufacture of Nike shoes and the stories of many more people who have left their mark, let me emphasize that leadership is only a matter of who you are or who you become. All of the above people had one thing in common: a vision. A purpose.

I will be honest with you. None of them was the same person at the beginning of their journey as at the end. All of them had to adjust their priorities, change their habits and evaluate their beliefs all over again for the sake of their purpose. At the same time, they made sure to maintain the same values and principles at every stage of their life, without separating professional from personal. They were the same person in both fields.

That is the main principle of the "Who I Am" philosophy. Based on what "success" means to you, the philosophy focuses on who you need to be to make it. What kind of leader you need to become and what your principles should be. It is based on whether you are one of those people who stand out of the crowd and you are a source of inspiration and creation or one of those people whose words are bigger than their actions. There will be a clear-out. History has proved that this is what happens.

The aim of the philosophy is to help those who will decide to follow it to realize what their habits and beliefs are and to re-evaluate them taking one thing for granted: their goal, or purpose if you will. The rest is a way already paved.

The six following Core Principles of the philosophy are based exclusively on developing your own principles for leadership. These principles are crucial when it comes to the "Who I Am" philosophy.

## The Six Core Principles of the "Who I Am" Philosophy

History has shown that people do not decide to follow leaders based on what they say but mostly on what they stand for, and their vision.

The most typical example of that was Hitler. When he first talked about the reasons that, according to him, led Germany to the difficult financial situation around 1930, how ashamed they were of their loss in World War I, and the lack of trust in the government, people disagreed with him at first. Soon though, he managed to talk them around thanks to his passion and his belief in what he said. He talked in a way that transformed peoples' reality, he twisted the facts and more and more people supported him. Hitler was a gifted speaker with exceptional intelligence and situational awareness of the situation at the time. He is, in my opinion, the most typical example of a leader who no matter what he talked about, he was the man behind his own words.

Hitler meant every word that came out of his mouth because that was his only truth. His only reality. And you can see that from the expression on his face and the passion that his words had every time he spoke. Not even one tiny sign of doubt or insecurity. He managed to create the German Empire (if you can call it that way) because he was by 100% authentic. The world, undoubtedly supported him because of his belief, his courage and his nerve, leaving aside the fact he was one of the most obnoxious people who have ever lived.

The latter would be proved later on when his authority was over and most of the people who had supported him "woke up" and took back their opinion about Nazism. This means that Hitler's influence faded away and his words were considered banned. It was his leadership skills that had influenced people who, at that point, needed to believe in someone. And something.

Of course, the fact that access to information was not as easy as it is today made things easier for him. Back then, people thought that Hitler's vision of a great Germany was the only reality that "made sense," no matter what it would take to turn this vision into a reality. Nowadays, in the fast way that information and knowledge in general, travels worldwide, I would not be surprised if that same man was an object of ridicule on Twitter or social media in general.

At this point, let me make something clear: I am not a fan of him. I do not even support a political party or a sect and I keep my distance from any political or religious belief. Not only for the sake of this book, but this goes to my real life too. The examples I use, whether someone likes them or not, are only used because I want to show the meaning hidden behind the examples themselves. Any kind of leadership is no longer considered to be leadership when deaths, tortures, or any other cruel attitude against humankind takes place.

People though support those who believe in one particular vision and there is no doubt that this was the case with Hitler as well.

### How Is a Leader Chosen

Throughout the years that I have been training salesmen, managers and leaders in general, I have always set one rule: "See things from the perspective of the one looking at you." In this way, I triggered their minds to "see" things from a perspective outside of their own reality and identity.

Listeners do not decide if they are going to support you or not based on whether the expectations they have from a leader are fulfilled while watching you. They decide to support you based on two needs. The first one is what you make them feel. How you trigger their *emotional* world. This derives only from the level at which you believe in your vision and from how passionately you get your message across. The second one is their *rationality*, which means that they judge if what you say is in accordance with their data and their truth. The two are not mutually exclusive, but since according to Dale Carnegie, people are creatures of emotion, the way you express your idea is more important than the idea itself.

So, if you take some distance and look at yourself, what are the traits you would like to see in you in order to support you? What are the traits you should have to become an attractive leader?

1. Leaders lead themselves, which makes them authentic, honest, self-confident and with integrity.
2. They are sure about their destination and have a clear goal in mind.
3. They have great communication skills and great use of the language.
4. They have high levels of energy.
5. They back up everything they say with actions that are easily accessible to a wide audience.
6. They know that they never stop developing and are based on data and personal experiences.

My experience in training people has shown me that the main traits you will love in yourself and that will make you support yourself are these 6 Core Principles of the "Who I Am" philosophy. Before you move on, hang a banner somewhere in your place so that you can read it again and again:

*It's not important what you do,*
*but who you are while you do it.*

### 1st Core Principle

A leader leads himself first.

It all starts and ends with you. It is about how you lead your own self. Who you *are* and what you do when you are alone. What your habits, your thoughts, your beliefs and your actions are when no one is watching.

Most people believe that what they do or what they do not do when they are not supposed to demonstrate their skills in leadership is not important. They think that what they need to do is only to set an example when they have to. It is a big trap. What they really need to do is to constantly set the example, simply because, sooner or later, the truth about who they are will be revealed one way or another. No one can escape their true self.

Take the example of a marketing and sales office that I visited in May 2020 in Greece. I met a manager who whenever talked to his team, talked about leadership, strength, determination and self-confidence. However, when we went to the meeting room to discuss, I realized that I had in front of me a quite insecure young man. He was not a leader when he left the office. He was like a scared child, his self-esteem was low and he had bad habits, such as smoking weed, having few social interactions, poor education on how he should treat the opposite sex and so on. Nevertheless, he spoke to his team about values such as vigor, nerve and respect.

I cannot help laughing.

His team had the worst performance in the company, as I found out later because none of the members of his team respected him. The reason for that was that he asked his team to have all the traits that would bring them to success, but he was far from having these traits. This is why the members of his team did not believe him and did not respect him.

Being able to lead yourself means that you represent at the highest level what you talk about in public. You need to represent the strength and the vigor everywhere and not only whenever you find it easy to do so. You need to have the right habits, the right beliefs and the right attitude before you ask to see that in others. The leader needs to completely come from within you, with modesty and honesty. You need to be the leader of yourself without making any compromises.

*If you can't lead yourself,
you are not worth leading anyone.*

Many people get confused and think that leadership is only about managing a group of people. I am sorry that you have to hear that from me, but you cannot be a leader only when you want to be one. You are a leader at any moment. You are a leader when you make everyday decisions, when you follow your daily routine, in your professional and personal life, when you are at work, when you play football with your friends and when the weather is sunny or rainy.

Be the leader of yourself. If you say that you will do something, do it. When you set a goal, make sure that it is realistic and achieve it, no matter if others will achieve it or not. When you are asked to do something, do more than what is enough. When you are scared of something, confront it even if no one is around. When you are bored, move. Maybe no one will learn about it, but you need to move anyway. When you have expectations from others, first you need to show them how it is done.

Evaluate your values. Know what your values are and stand for them. This is where a leader's integrity is based on. In fact, the extent to which you stand for your values when no one is watching is where you will be able to tell the difference between the person you are and the person you need to become.

**Self-respect.** Respect yourself first. Take care of yourself and protect yourself from any meaningless or offensive threat. Be mindful about who you spend time with, which media you spend your gray matter on and how you spend your free time. Be mindful of how much you take care of yourself, what you eat, how much you sleep, how much you exercise and the way you talk. If you do not respect yourself, you do not respect anyone else.

**Responsibility.** The only person responsible for what is going on in your environment, in your present and your future, is you. By accusing others of something that has happened to you shows a cowardly person who is afraid to take any responsibility. No one has the power to affect your present, but you. This is one of my main principles. What is sad is that I rarely meet people who have the same way of thinking. There are not many people who have the stomach to take full responsibility for their actions. If you do not admit your own mistakes, then you release yourself from your own responsibility, and thus, it is charged to someone else. Not only will you get off lightly, but you will also remain the same and will not make any progress whatsoever. You will be remembered as a loser.

**Action.** Demand from yourself to take action in a way that no one else does. It is only through action that you can get results. Rambling ideas that you might be listening to or, even worse, you might be saying, cannot replace even the tiniest action. Act to the extent that you will be judged as someone who is "too much" or obsessed with something. Act as if this is the last chance you will ever get.

**Results.** Demand from yourself to see the results. Learn and then teach that action itself is not enough. It is one thing to take action and another to complete a task. Most people care about the hours they spend working on something, while what they should care about is if they can see the results after all these hours. This is why they are in the same position for years, while others climb up the corporate ladder.

**Motivating.** I could send you an email with hundreds of examples that prove that people wait for someone or something that will motivate them to take action or take a step forward. All these people have one thing in common: they lack the self-confidence it takes to move forward. They are afraid that they might be wrong. Those who will take a step forward are those who have a stronger will and know that, in any case, they have nothing to lose.

**Integrity.** You need to have integrity. Your integrity is defined by the extent to which you stand for your beliefs and to what extent you negotiate or sacrifice them. Integrity is defined by the extent to which you stand for your beliefs at any moment.

Be the leader of yourself first. Do not expect others to respect you if you do not respect yourself. Only if you set the example for an action, an idea, or a situation, will others be willing to support you. Only if you run towards a specific direction first, will others be willing to follow you. Your speed and your vigor are what will define the quality of your followers.

In case you are not the person you need to be, then become that person. This is the aim of this book: to help you discover who you are and where you are heading and to become mindful of the former. No matter what your age, your financial or social situation is, you can always change your habits and become the leader that you would follow as well. It is never too late to achieve great things in life. It is never too late to become the person you want to be. It is never too late to become a leader.

You can become anyone you want to become. The only thing you have to do is to make your choice.

## 2nd Core Principle

A leader is his purpose.

This is the most important part of leadership. Ambition is important, but it is not enough. Your purpose is just as important as every breath you take. You can tell how important it is for you if you wake up or go to bed having your purpose in mind and thinking of ways to achieve it. Compromising for anything less than that, whatever the factors may be, shows cowardice and disrespect to the purpose itself. The greater your purpose is, the more important it is for you to achieve it and the greater leader you seem to be.

You need to understand that people, by nature, tend to follow others. Since the dawn of our species, people followed people. People followed Kings, Rulers, tribe Leaders, etc. Even nowadays, there are such examples. Shall we mention the devotion of some people to their religion? Shall we mention the devotion of some people to political leaders? To sects? To sales teams? People, regardless of the period of time, have always looked for someone who would be able to lead the way and with whom they would be able to share the journey. People have always needed to follow someone.

The criteria by which they choose who they will follow are very strict and, in most cases, a subconscious choice. More often than not though, the only criterion is who inspires them the most. As mentioned above, this is something that cannot be perceived based on reason. People choose to follow those who stimulate their emotions, those who fire their imagination and can lead them to unknown paths. They choose the leaders who will make them feel as excited as a kid listening to a great fairy tale.

Followers, even without realizing it, will take into account the extent to which leaders trust their vision, their nerve, their strength, their honesty, their modesty and how much they want it. Followers will support leaders who fully represent what they stand for, without doubts or second thoughts. At the end of the day, a leader who has not a purpose of vital importance in mind is nothing but an ordinary human.

Once, during a three-day personal development conference I attended in Budapest, I heard that "leadership is a straight line." This was told by the great Marc Accetta, Director of Training in the multi-level marketing company I was a member of. What does it mean? Simply that you are the beginning and the end of leadership. You are the one to set your purpose and the one who defines how great the need to achieve this purpose is. The greater the need, the greater the longing to keep on track no matter what. You should not deviate even slightly from your purpose, whatever the reason, the facts, the excuses, the steps back, your fear, or your insecurities. Any kind of procrastination or compromise is not an option. The only thing that matters is the result and that is it.

*No limit can stop the urge of a man with a purpose.*

On the morning of June 1st, 2018, I walked into the meeting room to meet the sales team I was managing. I saw five people with their heads down as on the previous day we had failed to achieve an important goal we had set. By looking into their eyes, I could tell how disappointed and exhausted they were, as we had all made a huge effort.

I walked in feeling strong and self-confident. After yelling at them for being so disappointed, I set the goal for the current month even higher and increased it by 20% comparing it to the one we had the previous one. Why? Because I did not doubt that we could make it.

Everyone stood still and stared at me confused. I am sure they thought I was a "dreamer," a "jerk" or whatever a mind full of imagination, like theirs, can think of. If they had the choice – because of course there is not such an option in a team of that caliber – they would have left the room immediately.

"Spyros, we did not even manage to achieve the previous goal. How the hell will we be able to achieve the new one?"

"I agree, Spyros. We are already exhausted and have gone beyond ourselves. We achieved things that, until recently, were beyond our imagination, even if we did not achieve the goal itself. That is as far as we can get, for real."

"We've made it so far because we promised that we would do everything possible to make it. The goal is hard according to objective criteria, but whether we can achieve it or not is something to be discussed according to subjective criteria. I have never seen anyone else trying so hard to achieve a goal as we did. Yesterday, we worked until 10:00 in the evening trying, but we failed. This time we are setting our goal and we WILL achieve it before the end of the month."

At this point, they had their heads down again. Not only had we failed to achieve the goal of the previous month, not only had I increased the current goal by 20%, but I had also asked them to achieve the goal before the end of the month to be sure that we would not fail once again.

I was so determined that I reminded them of the goal at every opportunity. Every single day in every single one of our meetings, either as a group or individually, was to remind them of the goal we had set. I did that for the whole month, every single day. Even on Sundays, I would "steal" a couple of hours from their day off to have a quick training, before they went to the beach and the coffee shops. The goal was the only thought I had when I woke up or when I went to bed. Once, I had food delivered to my office and I told our goal to the guy who had brought it. Everyone laughed. They had got the point.

Five days before the end of the month we managed to achieve our goal. In a spirit of celebration and excitement, everyone understood that any goal, big or small, is achievable as long as you really (really) want it. We were all over the moon and we could not stop joking around. It was a great day.

Until I called everyone in the meeting room once again.

"Congratulations, everyone. We have achieved our goal. We have covered the extra 20% of the previous month, five days before the month's ends. Well done! How do you feel about it?"

"I'm pumped! (Well, he didn't say the word "pumped")"

"I still cannot believe it!"

"That's nice. We have five more days left until the end of the month. The goal is now increased by another 20%!"

Everyone stood still. They could not believe I had just said that.

"What are you talking about? Are you insane?" asked someone who always shared his opinion.

"Are we at the top?" I asked.

"No, we aren't," one of them replied.

"If we get that extra 20%, will we be at the top?"

"For sure," said someone else.

"Great. So the goal is increased by 20%."

And I left the room.

Five minutes later, all of them went out of the room and it was obvious they were upset and angry. I waited to see their reactions. Ten minutes later, I asked everyone to go back to the meeting room. I do not remember what exactly I told them, but I am sure it was about how much I trusted our potential, how much I believed that we could make it and a great vision: to be the best team. The newest team in the company and the most successful one.

On June 29 of that year, at 5:00 in the afternoon, our team achieved its goal. A goal that led us to the top of the company's rank and we have never looked back since then.

I know that I pushed them to their limits, I exhausted them, they were angry at me and maybe some of them hated me for that. I yelled at them again and again and I kept pushing them, but I never took a step back. We had agreed that I would push them as much as it would be needed to reach our goal. I knew we could make it and I knew that we would. I believed it could happen and so did everyone else.

Of course, there were moments when my trust faded away for a moment. It will happen to you too and it is justified by our nature. However, even if you leave your path for a moment, it should only be for a good reason: to take a deep breath, clear your mind, see the big picture and go back more determined than ever. There will be days when you will feel depressed, regretful, scared, or disappointed, but you need to remember your purpose and how great it is, and get back on track. You need to bring back your action plan and keep implementing it from where you left it without further ado.

Read carefully this one: as long as you keep on track, which means that all of your actions bring you one step closer to your purpose, you have nothing to worry about. You will have a difficult time and you will find many obstacles on the way, but it is your attitude toward all these that will define your future. Have a positive attitude towards any problem that might come up, deal with it and move on.

As you have already read in the previous pages:

*Our actions define the magnitude of our needs.*

If at this point, you still do not have a clear purpose in mind, I would recommend you to review and complete Question 3 on your phone. If you keep moving forward without a purpose in mind, you will go where people who have one take you.

The greatest leaders were obsessed with their purpose. Most of them were questioned, but if you think about it, there is nothing wrong with being obsessed with something. Those who disagree are the ones who did not make it or those who needed much more time to make it. Being obsessed with something means to keep trying even when it seems to be foolish and meaningless to do so. Even when people make fun of you or think you are fixated on your dream. Being obsessed with an ultimate purpose is healthy, within the boundaries of common sense, of course. Your obsession is what will help you endure difficulties and what will prevent you from taking a step back.

### 3rd Core Principle

A leader is his communication skills.

Imagine that: you have discovered the drug for eternal youth. Who will know if you do not speak about it?

From my experience, the biggest challenge that those who want to create something big have to face is to communicate their plan and their vision to people. It seems to be extremely challenging for a manager to keep finding ways to motivate the members of the team to get the job done faster, without distractions. It seems to be extremely challenging for couples to figure things out when a problem comes up.

The unpleasant truth is that people do not want to communicate because they do not know how to do it.

You can find books on why and how you should be able to communicate effectively, but this book is not one of them. Regardless of how communicative I might be, it will take a whole book to explain. Since I have not even started writing that yet, I will provide you with the two main rules you need to follow to be a good interlocutor.

## 1) KNOW HOW TO LISTEN

Keep in mind that showing respect to others is quite important, even in communication. This means that it is one thing to listen to someone because you just want to say your opinion afterward and another to listen to someone because you want to get their point. Getting the point, to my mind, means "to be willing to resolve any issue," which means that you respect the other's opinion and you have the will to resolve any small or big issue. Even if you disagree with them and all you want to do is to interrupt them and say your opinion.

Keep in mind that if you know how to listen, you are open to receiving any kind of new information, thus knowledge, to process it and then to decide if you agree or not. Most people prefer talking over listening as they believe that their opinion is the correct one. In this way though, they block any piece of new information and with that, they block knowledge and progress too.

Without mutual understanding, there cannot be a solution to a problem and without solutions, there cannot be progress. And guess what, without progress, there cannot be success no matter how badly you may want it.

For me, my skill to listen is one of my main strengths. I believe that when people talk to me, they see their mirrored selves in me. This has proved to be helpful both when it comes to personal relationships and at work, since I can understand what people need and most importantly, who they are. Once I know who they are, I can immediately understand what they want. This process is always the first exercise I use in every training sales course in my company. I would call it a precious technique which is the only one that can provide me with what I want.

## 2) KNOW HOW TO SPEAK

Regardless if you are at work or home, your speaking skills are the ones that will shape the result. If you can put your thoughts and your beliefs in words in the right way, the other party will follow you even to hard paths. Only a few people know how to do that because most people are satisfied with the way they already speak and do not try to make any further progress.

You should never think that you speak in the best possible way. There are numerous courses, videos and books that can develop your speaking skills. If you aim high when it comes to your personal life or your career, how you express what you need, the words you say, your tonality and the way you use them are of vital importance.

All the leaders who have ever been, have always presented their vision and their needs in well-thought-out means of expression which could convince even those who strongly disagreed. So keep in mind that if you want to convince others about your vision and your trust in it, finding a proper way to express yourself is the key to showing why it is so important to achieve your purpose. This is the only way in which you will be able to inspire and motivate people. This is the only way in which you will be able to show who you are and what you are capable of.

Great leaders are aware of the fact that communication is the way to bridge the gap between opposing situations. Leaders are aware of the fact that by listening carefully to the opposing argument, their skill to understand such arguments is further developed. This skill is the one used when differences are resolved or negative influences are eliminated in the cycle of action. Either in professional or personal life, there is not a single disagreement that cannot be resolved with a nice conversation, after having carefully listened to one another.

After understanding what the opposing side needs, leaders have the skill to motivate their followers by providing them with new ideas and new approaches. They have the skill to make their followers feel excited, encourage them and congratulate them. Through communication, leaders can form stronger bonds, smile and show that they are proud of everyone around them. They can announce new leaders, train and stand for their beliefs. They can express their emotions, convince the indecisive ones, eliminate any form of doubt, make interpersonal relationships stronger, resolve misunderstandings and form relationships based on trust and mutual respect. Communication has the power to provide the solution to such problems and bridge any gap. Leaders know that there is no other way to do that.

*If you're not connected, you're disconnected.*

Even if it sounds difficult, leaders always find ways to develop their communication skills. They know that *the way* you say something is more important than *what* you say. They know that they should stand as an example of self-confidence, integrity and strength while speaking or when they have a discussion. They know that the way they stand, the tonality of their voice and their vibe are much more important than the content of their words. Jordan Belfort in his book *The Way of The Wolf* analyzes the significance of the way we speak. Read this book and you will find out about things that have never crossed your mind.

To sum up, communication is the greatest skill you have as a leader. The more developed and well-thought-out the way you speak and communicate, the more followers you will gain, the stronger the bond between you will be and the more connected they will feel with what you are looking for.

It is worth mentioning that 20–30% of leaders' time is devoted to social networking. This is the only way to boost your business connections, which are important not only because you can get inspired from them, but also because you can inspire them too, promote your products and form more intimate human relationships. The so-called networking defines how expanded your influence is. And guess what, the more developed communication skills you have, the more expanded your influence.

I read somewhere that "Your network is your net worth." With the right connections and acquaintances, you can reach the moon. There are no limits. Communication is your biggest ally.

**4th Core Principle**

A leader is his energy.

This principle has always been the Achilles' Heel of many potential leaders. And the reason is that they never actually believed in the value of energy while leading. They believe that the content of a lecture or a speech is more important than the way it is communicated. It is quite difficult to find leaders with this trait in the market but it is exactly the one trait that defines how expanded a leader's influence is.

I want you to put your feet in the shoes of a member of any team. Imagine that you have just been hired and it is your first day in the company. You are in the meeting room with your team and, once you have all met each other, the manager comes in. A manager is a person that the whole team must trust and depend on to bring the desired results. A manager is a person you must follow faithfully, with no doubt, showing respect and modesty.

Imagine that one of the two following managers comes in:

The first one walks slowly, steadily, shoulders falling down and lowered eyes. He or she seems weak and loose and does not smile a lot, maybe not at all. They are one of those people who almost always drag their feet across the floor because they had been sleeping until just before they entered the room or because they cannot lift the burden of their own souls. They pull up a chair and sit down slowly.

I want you to wonder:

What feeling do you get when looking at this manager?

How effectively can this manager motivate you?

How willing and motivated do you feel?

The second manager walks into the room, stops right away, looks every single person in the room in the eyes and says while smiling, "Good morning, team!" Standing up straight, with eyes projecting confidence, giving the idea that they own the whole company. They move fast toward their chair and sit down in an aligned position keeping their eyes at the same level as yours.

I want you to wonder again:

What feeling do you get when looking at this manager?

How effectively can this manager motivate you?

How willing and motivated do you feel?

Which one would you follow at the end of the day?

Your choice –I hope that it is the second one, otherwise this might be the reason why you fall asleep while working – is based on the energy of each one of these managers. Their influence fully depends on the energy they have and thus, they give off. This is because the content of words gets a different meaning depending on the energy of each speaker.

It is one thing for your manager to be an ordinary employee and another for your manager to be a boss.

*Your energy walks inside the room before you do.*

I do not want to focus too much on the importance of energy right now, so I will put it as simply as I can. Dale Carnegie in his book *How to Win Friends and Influence People* wrote, "*When dealing with people, remember you are not dealing with creatures of logic, but creatures of emotion.*" That means that more often than not, our choices are based on the way people make us feel. For example, if someone is dull, you get the same negative feeling. If someone is sad, you get that feeling too. If someone is smiling, you get a positive feeling and the same goes for self-confidence.

People choose their leaders based on the way they make them feel. The more powerful your attitude is, the more you will influence others. To put it simply, your energy, your way to express yourself, the way you walk, the volume of your voice, your smile and your body posture are only a few of the things that form your energy and allow people to decide if they are going to follow you or someone else. Based on the above, people will choose you or someone stronger instead.

When action and influence are a priority for leaders, then it is impossible to find either of them without power, passion and strength. People, even if they do not admit it sometimes, need to see a positive attitude in others. Leaders should passionately trust their purpose and communicate it in a way hard to be perceived by untrained ears. Leaders should inspire people to be productive and happy, they should inspire action and response, progress and diversity.

Besides, if you love something and you want to work on it, you will understand that the energy you give off and your actions are proportionate to your passion for that. Great things cannot be achieved without passion, and thus, without the right energy.

Tonight, watch a speech of a politician talking to hundreds of citizens. Watch the way they talk. Watch how they stress certain points, how they inspire people and how they seem to be addressing each one of us separately. Watch how they stand as an example of power and determination, vision and action. Do not worry too much about the fact that he or she is a politician or about the content of the speech. Just take it as an example of how things work. In fact, politicians have been trained in public speaking, in the body posture they should have and in using the right words to make their audience feel in a specific way. We might as well say that they have turned public speaking into a form of art. That is why they manage to convince us and we keep voting for them.

Leaders' vibes can also be shaped by their sense of humor. A good sense of humor shows self-confidence and, trust me, people who have a sense of humor are more attractive personalities than those who do not. Personally, I constantly use humor because I enjoy it myself and because this is my way to balance the pressure I put on people in my working environment.

As for those who never smile and only Eddy Murphy's humor would make them laugh, I can only say that they are boring, not only at work but in their lives in general. I cannot help laughing when I think of their partners and how miserable lives they must lead.

*The funniest people are the ones
who have no sense of humor.*

Nowadays, smiles and laughs can be hard to find, especially if you watch TV, which I do not. If you want to become a leader though, the energy you give off must be the most important thing. Without it, you will not be able to lead yourself or anyone else. Without it, you will not be able to take a single step forward.

**5th Core Principle**

A leader is his results.

And here we come to the most critical rule. Theory is good to know, but putting theory into practice is totally different. We will discuss this principle in detail, but let me make a short introduction.

Words have never fed anyone who was hungry. Theories and nonsense did not create any city and any empire. They gained none of Muhammad Ali's many victories, they built none of Dubai's skyscrapers, neither Steve Jobs' iPhones nor Ibrahimović's goals. Great leaders, whether working independently or in a team, prove their value through their results, regardless of the greatness and the power of the action. Leaders act daily, as fast as needed to achieve the desired results, having one purpose: to complete every single task.

Do you want me to be more straightforward? Let's do this.

Humans, by nature, always focus on the action itself, ignoring the result. They satisfy their need to complete a task, by focusing on "hard" work. Action, however, is a subjective condition, because there can be no measure of comparison as to which is good or bad, little, or enough. My perception of fast and good action is different than yours. I might think that action means sending 50 emails a day to promote my business and you might think that it means sending 20 emails.

Our difference lies in the fact that your goal is to send 20 emails a day, hoping that you will arrange some meetings and then close one deal. If you arrange no meetings, you will assume that you were not lucky that day and you will try again the next one.

My goal is to make one deal a week. To do this, I know I will have to arrange at least 10 meetings during the week. I also know that to arrange these 10 meetings I will have to send 20 emails a day.

There is one exception to that. If 3–4 days go by and I have not arranged at least 7–8 meetings, I will then increase the number of emails I send in order to have 10 meetings arranged.

For example, if I have scheduled 10 meetings, I just need to close a deal only with one of them to have the weekly deal I want. If I have arranged 5 meetings instead of 10, I have the half chances, so I will have to try twice as hard during the meeting.

In conclusion, most people focus on the action itself and not on the result of this action. They focus on the amount of work they do without caring about the actual outcome. Knowing they have worked hard satisfies them and allows them to sleep at night. Sometimes, they reward themselves for their hard work and make sure they find satisfaction in that. For them, seeing results is not important.

"Honey! I am home!"

"Welcome home, baby! How was your work today?"

"Well, it was a very busy day! I ended up having eight meetings with potential new clients."

"Good job, baby! And how many deals did you close?"

"None."

"Well, if you do not close any deal by the end of the month, you will get paid the basic salary, won't you?"

"Well… yeah… But I tried, though!"

Some people might think, "Well, he did try, what else could he have done?" and someone else might think, "Fine, since you tried and you are satisfied with it, do not whine about the increase of the cost of electricity bill because some people, *tried* to lower its price, but they did not make it. They tried, though."

Well, you know I am a bit sarcastic, so do not get upset. But as I said before, this is how the vast majority of people act. Do not worry. I was like that too, until I realized I was working my butt off but I still I did not get the result I wanted. And that was because I did not focus on the result that hard work was supposed to bring me. I used to focus on the fact that I had to work. That was what I had been taught, by the coaches, by all the books I had read (except for one or two maybe), and by almost every seminar I had attended about action. I had been taught to act, but I was not told about the importance of the results.

However, I find it somewhat selfish to have the skills but find an excuse not to use them to the fullest. Especially when you have to take care of your family. It is completely unacceptable when you can, but you do not do it, because you think it is beyond your limits. It isn't. You, I and the whole world are destined to achieve great things. We have been made out of materials that make us able to move forward, create people and achieve great things. Sounds a bit cliché but it's the truth.

Action is no longer my goal. My goal is the result. In the above example, I do not care about how many emails I will have to send. Even if I have to send 50 emails and then 50 follow-ups, my goal is to book 10 meetings and close at least 1 deal. Even if I have to do this twice a day, that is to send 100 emails, I will do it. Because my goal is to arrange 10 meetings that I know, will get me at least 1 deal. This is where my money will come from. This is what will shape my present, my future and my overall success.

*Action is subjective.*
*Your results are your true judge.*

As you will read further down, I am a big fan of a phrase I said back in 2018: "Everything begins at the finish line." Not only will you read a full analysis and where it comes from, but it also is one of the main foundations the "Who I Am" philosophy is based on. So, when you start working on a project, regardless of the nature of the project, the location, or anything else, always start with what you want to produce over a certain period of time. If you want to arrange 10 meetings a day for next week, it is not about how many emails you will have to send. The thing is to achieve your goal of arranging "10 meetings per day." Keep that in mind. Focus on that.

If you do not focus on the results, you will focus on the amount of action instead. And no one ever got paid for working hard. We get paid based on the results.

## 1) HAVE A PLAN

Williams sisters, some of the greatest tennis players ever, have expressed it in the best way: "If you fail to plan, you plan to fail."

Everything is the result of how great your actions are. Every action is the result of a well-thought plan that you know is the best possible, the fastest and the least consuming one. It is your strategy to success. It is the chessboard on which you put your pawns and get ready to attack.

Your plan should also include possible dangers, advantages and disadvantages, a schedule, market tendencies, competitors and the first steps. All these form several tasks you are expected to perform and with every task you complete, you get closer to your goal.

What I need to do first, is to specify the result I want to get once I do everything I have planned. If we take the above-mentioned case as an example, I might want to close one deal per week, no matter what. Taking my capacities into consideration, I know that this can happen if I arrange ten meetings during that week. I also know that if I want to arrange ten meetings in a week, I need to send fifty emails. This is my main plan for this task.

As I have already stressed, if at some point I realize that I am about to arrange five meetings instead of ten, then I am expected to increase the efficiency of the follow-ups and send twice as many emails daily. The goal here is not to send emails, but to close deals.

In their rush to succeed, people act without making a plan or research first. Thus, their actions are usually clumsy and have no impact. Sometimes, they find themselves facing problems that they should have predicted. They bang their head on the wall and then, they fail.

In these cases, it is the wall that takes the fall and the problem is the reason why they failed. Or at least, this is what people believe. However, if you think about it, if they had made a complete plan beforehand, the problem would still be there, but they would have been able to overcome it.

At least now, they have a bump on their heads to remind them of their past and of the 1st Core Principle of the "Who I Am" philosophy shouting at them via a megaphone that "leaders lead themselves first."

## 2) EXECUTE IT

It might sound silly, but 95% of those who set a plan do not put it into action at 100%. Most people take the trouble to make a plan but fail to put it into action. Why? Because they lack the discipline to do so. Or maybe because they choose to spend their time on something else or because they do not believe in it.

You develop a strategy to put it into action in every detail. Do not deviate even slightly from the plan as every time you do so, continuation is interrupted and so is its effectiveness. In fact, you will have to work twice as hard to get back on track and this might make you want to quit. Also, keep in mind that if you deviate once, you will do so again in the future. This is why discipline is so important.

If I close one deal per week and according to my initial plan, I have to send fifty emails per day to arrange ten meetings, then I will have to stick to it. The plan might show me where my system goes wrong and what I should change. For example, if fifty emails are not enough, I will have to send one hundred. If I also have meetings throughout the day, then I will have to redefine my plan because there are only 24 hours in a day. One idea would be to hire someone to send the emails instead of me.

*Sticking to a plan is more important*
*than the plan itself.*

It should also be noted that you should follow the plan even when you feel that you "are not in the mood today." Besides, this is the definition of "discipline." You cannot, for instance, send fifty emails in the first couple of days but then send only thirty because you have other things to do. What can be more important to you than closing one deal per week? If you fail to close the deal, then you will have to "close" yourself too. This means that you have to send fifty emails per day come rain or shine.

If you absolutely need to work on something else for a while, it does not mean that you will consider your plan to send emails as canceled. You will just have to postpone it for a while until you complete the other task, even if that means that you will have to work overtime. It is important to follow your plan in detail and consistently.

## 3) CELEBRATE SMALL WINS

Your plan should also include the achievement of small wins that will remind you that you are moving forward. This is as important as the breaths you take, for every small task that is completed has the power to make you believe even more that your plan is effective and that you are one step closer to its completion. Small wins greatly boost your satisfaction and thus, your self-confidence.

From my experience, I can tell that every time I completed a task, either big or small, I got the feeling that I had carried out something and that I had taken a step forward toward the completion of my goal. My self-confidence was boosted and I felt so satisfied that I was addicted to completing the next tasks. No motivational video or speech can make me feel stronger, more patient and more integral than the results of my own actions.

This is the reason why part of my role as a leader is to "push" the members of my team to bring the results that both parties want. I am aware of the fact that they will not push themselves as much as it is needed to succeed. I have been there and I too was pushed by another manager to bring the desired results. It is human nature.

Of course, this should be done in the right way and with the right practices. You should be conscious before you "push" and judge objectively being aware of the limits of each person. This is one of the most important skills managers should have and this is what defines their success and the success of their teams. A great leader and a great manager know that:

*Nothing and no one has the power to boost your self-confidence more than the results of your own actions.*

That's a law!

The time has come for you to learn something that few people know. Based on the above-mentioned, the fastest way to become as self-confident as you have always wanted is to complete your tasks and fulfill your goals. The results you see though depend on the *rate* and the *quantity* of your actions. This means that your productivity depends on these two factors. The more productive you become – meaning the more results you bring –, the more self-confident you become. The more self-confident you become, the longer you will be productive.

Let's face it, most people stop trying if they do not see the desired results after a while, they quit.

People who act slowly and/or produce a little are less likely to carry out a task than people who act fast and/or produce a lot.

Those who belong to the first group feel as if they take action, but they cannot see the result. They feel that they do their best but still, the results are less than what they would expect. This makes them doubt their skills and their plan. It makes them believe that they cannot make it, so they stop. They give in and they quit.

Those who belong to the second group are empowered by how productive they are. They constantly see the results that their actions bring and their self-confidence is boosted in no time. They can tell that they achieve their goals and this is perceived as a success by their subconscious. Once they experience it, they will keep longing for it because:

> *The satisfaction we get once we achieve a goal*
> *is the greatest driving force on our way to success.*

Imagine two friends who decide to start working out together, on the same day. In the first week, they both go to the gym three times. In the second week, one of them goes to the gym three times and the other one, only once. In the third week, one of them goes to the gym three times and the other one, not even once. Who do you think will keep working out and why?

The first one, of course. Because at the end of the third week, he or she will start seeing the results, while the other one will not. The second one will fail to believe that he or she can "build" the body of their dreams since they will not see any results at the end of the third week. Even if the second one keeps going to the gym once a week, the first one might start going to the gym even more often because of the progress he or she might see and with that, he or she might spend more hours there and follow a more challenging workout plan.

Six months later, it will be quite easy to see the difference between the two. The first one will get "shredded" and the second one will put the blame on his girlfriend.

This is what I call "Aggressive action." It is the action we take when we have no opponents. The action that is so fast and so overwhelming that it is the dominant one and it brings so many results so fast that you will be unable to count. Aggressive action will make you seem as if you are on fire and will make you different from everyone else.

If you want to become a great football player, go the training one hour earlier than everyone else and leave one hour later. If you aim at shining as a real estate agent, arrange twice as many meetings as everyone else. If you are at a multi-level (or network) marketing company, follow the principles of your company, speed up and arrange twice as many meetings per day as the most successful colleague of yours. If you own a business and want to make it widely known, hire a professional and pay them as much as is needed to get as many clients as possible. If you aim at becoming a famous singer, then do three rehearsals a week and play twice as many gigs as the best singer in town.

Make aggressive action a part of *who you are*. Take so radical actions that will make those who have no clue about what you do talk about you. Take ten times more actions than anyone else. Get to a point where you will have to pay people to complete your daily tasks. Act as if the whole world is looking at you. Leaders who are determined to win and have nothing else in mind but the achievement of their goal act way more than anyone else. They are addicted to carrying out tasks and when everyone else acts twice, they act ten times. When everyone else is asleep, they make plans and when everyone else is awake and starts thinking about what to do, they put their plan into action. When everyone else sets off, they are already halfway there. When everyone else finds excuses, leaders manage to achieve goals.

This is what brings results and this is what success is made of. Everything else is meaningless.

What about you? In which group do YOU want to be?

## 6th Core Principle

A leader is his growth.

This value is highly misunderstood because we live in a world where we speak more than we listen. By default, we tend to judge more than our experience allows. We share the knowledge we do not have, we get advice from people who are not experts in their field and we claim to know while we should be learning. This is the ugly truth.

## LEADERSHIP IS A MATTER OF ATTITUDE

*Learn everything so that you can be anyone.*

Great leaders know that they should focus on their mental health first and then on their physical one. They know that if their mind is not alert and in a positive state it is extremely doubtful that they will manage anything. Having the greatness of the achievement of the goal in mind, leaders should first focus on positive thinking, teamwork and consistency. They know that if a mind is not alert and ready to act, then it is in sleep mode and the body is tagging along.

The thing is that leaders who want to inspire others and find solutions to any problem should invest in their education and development. They need to find new ways of communication and innovative ideas, to widen their horizons, get a better perception of their environment, and react based on the kind of person they are. A book, for instance, can teach us millions of things that our minds cannot even imagine. In a book, we can find stories of people who have excelled, solutions to various problems and the values we need to have to become great leaders.

It is sad to think that the average person holds books in such low esteem. Most people think it is a cheap object that can be used to decorate the bookshelf or something to take pictures of on the deckchair on the beach. They do not think of it as something out of which you could make a fortune.

Nowadays, when the internet is deeply incorporated into our daily lives, most people prefer to be taught by random people who lack any understanding and knowledge. They are taught by people who write books or post stories without having experience and who cannot relate to current reality and the circumstances.

*People tend to follow those who have the most followers rather than those who have the most experience.*

Leaders do not do that. Leaders choose to learn from people who are proven to be at a higher level than themselves. In this case, leaders react smartly and allow others to speak. They "steal" knowledge, listen, observe, take notes and, in the end, choose based on *who they want to be*. But before anything else, leaders listen. Even if they do not believe the person speaking, even if they think that he or she is not as great as presented, they keep listening. Because they know that, in any case, there is something in it for them and they have nothing to lose. Leaders do not have to speak as their results speak for themselves.

Leaders are willing to pay to attend seminars on topics of interest that will contribute to their development. There are hundreds of seminars around the world, either in-person or online, courses offered by well-known Universities and podcasts of qualified coaches. Leaders take notes and implement whatever they believe will make their daily life better. They recognize the flaws in their character and use them as a means to further develop as entities, not because they want to increase their followers but because they want to become the kind of leader that they would choose to follow themselves.

Knowledge is power. Right?

Wrong!

*Applying knowledge is power.* Because what good is in knowing if it is not put into practice? It is useless. How are you going to achieve something if you do not use the knowledge that will help you achieve it? Let me repeat that and who knows, you might as well make it a tattoo: *Applying knowledge is power*, my friend. Read, take notes of anything you find useful and put it into practice, either at work or in your personal life, at every single minute.

Stop listening to people around you who have nothing to do with the answers you are looking for and stop taking advice from them. Stop taking advice about your long-term relationship from your single friends. Stop taking advice about your concerns from your parents who have no experience on that subject. Stop, at last, following people and ideas who have no value and no proven experience.

The greatest school for you is all the people who already have what you want and the experience you are trying to get.

Let me make something clear. There are many different forms of leadership. Each one of them depends on *who you are*, who you want to be, the kind of industry you are in, etc. You might read about leadership as presented by Maxwell, Hackman and so on. You will have to find your style of studying and, most importantly, work on it. Whatever you choose, make sure that they know what they are talking about. That they have put into practice their saying and have proven to be right. With damn results!

From my experience, I would say that the best and the most effective way to become a great leader is to find someone to show you and with whom you will work together. Either face-to-face or online, at least three times a week. You will work on core principles and values, either theirs or the ones you have acquired, you will talk about them and put them into practice at work or in your personal life, constantly providing your feedback. You will make mistakes, for sure. But having a mentor will make it easier for you to recognize them and further develop. An experienced mentor with powerful leading skills is way better than any book you might read or any seminar you might attend.

That is only if you have the strength and the fortitude.

> *Acceptable knowledge is only the one that derives*
> *from strategies already put into practice.*

Think about it and find someone. That could be someone in your inner circle or someone new. Until then, be the leader with the best and most flawless characteristics.

Be a leader who, even in the most difficult conditions, moves forward. Find a way to take a step forward, even when everything seems impossible. Do not take defeat as an option, no complacency and no compromise. Learn how to fight until everything is exactly as you want it to be. No matter how "romantic" or ideal it may sound, it is true. You will be considered to be a great leader once you understand that you are not but the result of your own actions. When everyone else stops or stands still, find a way to act, with no excuses, postponements, or restrictions.

Be a leader who shows up first. It is time for you to lead the way. Especially in crises, your calm, your certainty and your self-confidence is the key to finding a solution promptly. People tend to hide when controversies come up. You should be the one who gives the pulse to avoid any internal controversy, either at work or at home. The world needs people with a positive attitude, no matter what the problem is.

Be a leader who makes decisions, even in the most crucial moments. Nowadays, the average person finds it hard to make decisions, so be the one who does so. When everyone else is afraid of the consequences their choice will have, be confident enough to choose right. Regardless of the goal, the decisions you make will define the outcome of each situation. So decide correctly, having in mind the best possible result for the team, or do the right thing. Accept the situation and take action fast to find a way out of any deadlock.

Be a leader who acts even when the goal, big or small, seems unrealistic. Your strong will, your trust and your actions have the power to turn a dream into a reality. Take action as if tomorrow never came and focus on small wins. You now know that the strongest motivation is your own results. Nothing can motivate you more than your small achievements. There is only one way: the way of success, which leads to the finish line. Even if you decide to destroy everything you have built so far to lay the foundations to create something even better. Even if your decision does not serve the majority. Every single action is better than inactivity.

Be a leader who is responsible for his or her own actions. Few people accept they are wrong. Do not be one of them. Accept your mistakes and the consequences. You are not perfect and you will never be. But when everyone else blames it on others, acknowledge your defeat, accept it, take a stand and make sure that you are back in action as fast as possible, being aware of your failure. In this way, it is less possible to make the same mistakes and of course, you further develop in your field.

One of my favorite personal quotes is:

*Act fast.*
*Fail fast.*
*Repeat.*

Be a leader who takes advantage of the result of their action and is confident about their skills. Your activity levels should be so high that will be visible from the moon. This is how self-confidence is built and how you start trusting your skills. This is how experience and success are built. No matter how many books you read, how many seminars you attend, or how many excuses you find, this is the only thing that matters.

Be a disciplined leader. No army has ever fought with no discipline. By discipline, I mean the constant repetition of small habits and actions no matter if you are in a mood or not. If you are disciplined with small things, you will also be disciplined with bigger things. In this way, you will be able to achieve your goals faster than anyone else. Along with the good outcomes, there will also be bad ones. The faster you see the bad outcomes, the faster you will learn and lay the foundations for the good ones.

Be a leader who monitors his or her past, sees what went wrong and changes it. Every bad outcome can be a reason to do research to avoid in the future what brought you to a standstill in the past. If you act in the same way as you did back then, you will get the exact same results. Each time, choose what you want to keep and what to change. Do not get stuck in situations, ideas and similar nonsense. There is nothing more important for a leader than the achievement of his or her goal.

Be a leader who can tell the difference between being lucky and unlucky. Sure, you need some luck to succeed, but it does not work the other way around. Bad luck is never to blame for your failure. Bad luck is not a thing for leaders as they know that if it were, that would mean that the outcome would be based on luck. The same goes for you. You are responsible for your actions and your fate. You are responsible for the results, good or bad and not luck. There is no one to blame for your misfortune but you. Not the government, the economy, your neighbor, the traffic on the streets, nothing whatsoever. Every single action of yours is the result of your own choice.

Be a leader who is modest in front of knowledge. Become the greatest mental bookshelf that has ever been. Read at least one book per month, with discipline and consistency. When people who know more than you do talk, be silent. Do not interrupt them. Listen, absorb and learn. When your mentor, the speaker of the seminar, or the book "talk," listen. The most incapable people are those who have not learned to listen further than what their own mouth has to tell.

You did not misread. Yes. Incapable. Learning is the only way to develop your skills.

Be a leader who knows how to handle his or her ego. Keep in mind that the way you handle it might turn it into your strongest trait and your greatest advantage. If handled correctly, your emotional world – and especially your ego – might offer you a whole empire, and at the same time, destroy it. Your ego might become your best friend and at the same time, your worst enemy. Learn how to handle it. Be mindful of the situations that led you to a deadlock and the ones that led you to success, and learn how to handle your ego. I know it is difficult, but a true leader must be able to do so.

Be a leader who takes personally every single defeat and works to make sure that the next outcome will be a victory. A leader who knows how to lose but never quits. Be a leader who has the attitude of a winner, not a loser. The world is full of people who do not mind being average, as long as they do not have to leave the couch they are sitting on. People who quit after every failure and find weak excuses and random thoughts to justify their failure. Represent success and victory. Even if you lose, try again. If you lose once again, keep trying. The biggest difference between successful and unsuccessful people is that, despite failing the same number of times, successful people keep trying until they get it done.

Be a leader who does not care about who they have in front of him or her or what the situation is. Never discriminate based on sex, culture, title, color of skin, political or religious beliefs, or sexual orientation. Promote ideas of equality. Recognize people's values and do your best to help them. Provide them with as much knowledge as they can take in. Shake their hand and allow your actions to prove that you are fair and honest. Show that everyone gets the same chances under the same circumstances. Equality is not a luxury and it does even not require special education. Equality is a self-evident given reality.

Be a leader who does not judge people around him or her. All of us carry our burdens and make our own choices. People will not change only because you judge them. On the contrary, whenever you judge others, it means that you look at their hump instead of your own. Which means that you care about what others do and not about what you do.

Be a leader who is in full control of his or her emotions and thoughts. Even in crises, keep calm and patient. You will often find yourself in situations that will piss you off and that is exactly when you will be expected to show your real leadership skills. People get caught up in their emotions and, usually, once they calm down, they leave a mess behind and it is difficult to pick up the pieces afterward. Do not allow yourself to do that.

Be a leader who always sees the bright and positive side of everything, but is, at the same time, prepared for the worst. Always keep in mind that a positive attitude is not a utopia. There are many sides to every situation and if you choose to see the positive one, you will find the motivation to move forward. Even if a situation seems black, find the white side and move on, while everyone else is convinced beforehand that it cannot be done. When you are negative, you are also a whiner. You find darkness in the light and you freeze. You stand still. Mark my words: The positive side is brighter. You will be able to see where you are going.

Be a leader who knows how to communicate. Get a master's degree in communication and understanding. Take advantage of communication to find solutions and bridge gaps. First, listen and then talk. Knowing how to listen to what your interlocutor is saying is a skill hard to find. Few people are willing to listen nowadays, as they prefer to impose their opinion rather than learn something new. Listen. This is the only way that will lead you to the solution once you understand the essence and the source of the problem. This is how great leaders get their message across to those who can listen. This is how the number of leaders' followers increases. This is how leaders show their strength, their belief, their integrity and how they influence their followers.

Be a leader who will inspire others. Inspiration means leading people to roads that they have never imagined. Ways that lead to the establishment and uniqueness. Ways of power and strength. Ways that allow people to create the world and the life they have dreamed of. Everyone is looking for someone to inspire them, even if they do not admit so. You now know though. It is time you made a difference.

Be a leader who will be changing his or her approach according to the situation. Transform from the easy-going team-spirited leader to the tough and result-oriented leader. "Read" your environment and adjust your attitude to the current atmosphere and the results of your team. Do not be afraid to change and become more authoritative if required. Do not be afraid to learn yourself through such situations. You should only be afraid of the possibility of your goal not being achieved.

Be a leader who does not care about what people say behind his or her back. Each of your decisions will be followed by supporters and opponents. It is impossible to have everyone satisfied. Stop caring about those who spend more time watching at your hump than at their own. Stop caring about foolish people. You cannot know what might be going on with their lives. People will judge. The greater you become and the more you expand, the more they will judge. The calmest people in the world are those who have never met anyone. Those who have never left their cage. Anyone who takes life in his or her own hands knows that there always be people to sling some mud. Ignore them. Turn your back and leave. They are not worth it.

Be a leader who realizes that he or she is not perfect or imperfect. Perfection is an illusion and you do not need to be perfect to make it. Know and keep in mind that you are enough. You will have the chance, here, to see where you need to further develop and I am sure that if you are disciplined and patient, you will get to the point you want to be. But you will never be perfect.

Be a leader who creates new leaders. A leader who promotes values and beliefs that only a few have. Do not settle with a group of simple employees and just a bunch of salesmen. Do not see them as simple humans. Teach them how to do great things and how to become great leaders themselves. This is the key to gaining the respect and the support of those around you.

Be a great leader.

## SUCCESS

*Success is the result of the actions of a great leader.*

This is my definition for success. Every lesson I have learned, every failure, every bump, disappointment, disagreement, achievement and joy made me reach this conclusion. My very first understanding, my first work in a construction site, when I quit my father's job, every step I climbed, every chance I took for a new position, every young person I trained and every 15-hour-shift I did to become the best made me reach to this conclusion. You cannot be successful if you are not the leader of yourself first. That is the 1st Core Principle of the "Who I Am" philosophy and the most important one.

Begin to change and be the leader you would blindly follow, without hesitation, without doubt and without further ado. Leadership, just like success, is easy to talk about but challenging to put into action. However, since you are reading this book, you are not one of those people who say "No worries, this is enough" even if they know that there is more than that, whether financially speaking, the quality of life, or anything else they might desire.

You are here because you know that you can achieve more. Because you aim high and have exciting dreams. You want to reach even higher, even farther away.

*Most people settle for few things.*
*Few people desire more.*

At this point, I will tell you something that you need to know. Many people will follow you on the way to success, but there will also be people who will try to stop you. Do not allow them to. Be understanding, as they do not know what the achievement of your goal means to you. Ignore all the judgments and keep going. It is just one of the obstacles you will have to overcome. From my experience, this is the most challenging one.

We all want to be likable, but no matter what you do, you will never be able to satisfy everyone. If you try to do so, you jeopardize losing your identity and get off track. If you try to satisfy others, you might become one of them and it will be too late when you realize it.

Stay focused on what you want to achieve, no matter what.

First, you need to focus on finding your purpose. If you do not find your purpose, if you do not find what you are destined for in this world, everything you are about to read will be useless. It will just be some theoretical knowledge in a book you have read and will be getting dusted -just like you.

If you find your purpose though, then I can help you. You are setting off for a long, yet great journey. I will show you how to find your "Identity" – that is *who you are* – based on some of your main characteristics. I will show you which habits you will have to change.

We will then take action. You will learn to change some of your main habits and start the process of your transformation. You will create a personal map and, if you strictly follow my directions, with discipline and consistency, you will come to understand that everything is up to you, your purpose and how badly you want to achieve it.

Your success has to do with the person you are. If you want to call yourself a leader, then you will have to put into practice what you are about to read. You will have to do some real soul-searching with modesty and responsibility. You will have to put up with whatever might throw you off balance or even insult you and get the "meaning." This is how you will know if you are a true leader or just a barking chihuahua. If you are strong or a coward. If you are just another one among the crowd or if you stand out.

On your way to success, you will have to go through Clashing Rocks, doubt strongly and dramatically change your habits. This is the only way to success, but it is worth it. It is worth it to go the extra mile and become the person you have never imagined in order to succeed. There is no doubt that you can succeed.

My goal here is to offer you some help in your effort to reach the top and give your story the ending you have always wanted. I will help you carry out your most important mission. The one you put yourself into and carry out better than anyone else.

Change is not hard to achieve. It takes though a strong will, discipline and stubbornness. You will just have to follow the below steps:

1. Understanding
2. Acceptance

3. Decision
4. Action

In case the above words are all Greek to you, do not worry. You will be fine. You will understand their meaning and their value later, as long as you keep your mind open as there is no one to judge you here. You will be the only judge of yourself. The ball is in your court.

Your success depends on how a great leader you are, or you are about to be. Once you prove to yourself that you follow some fundamental habits that can lead you to your purpose, you will understand that the way to success is not that challenging. It is just you constantly putting into practice your main habits. The greatness of your success depends on *who you are* and the kind of leader you are. In the end, you will understand that success is the ultimate feeling that you create yourself when you finish your version of a Marathon race, when you finish the race and cannot believe you made it. It is the smile of satisfaction you have while crossing the finishing line, when you realize what you have done, the first tears of emotion and your friends who will show up to admit how integral and strong you are.

Success is absolute freedom. Your own absolute freedom.

# Chapter 6
# Who You Are

## Part 1 Understanding

*Who you are is defined by what you do
when no one is watching.*

Did you know that you, just like everyone else, can control only the 5% (approximately) of your movements and decisions? Yep! Only 5%. This is as far as your so-believed "free will," that is every choice you make, can get. The remaining 95% derives from *who you are*. That is your habits, your personality, your experiences, whom you are influenced by, the people around you, etc. You make all these choices *unconsciously*, without even realizing it. Like an answering machine that decides for you based on old habits that were at some point built because of some stimuli. You might as well build a new habit today or develop a new belief without even realizing it.

As time goes by, every new habit becomes stronger, if we never doubt it or if it is not replaced quickly with another one. Habits go deeper and deeper into our subconscious until they become our way of life. Regardless of their nature or where they come from, they become our everyday life and our perception that "it makes sense to be this way." If we get to this point, it is difficult to get rid of them in case we want to, but there are some ways to do so as we will discuss further down.

I never make my bed when I wake up in the morning because I do not care about what it is like when I come back home in the evening. I do not give a damn. I have more important things to do in the morning, I want to drink a cup of coffee and be where I need to be – to an appointment or at the office – on time. Some people cannot leave their house if they do not make their bed first as they think it is messy. Fair enough.

Some people walk around their houses with their shoes on. To their mind, it makes sense to walk around their house wearing a pair of dirty shoes that God knows what they have stepped onto. On the other hand, I get shocked if people do not take their shoes off right after entering my house. I want it to be as clean as possible, not only because I always walk around barefoot, but also because I do not want to spend a lot of time, or money, cleaning it.

Some people honk within 0.02 fractions of a second when the traffic light turns green as, I guess, they think that the drivers of the cars in front of them have the option to fly. Or teleport! (Oh! That would be really amazing! Right?) Well, the truth is that they actually think that the driver in the car in front of them is the one to blame for being late while they could have been on time if they had simply left the house five minutes earlier. Of course, they know that but if you ask them, they will deny it. I never honk at the traffic lights as it creates a sense of tension that I want to avoid. I do not need that, nor the fuss, nor the bad mood, nor the desperation. It also reminds me of my father who always used to honk even when he parked his car. It is a habit that I do not want to have and seeing my father doing that makes me want to break the habit even more.

You know what though? We are all right whatever we do because this is our truth. This is *who we are*. This is how we grew up and what we learned. Anything else would not make sense.

I could give so many examples of such habits, that I could write enough books to fill a library but I think you got the point.

## Criticism

At the beginning of the process to change and while aiming at the first step, the one of "Understanding," we have to agree that one of the hardest things to do is to accept criticism or do self-criticism. I am talking about the kind of criticism that can shock you. The one that grabs you and shakes you so intensely that your mind gets so fuzzy that is forced to restart.

I must admit that I find it difficult to accept any kind of criticism. I can only take it when it is from my mentor or from those who are close to me. The latter is a bit more special situation since, even though I like the criticism in this case as I believe it is an extremely effective way for me to develop, I demand that it is done in a non-judgmental way and speech. If it is done in any other way, it can drive me crazy, it gets on my nerves and I start to steam. Even in this case though, I make sure that I take the criticism home so that I can process it afterward once my heartbeat goes back to normal. Then, I will handle it as a matter under investigation. I will listen to it, I will process it, I will place it next to other criticisms, I will evaluate it based on facts from the past that show me if it is powerful or not and I will store it.

However, you must admit that no one likes criticism. Whether it is self-criticism or criticism from others, why is it so hard to deal with?

Dale Carnegie in his book *How to Win Friends and Influence People* wrote that *"When dealing with people, remember you are not dealing with creatures of logic, but creatures of emotion."* This means that the way we live and act daily is such because we are used to it. Some habits are so deep-seated in our minds that any intervention from our environment can make us feel frustrated. It feels like a part of our soul is taken away. Our mind feels that a new force is trying to get into our world and, depending on how powerful our world is, we tend to deny access.

Let's use the example I mentioned above. If you come to my house and you do not take off your shoes when you get in, I will just ask you to do so. I do not want people to walk around my house wearing their shoes because I cannot even imagine what they have stepped onto. Since you are used to walking with your shoes on in your own house, If I ask you to take them off, you might just accept it and go with it or you might roll your eyes. You might think that I am weird or hypochondriac. You might get so upset that you will not eat the pizza I ordered.

What a shame… #not

But if you refuse to take your shoes off and you tell me, "Come on Spyros, we're buddies," in a judgmental way, I will get pissed off and will reply accordingly.

"How can I know if you have stepped on cow or dog shit, man? Why should I have it in my house? To match the brown carpet?"

And so on… You will think that I exaggerate, I will think that you are disrespectful, you will try to explain your point of view, I will do so too but differently and it will not take us anywhere. The most we will get from this is to be in a bad mood, eat cold pizza and drink warm beer.

I am sure that you have found yourself in a similar position a lot of times and that you did not have a good time. It might have happened at work, at home, or with your partner. How did you feel? Did you feel that someone was trying to convince you that he or she was right when this was not the case? That they are judging you without even knowing you? That you are too old to listen to them? That they are full of crap?

Regardless of how you felt, I am sure that you did not have a positive feeling. Do you know why? Because, at that moment, you are not just listening to someone saying something. You are listening to someone trying to doubt the reality you have believed and lived in your whole life so far. It is as if someone told you in your 40s that you were adopted. The possibility of that being true, calls everything you have known into question and your denial makes you want to stand up for your truth, and thus for yourself. You will deny that this is true and will question it.

So you are reflected in any kind of criticism, right or wrong. Ugly parts of yourself that you had always thought were beautiful are highlighted. When you see the ugliness, you question whether it is real and you step away. Just like Quasimodo did when he first saw himself in the mirror.

This is why we do not want to be told what we must do or how we should behave. We cannot accept criticism. Our habits are questioned and if someone tries to change them in any way, we resist and it bums us out. It is in human nature and totally accepted. This is why I never spend a lot of time arguing. I recognize the fact that the other person is the way he or she is, I express my opinion a couple of times and then I stop as I know that it will not take us anywhere. Besides, I am bored with the process of trying to change the world. I tried that when I was younger and I completely failed. If someone does not want to change, I am not going to play God. That is their own problem.

I believe that those who believe that they can make someone adopt their way of thinking are dumber than an empty can of Coke that has been left in the fridge for 9.5 weeks. To be honest, "dumb" is not even the word I had in mind. People cannot change unless they want to. The more someone is trying to make them change, the more unlikable he or she becomes.

## SELF-CRITICISM

Self-criticism on the other hand is different. It arises first from our desire to change, having at the same time the right attitude to do so in the right way and consistently. Then it is time for research. Based on my experience and practice, I can tell that self-criticism is the result of constant, thorough, and objective research. Research regarding your actions, your environment, your thoughts, your choices and their consequences. Research about what happened in the past, the reactions of your environment, other people's findings and the criticism you are subjected to.

The latter, in particular, is the most difficult to deal with as, as you read above, few people take in criticism to process it. This is why self-criticism is something that very few people are after. Very few people admit that they have a bad habit because very few people are strong enough to look at themselves in the mirror. Very few people understand and accept their nature. This is also the reason why they are happy to highlight everyone else's flaws but explicitly deny their own.

If someone chooses to become subject to criticism or decides to do self-criticism depends purely on the reason (or the purpose) of the criticism. Some people might see it as an insult and others might see it as a lesson. People who are extremely attached to what they are and cannot be subjected to any change will remain the same until they die. The rest will be developing until they triumph and then, they will die. The way we take in criticism or we do self-criticism is totally up to us. It is totally up to us to decide if we will do something to change. And this is the purpose of this chapter.

This is the purpose of the whole book.

Personally, my self-criticism is harsher than anyone else's s criticism because I know that this is the only way for me to move forward and evolve. I have high expectations of myself and this is the only way to get the best version of me. If something is regenerated after criticism I have been subjected to, I rush into change.

This is how I show that I respect myself and I also prove to myself that I grow. I move forward.

Before moving on, I want to make something clear. I have not studied psychology or anything like that. In my career in sales, I have met many people from different sides of the world, with different mentalities, cultures, financial statuses, mental health, or class positions. Since I was a kid, I have been analyzing facial expressions, body language and voices, along with the actions of each person. In this way, over the years I have reached a point where I can "guess" people's thoughts, their character and possible next actions. It is like I am in a well-played game of chess, I can guess your strategy and adjust my next move.

One afternoon at a sales conference, I spent many hours discussing with a great therapist and writer. She told me that in this way I managed to strongly develop my emotional intelligence. Up to this day, I keep practicing daily, not only because I can understand who someone is, but also because, if they want to, I can also help them change. Especially in the industry of sales where I work, it is extremely helpful when it comes to understanding the salesperson and the potential client. If you remember, I mentioned in the previous chapter that my superpower is to listen. Now you know why.

## YOU WILL RESIST

Putting aside the attitude you need to have when you are subject to criticism, read below about some main types of people I have met in my life that are, let's say, red flags. You will read about their positive and negative traits. Especially when it comes to the negative traits, you will need to let go of any limiting beliefs and selfishness. In case you identify with this type of person, you will need to accept that you too have the same trait, either at a small or a large scale. I know that it will not be easy for you to admit that since, as we have already mentioned, you will deny it before it even gets close to the "wall" you have raised, but this is the only way to do it.

Before I move on, I would like to stress once again that, while reading this chapter, you will resist. You will deny that you are identified with any of these identities. I am sure that you will, stubbornly and with ego. In fact, your ego will try to protect what your habits have built up to now, to protect you from the criticism you will be subject to. You will deny seeing your true *you*. Your ego will try to cover up the ugly part of yourself. You know… ego holds a mirror, showing you a distorted reflection of yourself aiming to protect your feelings from that. Ego helps you deny your true self.

So, at times, you will think "I am not like this," "This is not how I do that," or even "What kind of bullshit is that? Who gave you the right to judge me, Mr. Writer?"

Exactly! You do not know me and I do not know you. It is up to you whether you decide to take in everything you are reading because you want to understand who you are and change. I will not try to make you change. Even if I wanted to, I do not even know you. What I can do, for now, is only to show you the way and you will decide if you will follow it or not. As we have already said, the ball is in your court.

This is why, in the first chapter of the book, I wrote proudly that my goal is to show my journey from being a salesperson to becoming the CEO of my own company in Bahrain in 4.5 years. It is not my business if you decide to follow the same journey. Everything you have done so far and everything you will do from now on is your problem. Let's say it once again to make sure we will not forget it: The ball is in your court.

Or in your hands. Whatever!

The bottom line is that if you really want to take matters into your own hands, if there is something missing from your equation and you are not exactly where you want to be, if you pursue change to reach further than you have ever had, you will need to carry the burden and let yourself go. Do yourself a favor and trust me, you have nothing to lose from this process. Allow yourself not to be perfect and know that you will never become perfect. Otherwise, you will not manage to get where you want to be. Self-criticism is the first step you need to take. Read about the following types of people and act accordingly.

*Who you are is defined by what you do*
*when no one is watching.*

This is how you will understand *who you are*, based on the evening routine you have after work, your morning routine and the way you drive. Your thoughts when you are alone, your actions, your spontaneous movements, the words that come out of your mouth about anyone and your deepest secrets will show your true self. Your cultural and political beliefs when there is no one around to judge you. When there is no one around to say a single thing about you. When you have the freedom to do whatever you want, whenever you want for as long as you want to.

This is who you are.

Hasan used to work in my company in Bahrain and this is the perfect example of how a typical person behaves. At first, he was eager to work. He used to smile, he was polite and he had a positive attitude when he was trained.

When I asked him what he wanted to do in the future, he replied that he would like to build his own company. He was already running a small business on Instagram and he provided computer-related services. His account had 55000 followers. I thought that this was a great achievement, considering that he was only 21 years old.

One day, he told me that I was a good role model for him as I had the professionalism and the attitude he would like to have. What he left out of the picture though was his attitude. I called him in my office and told him:

"Hasan, what do you want to do with your life?"
"I want to build my own business."
"Do you want it to be successful?"
"Of course, Mr. Spyros."
"Then why do you act like a child?"
"What do you mean?"
"Let me tell you what you did today and what you do every day without realizing it.

"First of all, you made ten phone calls in 2.5 hours, while others made twenty-five. Which means that you gave yourself fewer chances than the average.

"Secondly, you stopped working for ten minutes when you were trying to decide what you would have for lunch and you kept checking your phone to know when your food would be delivered. During that time, your colleagues were working trying to achieve the goal they had set for the day.

"Finally, you know that the training starts every day at 10:30, but you chose to go to the restroom at 10:25 and come back at 10:35, while you know how typical I want everyone to be with the schedule. This shows that the limit between being ignorant and disrespectful, towards me or yourself, is not clear to you.

"To sum up, you bring fewer results than the rest of your colleagues, you spend time on your phone, but only because you do not want to miss the call from the person who delivers your food, while everyone else is working to get the results that you do not get. Not to mention how disrespectful you seem to be when you do not care about the schedule of the company that pays your salary and you go to the restroom, while you should have gone ten minutes earlier and been on time at the meeting.

"Does it sound to be the attitude that a wannabe entrepreneur should have? How do you think I feel when I see you working like that? Do I get the feeling that you respect my company? Do I get the feeling that you value the training we offer or your salary? How do you expect me to react to such an attitude? How would you feel if you were the CEO of the company and you had an employee with such an attitude? Is this how you will behave when you will start your own business? If so, do you think that everyone else will respect you?"

He remained speechless.

"I thought so," I told him and I drove him to the core of my philosophy...

"Hassan, If you **really** want to become an entrepreneur, stop acting like a baby and act as if you were an entrepreneur. If you keep acting like a baby, you will never become anything more than that. I used to be like you – that is very true – I wanted to achieve something great, but I did not have what it takes to achieve it. I had not realized it until it was late. Do not make the same mistake. I will not pretend to be your dad and spank you. If you do not know what you need to do, then put yourself in my shoes and see what I see. It is the best way to understand if you like to treat yourself in the way you do and to see how you would react. Only if you put yourself in my place, you will understand what is the right way to think and who you need to be. It is the only way to become a successful entrepreneur."

Some people might think that I was too harsh on him. But the truth is that he got the point. From that day, he asked me to watch every move he made and he changed. I cannot stress enough how much that guy changed. He became an example to everyone else because of his attitude, the respect he showed and his good manners. Of course, it took some time and patience from both sides, but Hasan got the point. He already has the attitude of an entrepreneur and taking into consideration how young he is, I am sure that this guy will shine in the future.

This is a perfect example of daily life. All of us, without exception, have behaved like Hasan at some point. We have all acted in a way that was not appropriate considering our expectations and ambitions. Some of us understood along the way what we should change. Some of us never did...

Before I start, I want to open a parenthesis to tell one more short story. In August of 2021, when I had written a rough version of this book, I was in Athens for a few days of vacation. One day, I talked on the phone with my close friend, Giorgos Lebesis. He is one of the greatest authors of children's books of our generation. Giorgos and I have been friends for ages since we were both members of the music band "Petrines Psihes," back in 1999 and to this day, he is still one of the most important people in my life. I love him and I respect him.

After spending several minutes on the phone and since his wife and their two kids were out of town, we started talking about the book I was writing at the time and you are currently reading. He got excited with the topic of the book and then he said:

"Man, when are you flying back to Bahrain? I'd like to catch up with you and talk in person. The topic of your book sounds amazing, but it can also be a touchy subject"

"I'm going back in seven days."

"Too bad. I'd like to see you and talk in person."

"No worries, man. In any case, when the draft is ready, I will send it through because I'd like to hear your opinion."

"For sure! I want to read your book because, considering your character and your personality, it must be spicy."

"Well, you know me."

Then, he told me something that I will never forget:

"Spyros, be mindful about everything you write. Keep in mind that people who don't know you can easily get you wrong. They might be offended and turn you down. The written word is different from the spoken word, as readers can't see you and they don't know you. This is the only piece of advice I have to share with you after all these years I've been writing books."

What Giorgos told me was entirely true and I kept that in mind as a guide while writing, following his advice. However, my opinion is clear. Written or spoken word, those who tend to get things wrong will do in any case. Nowadays, people deny any kind of change and growth. They choose to live in their bubble over understanding reality and taking a step forward. It goes without saying that we all have to deal with our own burdens. People all over the world have suffered a lot because of Covid-19, and various political or financial disasters that caused inaction. In fact, inaction became the new reality and a way of life. This is why the general population, who is sunk into oblivion, explicitly denies changing their minds.

I have many old friends too who have not changed at all for the past 10–12 years, as if time has stopped for them. They still have the same jobs, the same daily lives, the same hobbies and the same opinions. They are still the same as they were on the first day we met. They have a passivity that cannot be justified in any way. This is one of the reasons why friendships sometimes fade out. Because some people move forward, while others stay the same. It is really sad to see that the same people you used to travel with when you were younger, have not moved forward, even after all these years.

To put it simply and to be honest, because this is *who I am*, I have also cut off relationships with people who have not taken a step forward in the past few years. I do not choose to avoid them, it is an unconscious decision. On the other hand, even though I try to promote ideas with a positive attitude and I run leadership Masterclasses, I will never work with people who are not willing to do self-criticism. The same goes for you. If you are not willing to take a step forward while reading this book, I will not be able to help you further. If you are not willing to overcome the limitations of your ego, it is only up to you.

The way I see it, my purpose is to share everything I can, based on my experience, not to knock sense into you. Whatever you do will be for yourself. Keep that in mind: what is written in this book is not something I have read in another book or quotes I have read online. What is written in this book is not romanticized or ideal. Everything is real and I am the only one responsible for that. Because I used to do harsh self-criticism and I still do, as I refuse to be controlled by my strong ego and my stubborn temper.

So far, I have never read a book that comes on so strong and you should consider yourself lucky that I am doing so in this one. If I had read such a book, I would not have had to go through all that in my 40s. I would have done everything earlier when I was stronger and had more time. But when I can see that seconds and days pass by so fast, I cannot afford to postpone it. At least not as long as I want to make my mark on the world and create more than I have ever imagined. I am sure I will because this is *who I am*. I might not be perfect, but I am the version of myself that has been created after self-criticism and actions, constant, persistent and nerve-wracking actions.

Let's take it a step further and talk about the Identities. The goal here is to bring out traits of yours that you have always thought healthy and right. You will come to understand their nature, and what they can cause, and get rid of them, if you choose to. Understanding and letting go of bad habits is the first step toward development. This is where purification begins.

This process is the starting line, the point 0. You will see *who you are*, as this is the beginning of everything. If you refuse to accept the real you, then the 0 point is useless. It is as if you have a treasure map, but you start off from the wrong starting point. It is as if you start from New York instead of Athens. You might think that you are a few hours away from your destination, but you should cross half of the world. You will never get there.

Your reaction once this process is complete is also something that no one will ever know. *Who you are* will be defined by the actions you will take while reading this book and by the way you will choose to use the "Who I Am" philosophy.

You can never escape from yourself.

Keep that in mind.

## IDENTITIES

Let's analyze some of the most typical identities of people whom I come across daily. The reason I am doing this is that, as I mentioned at the beginning of this book, I want everything that is written in this book to be close to your reality. In this way, the message I want to get across becomes clear. It sounds familiar to you and you can put it into practice right away.

Take me for example. I could have been your neighbor once or maybe, we used to play football at school together. Maybe, I am that guy that you met at a party or maybe, we have had a few drinks together. I am not far from your world. This is why my philosophy will be easy for you to understand and if you decide to put it into practice, the outcome will be right across the street. This will not be the case if you follow Elon Musk's or Jeff Bezos' philosophies. In fact, the stories I have used are real. It has all happened to me and I cannot think of a better way to get my message across. These are stories that could have happened to you as well.

Regarding the identities, keep in mind that they are all related to each other. None of us can identify with only one of them. Our traits are interchangeable and depend on the environment we find ourselves. The tricky part here is that most of the following habits are habits that you have never spotted. Some habits are so real and common that you might want to write them down in the text you have started writing down on your phone.

So, let's begin. Shall we?

## THE SATISFIED

I decided to use this name because I refer to people who are satisfied with what they already have. They do not long for anything else. They have their job, their family, and probably, a salary. They do not need anything else. They are happy with a simple life, without many responsibilities, and without challenges. They are calm and you can easily have a beer with them once in a while. They might talk about a trip they recently took and they might invite you over for dinner. On Sundays, they might watch a game or take a walk in the mountains. Then, they go back home, have dinner and wake up the following morning to go to work. They appreciate the small things in life.

They hardly ever complain about taxes, the government, or anything else. It is not that their life is problem-free, but they choose to have a positive attitude. They use social media to catch up with friends or to post a photo once in a while, and they do not care about how many likes they will get or about drawing attention. They feel that they are enough and are satisfied with themselves. Good for them.

I like this type of person. They make my heartbeat slow down for a while and I cannot help wondering if I would like to be this type of person myself. Free of worries, healthy and without many responsibilities. Sometimes, that might be enough indeed. It depends on the goals we have set in life. It might as well be the purpose of life itself. Of course, people who belong to this category cannot have great expectations from life. In fact, in case they do not earn a decent salary, they will probably take some hits money-wise in the future, especially if they start a family when responsibilities and expenses add up. But this is completely up to them.

The big challenge for those people is to handle situations when things get bad, mainly financially and mentally. This is because people who do not push themselves daily, cannot easily handle difficult situations. They are fragile. They get too comfortable and they never look for new challenges that will take them out of their comfort zone. They do not build character and integrity and in difficult situations, they have to redefine their needs and their priorities.

Difficult situations make us grow and make a difference.

*The more time you spend in your comfort zone,*
*the more exposed you get.*

This is the greatest quote I have ever put into words. I remember a special moment with my team when everyone thought that the game was over and I put myself out there. I told them how feeling comfortable is a sign of weakness and that our team was a team of winners who can go beyond all bounds. What happened next is part of my non-negotiable reality. We went beyond our limits, once again and we achieved our goal.

I believe that a lot of people wimp out at this point and that this is one of the biggest problems of people. We deal with difficulties according to the stamina we have developed, either when it comes to the quality or the duration. The Satisfied is the most typical example of people who do not broaden their horizons. They think that a stress-free life is a nice life. However, when things get rough, they fail to cope with the situation.

Finally, the Satisfied do not have goals. More often than not, they live their lives day after day without heading anywhere in particular. In case they do find a goal, they rush back to their reality once they realize that it will not be easy to achieve that goal. To back up their theory of an easy and problem-free life, they go back to their cage and spin the wheel.

The Satisfied desire success, but they can also live without it.

## THE LOST

I used to be a Lost myself back in 2011 when I wanted something, but I did not know how to get it. I was surrounded by people who did not help me move forward but held me back (because I allowed them to do so, of course). It was the time when I was looking for something more, something to hold onto and someone to help me succeed in everything I had in my mind.

The Losts usually stand out of the crowd. They keep trying to fit into their current environment, but they fail to see that this environment will never be enough for them. Thus, they never feel satisfied. They remain "average" for the rest of their lives as even if they want to escape, they do not know how to do it and what their destination should be. People around them judge them, marginalize them and underestimate them. They are said to be unreasonable, dreamers and selfish.

What happens in the end? The Lost feel that they do not fit in. They do not see it, but since they are trapped, they do not leave any space for development. In fact, the Lost often have extraordinary skills, but they have not got the chance to use them. If they do not find their inspiration that will show them the right direction soon, they might get lost in "normality." They might disappear into the "typical" reality, which seems meaningless to them. They might remain trapped for the rest of their lives.

I do not have much to write about the Lost. What they need to do is to live life to the fullest, whatever that means. They might need to find a different job, break up with their partner, join a different social group, go for more, read leadership books, or – the best thing to do is to – find a mentor. The Lost are people trapped in everyday life and must find their way out as soon as possible. They need to differentiate themselves from the norms set by society, to search, to experiment, to fail and all over again until they find what they want.

The Lost will not find the answer nearby. They will need to search a bit further away, either literally or figuratively speaking. They are the hope of humanity and the crazy ones that Steve Jobs was talking about. They simply do not know it.

The Lost desire success and they cannot go live without it. They just do not know that they can achieve it.

## THE HYPNOTIZED

This is a strange category of people. I call Hypnotized those who care only about the way other people see them. Those who wake up in the morning and go to bed at night thinking about the opinions of other people. Those who spend their time promoting themselves on Instagram and Facebook, by posting hundreds of photos and stories trying to be considered (but not to be) likable. Those who post again and again filtered pictures of themselves to get the – crucial for them – number of likes only to find new ways and filters to further increase the numbers of likes afterward. They draw satisfaction from that, only to do it all over again the following day.

A positive trait of these people is that they are experts on social media – they can use it better than me – and they are always a good source of advice.

A negative trait of these people is that they spend their time and their attention on social media and they are distracted from what should typically be more important to them, such as being specialized in the sector of their interest.

They cannot tell how much they miss due to their way of life. As they spend their time following new trends, they are consumed. Time flies right there in front of their eyes but they are too busy to see that. They are hypnotized by their need to feel accepted. In some cases, this might also be called an addiction. When people get addicted to something, it is really hard to get their attention off that. For the sake of social media, someone has even jumped off a cliff to be cherished. This is not trendy. It is just stupid.

It has also become fashionable to have fake followers. The Hypnotized "gets high" when he or she buys millions of fake followers to make the audience believe that he or she is important. It is as if someone "goes on a date" with a blow-up doll that he calls Jessica Rabbit. If it is not deflated fast from the constant and aggressive use, he will have a great time, but no one else will.

Biologically speaking, it is justified that a big number of likes can make you feel great. This happens because of dopamine. Dopamine is a neurotransmitter in our brain which affects the way we feel. In fact, it has also been linked to addiction. Every time we get a lot of likes, a large amount of dopamine is released and our brain receives that as "Cool feeling! I love it! I want more!" Well, this is exactly the effect of dopamine on psycho killers too, but let's not go there.

Another trait of the Hypnotized is that because they spend too much time on social media, they get into a vicious cycle that is difficult to break. When they are not preoccupied with themselves, they look at other people's profiles, in the search of perfection. The more time they spend observing other people's lives, the more imperfect they think they are. The more imperfect they feel, the more they need to replace their image with something more beautiful. So, they are consumed, with making themselves look good, and then, they promote themselves once again, in an even better way. There are always new models, new ways of life, new luxuries, and new trends, and the ultimate goal of the Hypnotized is to keep seeking ways to change. They are addicted to beauty and perfection. They need attention and adoration. In other words, they are addicted to nothingness. This is why most of them are constantly unhappy. In fact, some of them might also be depressed, which is sad.

In case I came off as too judgmental about social media, let me say that of course, I am not against it. On the contrary, I think that it is quite an advanced way of communication, advertisement and promotion. Since Facebook, Instagram, Twitter, etc. entered our lives, we have been able to get in touch with people we had forgotten they existed. We have come even closer to our friends, we can speak with friends who live abroad and so on. We can express ourselves through music or cultural and social beliefs, we can promote our products and share nice moments.

However, I believe that there is a sort of red line that should not be crossed. I agree that if you have to promote your business or whatever it is that will increase sales, you must spend thousands of hours and dollars on social media or hire someone to do the job. But when your only goal is to promote yourself without serving any purpose other than getting likes, then there must be a boundary.

Now, watch this: if your mind is on your phone even when you have a conversation with a friend of yours, if you keep checking for messages or notifications looking for an excuse to pick your phone up once again, then you might be a Hypnotized as well. If this is the case indeed, it is time for you to admit it, otherwise, only one thing can happen: you will remain hypnotized and you will never wake up.

The Hypnotized come off as people who have achieved success, but they lack the integrity to do the work it takes to actually succeed.

## THE EXPERTS

The Experts are those who know everything. Those who see conspiracies everywhere and think that everything is just another evil plan against themselves and their kind. They think they can be educated by reading Facebook posts and then they question people who actually have knowledge on a topic. Alright, let's take it step by step. The Experts are:

– Those who have an opinion on everything and would not accept any opinion different from their own.

– Those who, regardless of whether they have knowledge on a subject or not, are not willing to hear that little something extra from someone who might know more as they deny that there is someone who indeed knows more.

– Those who, even if they are wrong, do not admit it because they cannot accept that someone else but themselves might be right.

– Those who will not hear you out if you express your opinion first. Even if they agree, they care more about who said it first.

You can recognize the Experts from the frequency they speak when they are in a group of friends or acquaintances. You will understand that they do not have much to say, but they want to speak nevertheless. People might become Experts because they were not adequately breastfed as infants (at least not as much as they needed to) and have abandonment issues or inefficiency. They need to show off, but they have no experience or knowledge to share. They think that this is a way to be likable. They do not do that on purpose, but they do it.

They have the same attitude in real life and on the internet. It is funny when I come across topics on Covid-19, the fact that the earth is flat, and how the height of a mountain is defined by the point you are standing instead of the distance from the sea, sad is that only a few of them will manage to let the feeling of weakness go, simply because most of them do not see themselves as weak. Only if they go into a big shock, they might get their head straight. Sometimes, not even then, they will admit that they were wrong and they remain as weak as they were.

So:

1. If you find yourself advising people who have not asked for it just because you are trying to help, you are an Expert. No one wants to hear your opinion. In case they do, they will ask for it.
2. If you find yourself advising on the "ideal relationship" and you are single, you are an Expert.
3. If you find yourself rejecting the opinion of someone who knows more than you on a certain topic, you are an Expert.
4. Finally, if you try to convince a friend of yours who dares more than you do that he or she is wasting their time, you can be sure: you are an Expert.

Well, Expert is the polite word to use in this case, because otherwise, I would need a "Parental Advisory" sign on the cover of the book.

# THE ANALYTICAL

Mark Twain said, "I've had a lot of worries in my life, most of which never happened."

One thing is certain when it comes to the Analytical: they need to know the slightest detail before they do something. They are easy to recognize but difficult to understand. They are the type of people who will analyze every single detail they will see or hear. Their brain has a capacity for useless information 98 times larger than a typical person's. A capacity that equals the capacity of 16 football fields, including basketball and tennis facilities, swimming pools, indoor halls for artistic and unartistic gymnastics (yes, I know there is no such thing, smartass), canteens, clothing stores, supermarkets and parking areas for cars and garbage trucks! They are consumed with analyzing details as they try to predict every single bad thing that might happen, regardless of the fact that the odds of it actually happening are zero.

You might think, "What's wrong with that?" So far nothing. On the contrary, the analytical can predict reactions and possible scenarios better than the rest of us. They can see smaller or bigger disasters coming and for them, every single detail is worth observation, mentioning and further analysis.

In case the people around them fail to understand, they analyze the issue even deeper in order to convince their environment that something is worth mentioning and repetition. And just when you think that this might be coming to an end, they find one more aspect worth analyzing and explaining. It can get tedious, but for the Analytical this is a way of life.

From my experience, the Analytical go down such paths because they try to avoid any sort of failure, rejection, or worry. They believe that if they analyze every single situation, they will be able to control everything and take care of everything. They think that they can protect themselves from anything bad. Having this attitude in life, they feel safe and strong. They feel untouchable.

But this is only an illusion. No one can control everything. No one can predict what is going to happen and no one can avoid all the challenges that will come up. You cannot be always happy and have everything settled. It is just impossible.

Some of the Analytical take it too far. Some books refer to it as "Paralysis by over-analysis," which is the situation they find themselves in when they are drawn by all the possible scenarios they make up when they face a problem. Not only these scenarios do not lead anywhere, not only do scenarios that seemed impossible to happen before now seem to be an option, but also they forget where they started in the first place. They are trapped among all these scenarios and branches, the branches now have thorns too, and the Analytical refuse to escape because they think they are coming to a conclusion. The truth is though that they only get even more trapped. They reject any opinion or theory that is different from theirs and they can even reject the most solid theories.

At the end of the day, what makes the Analytical analyze in detail and then, reject what they wanted in the first place is fear. It is the fear of failure. They think that analysis helps them be prepared, while in fact, they are doomed. As they look for negative aspects, they only manage to discover even more and thus their fear is reinforced. Instead of looking for ways to succeed, they find reasons to fail.

What is the result? Nothing at all. Just a tangle of thoughts and possible scenarios which lead to absolute idleness. They are so afraid of all the possible negative scenarios and the fear is so realistic (at least in their mind) that any step forward seems to be a failure.

My friend Analytical, you get bummed out for nothing. You only manage to let fear pull you away from all the great things you can create. Your obsession to control everything is nothing but your fear of failure. But the more you analyze everything, the greater your fear becomes and the more away you fall from action and success. Go for it. Take action right away. The circumstances will never be ideal. Keep in mind that:

> *Fear is a 75-year-old crippled bodyguard*
> *who is selling you protection in the land of opportunity.*

That's what fear is!

The more you analyze a situation, the more you focus on the negative aspect of things. You tend to focus on the problem instead of the solution. The more you keep analyzing the problem, the further away you move from the solution and the more you destroy yourself.

A special feature of this identity is that if it is not recognized and handled in the right way, it might turn into something more repulsive.

**Drama Queen/King:** No introduction needed. We can all recognize those people by the frequency they create drama in situations that need to be handled objectively and calmly. We can recognize them by the pathetic and grumpy way they handle any situation depriving us of vigor. They keep projecting the negative aspect of everything to such an excessive extent that they almost become self-destructive. Just like all analytical people though, drama queens/kings can be ingenious. They just need to work a lot with themselves to learn how to deal with their feelings.

**Possessive/Manipulative:** Over-analyzing might make people extremely afraid of losing something they have. While trying to think of every possible way they might lose something, they bend reality and believe that they possess it. Thus, no one can take it away from them. This might be considered a violation. Here is what I once told my friend Alexandros who, as he has admitted himself, has shown signs of possessive behavior, "Man, people are beings of free will. By thinking that you possess whoever is around you, you deprive them of the choice to be free. At the end of the day, you only care about how you will be happy making other people stay only to make you happy. If you deprive them of their freedom, how can you say that you love them?" "You are right" is what he said while having a sip from his drink and he immediately changed the subject.

**Angry:** Angry people are those who easily lose their temper and the worst feeling is created: anger. Anger is their emotional reaction every time they expect – or demand to be more precise – from other people to handle a situation in the way they would handle it. Since they do not have the clarity to understand that everyone else cannot act and think the way they do, they get angry and object to that. For them, it is easier to get angry than to understand that other people are different entities and act in different ways.

To sum up, the Analytical desire success, they know what they need to do, but fear of failure makes them lose their way.

## THE LUCKY

Let's talk about the Lucky. Once they put something in mind, not even a lobotomy would be able to take it off. These people will prefer to go the extra mile which will take them one step closer to their goal instead of having a cup of coffee with a friend. They are the ones who take over any conversation talking about their goal, no matter how unreasonable it might sound to everyone else. They are the ones who set the bar high, the ones who disappear for a few days and they tell you afterward that they have done the craziest thing in the world only because that would bring them closer to the goal.

All those people who have done great things in their lives belong to the Lucky. Simply because theories, plans, and catchy quotes were not enough for them. They took action. Any form of action is crucial because, for them, this is the only way to move forward. Inactivity makes them feel insecure. They feel that their feet are tied up. They feel trapped. They feel that someone is holding them back and preventing them from running.

The Lucky are weird creatures and difficult to understand. They only need one thing: to trust their skills, confidence that they will make it and open roads to run. Usually, if they ask for guidance from someone they trust and who is confident about their skills, the Lucky can achieve great things.

On the other hand, if you try to "set them straight," you will only manage to feel satisfied for a few minutes thinking that you are doing what you think is "right." It will not work though. The Lucky are persistent and they know they can count on themselves.

The difference between the Lost and the Lucky is tiny. It is so tiny that most people cannot tell the difference between the two. The distinction between the two is a fine line of self-confidence, which can be deep. This is what makes them move and shine. Once a Lost finds a purpose and self-confidence, he turns into a Lucky and nothing can stop him anymore.

The Lucky desire success and cannot live without it. This is why they move towards success every day.

## THE INSUFFICIENT

The Insufficient talk but do not act. They always talk about their plans and desires, but they fail to take action. When it is time to pay the price, they avert their gaze and go back to their cage, just like the satisfied ones do. The Insufficient are extremely ingenious when it comes to finding excuses for why they did not do something and they convince themselves daily that everything is fine, even if it is not. There is no hope for the Insufficient.

## THE "GIVEN UP"

The Given-Up is the saddest identity. These are people who have abandoned every hope in life and their only goal is to make it through each day. They go from work to home, home to work and all over again. A monotonous survival contract signed by themselves at a point when they decided to back off and give up. They simply never found the guts to move forward afterward. These are the people who do not know that they have always been coward and insufficient. In fact, if they do not realize that they will die and no one will notice, not even their cats.

## THE BRASH

The Brash are those who still believe that women should have fewer rights than men and they prove it daily when they go home and expect to find their food on the table. Yes, there is still such trash around. They should reconsider their view on all kinds of equality because they are the ones who raise all these murderers and rapists we see on the news. Someone should tell them that without women, they would be nothing more than an idea. A bad idea, but still…

I would not like to expand on this type of identity. I think you got it.

## THE KIDDOS

The Kiddos are those who convey an attitude of superiority towards everyone else, even though they lack any form of experience or knowledge. They think that a small win can turn them into champions, polished nails can turn them into models, 10 seconds of air time can make them famous and 20 minutes on stage can make them stars. The thought alone makes me laugh. I have met a lot of Kiddos during my career, whom I hired just after they had graduated college. Some of them though soon concluded to the fact that the sales structure and system we used did not work. The same system that got me to where I am today and that has been used by hundreds of successful people before me. All of us have made our fortunes with it. Some smaller, some bigger.

You know, some people have a great sense of humor without realizing it. They deserve to be given a microphone and a stage so that they can perform their comedy acts to a wider range of people. Everyone deserves a good laugh these days!

Or, they could have simply said that they were not able to do it. It is better to admit your weakness than question knowledge that might help you move forward – if you want to.

## THE NARCISSISTS

Narcissists are the most complex and difficult to handle identity, as it is made of many of the traits that we have already come across in two or more of the above-discussed identities. According to Greek mythology, Narcissus was a guy who had not loved anyone, until he saw a reflection of himself on the water and he fell in love with his reflection.

This means that the Narcissists love themselves (you can easily tell that from how often they take a selfie). They think extremely highly of themselves, and thus, they constantly seek attention (whether admiration or pity) both in their personal lives and at work. They think they are better than anyone else and only extraordinary people deserve to be around them. They dominate conversations and diminish or despise anyone whom they see as inferior to them. They tend to tell lies, with no meaning or sense, they lack the skill or the will to see other people's needs and emotions and they envy anyone who has more or better things than they do.

As I mentioned above, this is a complex identity. Handled in the correct way though, they can become No1. Provided that they manage to control their ego.

It goes without saying that there are even more identities out there or even a mix of them. The ones mentioned above are those I come across more often and that I wanted to talk about. You might see in yourself some traits from two different identities. You might as well think that you have nothing in common with everything that you read above. This might be either because indeed, you do not have any of these traits – I doubt it – or because you have some of these traits, but you do not want to admit it.

The deeper purpose of this book is to allow you to find out *who you are* and also if you are whom you want to be. Just because you always act in a certain recurring way, it does not necessarily mean that you act in the way you want to or you should. It is just the way you are used to acting. Since no important reason to change your habits has come up until now, you have unconsciously stuck with them.

What I want you to do now is to go back to what you have written until now and answer the following questions:

4) Which of the traits or the identities I read about above is closest to me? Which of all these identities am I, more or less?

**TIPS**: Start by numbering some of the traits you know you have and that you share with the above-mentioned identities. I want you to read again all the identities and think about which of these traits you have along with any other traits you may have. I want you to number them and analyze them. At this point, it does not matter. Do not be ashamed. Write them down. In any case, no one will ever know, not even me.

The analysis of each one of the traits should start with "I recognize that I am..." and write explicitly and in detail about the nature of this trait. The more you accept your nature and the deeper you search for every trait, the more effective this process will be. Even when you take a personality test, write down anything that you would like to change.

Something else that might be helpful is an exercise I learned at a psychology conference. Pretend that you call yourself on the phone and talk about some of the main traits that you want to change. Talk about the incidents that led you to develop these traits, and the situations that have caused them, and explain how important it is to change them. Along with yourself, you can face even the most difficult situations.

5) Interview two friends of yours and ask their opinion on some main traits you might have. It should be at least one hour with each one of them. Your phones should be in silent mode and your environment should be free of distractions. Let them know that you are doing research on yourself and that you are trying to develop and become the best version of yourself. You might need to record the interview. In the end, write down the answer in the text you are writing. No fooling around.

Once you are done, if you have written more than 15 traits, jump off the 15th floor of a building. There is no salvation for you. Or for us...

Complete the above exercise before you move on. Start right away. There will not be a better moment.

## UNDERSTANDING

In order to understand *who you are*, you can easily begin with the identities I mentioned above. Find the main traits of each one of them and see which of them you share, more or less. As I mentioned earlier, you form a separate identity on your own. You might share the same traits with many others or with no one else. So do not mind the labels I used above. You should only pay attention to the way each identity might act or think.

Read again the above-mentioned identities. Of course, you will need to write down your remarks and it will take some time before you will be able to move on. If you do so with patience and modesty, you will understand much more than you thought you would. So read them, again and again.

If you are thinking "come on, I'll do it later," you are at the wrong place. Close this book, turn on the TV and post something on Instagram. I am sure that your followers would like to see a nice story of yours. Besides, how long has it been since you last posted a story? You know, I am talking about the cool ones you usually post.

Way too sarcastic? Come on... Have some sense of humor. But let's be honest. If you want to achieve your goal and actually make it this time, you first need to understand yourself. It takes time, effort, discipline, patience and persistence. What did you think? That it would be easy? Nope. It is going to be hard. You must have the guts and the discipline required. You must let go of the limits set by your ego and face reality.

So just grab your phone and do the above exercise. Do not be an Insufficient...

## **CONSULT AN EXPERT**

Another way for you to understand *who you are* is to consult an expert. Yes, you got it right, to go to therapy. There are millions of professionals out there who can help you understand *who you are* and sort things out together. The best thing about this option is that you get to talk to someone unknown to you. This makes you feel free and you can share even the most personal aspects. You can share every single thought you might have or your deepest secret. Psychotherapists will know what to say, where to focus on and will help you understand what you had never thought you would. They can help you let out even your deepest truth.

The best thing about psychotherapists is that they can see outside of the box. When you are on your own, you cannot understand everything and that is exactly what psychotherapists do. They will explain what consequences your actions might have, the connection of your thoughts and where it all comes from so that you can change it. With their help, you will be able to shed light on aspects that you had never thought you should. You must know that you might leave the session in tears, after seeing some of your traits and their consequences, but this is part of the process too. You cannot take a bath without getting wet.

If you are one of those people who think that therapy is for those who are "ill," you are further away than Neverland. If you are mentally ill, you go to a psychiatrist. Psychotherapy is about exploring. You explore in detail your past or your present, depending on the kind of therapy you choose. Every therapist's work is different and the outcome is insane.

Keep in mind that humans are complex creatures, but quite simple at the same time. Psychotherapy is one of the most effective ways to understand *who you are*. It is no wonder that so many people today consult a therapist. Especially nowadays when everyday life constantly distracts us. For some people, it is necessary to consult an expert to keep their mental clarity despite all this madness. In fact, some people take it one step further and do the same with their families. I happen to know couples who have 2–3 sessions a month to take advice on what approach they should follow to raise their children or on how to keep their relationship healthy.

I believe that psychotherapy is a truly amazing and effective way to understand *who you are*. No one else can help you find your true self, not even you. Because I am sure that up to a point, you think that you know yourself well and you have accepted yourself. Good for you. I mean it, good for you. But I must say that a therapist will broaden your horizons and will help you see who you are.

## BOOKS

The most common way to explore and understand *who you are* is to read books. Yes, these weird things that decorate the bookshelf and are made of written sheets. Read them! If you do not like reading, I can tell you that 10 pages per day before you go to bed are enough. It is a habit you need to build if you are interested in finding out new aspects of yourself.

There are hundreds of books available about any kind of success, psychology, business and general growth. There are books about personal development, books about leadership, books about sales and so on. You will find among their pages the answers to questions you did not know you had. You will be surprised by the wisdom they can provide and some of them can show you the way to your definition of "success," just like the book you are holding. Words have the power to unlock your mind and show you paths that your brain would not have found. A good book is the most straightforward way to get out of any deadlock you may find yourself in.

The magical ability of books is that they include the knowledge and the experiences of other people who found the courage to write them down. They had also read other books written by someone else and they helped them become *who they are*. This transmission of knowledge which is the outcome of years of experiences is written down and broadens your spiritual horizon and allows you to move forward. It is the knowledge that you could not have acquired if it were not for books, because of your social circle, your experience, or even your education.

There is nothing healthier than consulting people who have already achieved what you are after.

Around the beginning of 2012, someone suggested that I read Dale Carnegie's book "How to Win Friends and Influence People." To this day, it is one of the TOP5 books I have read. Reading this book, I discovered something that was very true to me and it was one of the greatest lessons I have ever learned.

Carnegie's book is mainly about dialogue. It refers both to good and bad approaches. It is about how to speak, listen, understand other people's needs, make others think the way you do, etc. While reading the book lying in my bed one night, I read the following quote, "A person's name is to that person, the sweetest and most important sound in any language." At that moment, I stopped reading and put the book on my chest. I lit myself a cigarette and stared at the ceiling, having in mind the quote I had just read. *What a great quote,* I thought to myself. *When was the last time that someone heard his or her name from me? Why do I keep calling everyone "man" or "brother"? Is it possible that I might make people lose their appreciation and respect for me?*

That was when I realized that if I wanted to make progress, I should stop using these words. Today, I rarely use them and I find it frustrating when some people use them as if there is no other word in their vocabulary. When I come across people who overuse them, it is a good sign to partially understand what kind of people they are. Because they also remind me who I was.

## A MENTOR

My favorite way to understand and develop myself is to have a mentor. It is the most effective, the most powerful and the faster way to go where you want and be whom you want to be. It is a sensitive issue as it must be done following very strict criteria, but it is an extremely effective and fast way to develop. The criteria that I find important are the following:

1) You must choose consciously and sensibly. You must choose someone who has proven results to demonstrate and not someone who has just graduated a college or someone who seems reliable just because he or she has many followers on Instagram. You must choose someone who has worked a lot, who has many experiences, good or bad, who has the right values and ethics and who is able to share their knowledge not only in theory but also in practice. They should also be inspiring so that you are motivated.

2) Once you choose someone, he or she will also need to accept you. You must make your intentions clear beforehand and explain how important their guidance will be to you. The relationship between a mentor and a "mentee" is close and should be shaped by mutual respect and admiration.

3) You will have to be able to commit that you will do whatever you will be asked to. Military discipline is the only thing you will bring into this relationship. You will need to understand from the beginning that you are the one who went to the mentor asking for guidance, so you will have to do whatever he suggests, no matter how difficult it might be. Loyal followers are the greatest future leaders. The respect you have for your mentor is the same respect you unconsciously ask from your followers.

One of my mentees in Bahrain was eager to work when he started and he could not wait to learn everything about sales. We had met at some events, and he respected me a lot. When we first started, I told him to work on a small project. This is part of my philosophy, to guide people through "On the job training." This project worked also as a source of inspiration and motivation for him. With my guidance, he completed the project on time and he was excited when he made it. He knew that I was the right mentor for him.

A week later he got fired for some unimportant reason. Even though I tried to convince him that we should continue working together, he chose to isolate himself and find a job with the salary he had in mind. I did not do anything else and neither did he. Even though a month later he said he was sorry, he never found the courage to decide that he wanted my guidance. Shortly after that, I heard that he had to go back to his country because he was not able to find a job.

So he did not follow the third criterion. He had no discipline and no respect. I understand that he was probably going through tough times back then, but the thing is that there is no exception when it comes to the relationship between mentors and mentees. If he had let me work with him, I might have managed to broaden his horizons and he might have had the chance to live here. He made the wrong choice.

It might be difficult to find a mentor, but as I mentioned above, it is the most effective option. You are not on your own anymore. There is someone who keeps you accountable. Depending on your mentor's character, you will have to deal with how self-sufficient you will need to be. So what you will be doing while you are together might not be the most challenging part. The biggest challenge might be that you will have to deal with the psychological and emotional pressure that comes with development. A mentor help you see that and if he is good, he can do it very fast.

Mentors have the power and the freedom to be completely honest with you about who you are. They will make you accept your nature and will demand you to change, with no hesitation of pity. Right mentors can be your best allies.

At the same time, they see how efficient you are during the process of change. They evaluate the results. For example, if the result is not enough compared to your initial goal, the right mentors will push you forward and help you submit the desired results on time. You can be sure of one thing: you will be quite efficient and you will find out things about yourself that you have not even imagined. Along the way, the word "procrastination" will disappear from your vocabulary and so, you will be efficient quite often. Each day will be twice as effective as the previous one and your life purpose will become your daily life.

You will become who you need to be. You only need to let yourself go.

## A BIG SHOCK

The last and the hardest way to understand who you are is what I call a *"big shock."* An incident that is so tough that you learn a lesson you will never forget. A lesson so powerful that will make you quit a strong habit and change the way you think. A lesson so "unfair" that will help you reevaluate the values in your life and redefine the way you live. A big shock might make you readjust your priorities and leave dangerous situations, that until then you thought were safe, behind. Even if this has not happened to you yet, be sure that life is extremely strict when it comes to "giving a lesson." One way or another, you will get your fair share. And when the moment comes, you pay the price.

My mother used to smoke three packs of cigarettes a day. As she was in her 50s, my brother and I tried to convince her to quit smoking but she would not listen. She knew that it was unhealthy, but she always had an excuse for this bad habit. Usually, it was something foolish, such as that she smoked because we were watching a movie, or because we were having lunch altogether, or just because it was raining. She would not quit simply because smoking had become a habit. Habits of that nature, which are considered to be addictions, are really hard to quit.

The weird thing was that every time we brought the subject up – which was daily – she kept revealing her ego and denied everything. Her ego did not let her take advice or "orders" as she used to say from her two children. "Do your self-criticism first and leave me alone" she used to say and we were getting upset that she would not change her mind.

Years went by and she did not change anything, we had the same discussions, the same arguments and the same results. A vicious cycle that ended up being tiring and meaningless. We were sad for our mother, but she did not want to quit smoking even though she knew it was really bad for her.

At some point, she got very sick. She had a high temperature and a severe cough. It was an unbearable and unstoppable cough. It was so dry and intense that sometimes she could not take a breath. I remember that she spent many nights on the couch because she knew it would be difficult for her to get up from her bed. She also said that if she spent so many hours in her bedroom, she would go crazy. So she slept in the living room, a room with a big TV and large windows. She did not get any better though.

One evening we decided to call a doctor, who said that she was suffering from acute tracheobronchitis and that if medication would not make her feel better within six days, we should take her to a specialized doctor. The following six days went by quickly, but it was a real struggle for my mother. So my uncle took her to a doctor he knew.

My brother and I almost went crazy while waiting for them to come back. A few hours later, I heard a key turning in the lock. It was my mother and my uncle. They came into the living room and my mother burst into tears right away.

"What is it?"

No reply. She was crying as if someone was long dead.

"Well, the doctor told her something that was a big shock for her," my uncle Manolis said.

"Tell us what it is, damn it! I'm scared to death!"

"The doctor said that I must quit smoking, otherwise I will have to say goodbye to my children in six months," my mother stuttered.

I was freaking shocked!

I hugged her right away and she cried as if she were a small girl. I must admit that I was so upset that a doctor had said something like that to a patient who was in such a difficult situation that I started yelling at my uncle, asking for the doctor's address. My uncle refused to give it to me, trying to make everyone calm down as things had gotten intense. I thought that it was unacceptable for an educated person who is responsible for people's health, or even their lives, to say something like that to a sick woman. I did not doubt that we would get into a fight if I met him.

After this incident, my mother quit smoking cold turkey after 20 years.

This was the only way she would be able to quit.

*Passions turn into lessons only for those who have the guts to read between the lines. Anything else is mediocre.*

The "Who I Am" philosophy starts from understanding *who you are* and what your desires, your fears and your insecurities are. It is the way you drink your coffee, the way you brush your teeth or the way you treat stray animals. You *are* your disagreements, people you envy and any kind of attitude you hate. You *are* your father and your mother and the reason why your partner is jealous of you. You *are* the outcome of all these people who never showed up, of the ones you waited for, and of the ones you left waiting in the rain. You *are* the result of every single choice you make at every single moment.

People tend to be on the point of falling apart before they decide to take action or make a change. Humans procrastinate by nature because they do not realize the significance of the consequences of their inaction. In some cases, people decide so late to make a change that it can make you question the intelligence of humankind in general or if it is due to some kind of sadomasochistic behavior.

It would be an underestimation to say that you are irresponsible if you recognize a problem but do nothing to change the situation. Some things in life should be clear even without the help of psychotherapists, books, or after a big shock. It is a matter of how strong a personality you have, your character, your integrity, your willingness and your leadership skills in general. Everyone else will keep sitting on the bench because this is where they belong.

I am sick of meeting people who do not have a destination. I am sick of meeting people whose only thought is how to get away from work. I am sick of meeting people who choose simple things over great things. I am sick of meeting people who stick to their habits and refuse to develop, move forward and see different aspects of life. I am sick of meeting young people who waste their time on social media and are ignorant of all these beauties of life that will not have the chance to see ever again. I am sick of misery, greed, judgment, omniscience and of people who find hundreds of reasons to justify why something is impossible to happen while they cannot find a single reason to explain why something is possible.

People disregard change and sink into oblivion, into their daily lives, into boredom, mediocrity and compromise. The more they compromise, the more they sink into all the above.

The more they sink into all the above, the more they forget.

The more they forget, the more they sink into the above.

The more they sink into all the above, the more time goes by.

Time goes by so fast that people do not even understand it.

Time flies at top speed.

And people just sink into all the above.

Until they die and only then do they remember. Only then do they understand.

"What an asshole have I been…"

But it is too late.

*The more time you spend in your comfort zone,*
*the more exposed you get.*

I hope that you keep that quote in mind for the rest of your life. Because if you do not "eat" life, it is going to devour you.

# Chapter 6
# Who You Are

## Part 2 Acceptance

*Change can only come when we are aware of the present situation.*
*Jorge Bucay*

### FROM UNDERSTANDING TO ACCEPTANCE

I cannot stress enough how right Bucay is. In order to change something or to find the solution to a problem we first have to be conscious about where we are or *who we are*. And when I say conscious, I do not only mean that we are aware of it, but that we have also accepted it. Nobody will manage to make a change if they have not accepted their present situation.

You know, it is exactly what most books ignore. Because most people believe that the brain, as long as it has understood a situation, will automatically accept it and will make sure to change it. It is not like that. The human brain does not know the next step unless you tell it what the next step is. The same goes for understanding and accepting. The fact that you know *who you are* and which of your basic traits keep you from succeeding does not mean that you also accept them. Moreover, it does not mean that you embrace change.

This simple condition, going from understanding to acceptance, reminds me of a story that happens almost daily in my company. When I train new salesmen, it means I instruct them on what exactly I want them to do. During training, everything is clear to everyone. At least, this is what they claim. But when the time for action comes, almost every new employee finds it very difficult to execute even my simplest instructions. Things that seemed easy, simple and achievable suddenly become gibberish, hard and often nonsensical.

What happens in these cases? It is simple. Understanding seems easy on paper. However, acceptance will show if it is easy or hard to digest. When it becomes clear that things are not as easy as they seem, some people back down and some – usually only a few – continue. This is when people show *who they are*. If they are leaders or *Insufficient*.

How many of us haven't taken important decisions that would improve our life quality? How many of us haven't said "Enough with late-night eating!" or "I gained weight during Easter because I ate two whole sheep," or "I'm going on a diet from Monday!" "I cough like a donkey. I had enough of smoking!" or "We crossed the line again yesterday. I'm never putting a drop of alcohol in my mouth!" or "It's over between us!"

All of us have taken such bold decisions. But why do these decisions often last less than they should? Why are we on a diet for a week but at the same time we secretly open the fridge at 3:00 am because we got hungry and eat two sandwiches? Why do we continue smoking when we know that it is bad for our health? Why do we stay with our partners when we know that they are not ideal for us?

Because simply, we do not accept the truth. We understand it, but we do not accept it because we ignore the size of the damage that it can cause us. The line that separates understanding from accepting is very thin and in essence, it separates theory from practice. It separates those who will remain inactive in a situation from those who will act on it.

## THE REASON WHY WE DO NOT ACCEPT A SITUATION

Then why don't we accept it and get it over with?

Very funny…

Tony Robins says that the need to avoid pain and seek pleasure drives everything we do. Pleasure and pain, pain and pleasure. Nothing else.

When we choose whether we will cut down on food to be healthy or whether we will keep eating, we always choose the one that will bring us more joy. Even if it is temporary. We only care about not suffering *now*. Hunger is a kind of pain that we smooth out by eating. We choose to eat because it eases our suffering. We choose the action that will bring us joy. It is as simple as it sounds. Robins knows what he is talking about.

And someone will now make the million-dollar question:

"And how do we change this?"

I was sure that you would ask something like that, dear reader and I commend you for your courage!

It is simple. It will change when you focus on the long-term and not on the short-term pleasure. When you decide to be healthy tomorrow instead of devouring a pile of sandwiches today. When you ignore temporary happiness because you know it will lead you down the wrong path and you decide to choose the temporary difficulty for a better tomorrow. When you decide that what is important is not what you are currently doing but what you will have in the future.

When you choose the future over the present, then you will already have accepted your current situation. If you choose health, then you will have the guts to look in the mirror and realize that you barely treat yourself with respect. Then you will accept that this situation needs to change. If you DO NOT accept it 100%, then your wish for change will be overshadowed by your need to eat. So, you will be back to the beginning.

Do you remember the story about my mother who decided to stop smoking? Did you understand what exactly happened? My brother and I had been trying to convince her to quit smoking for many years. She understood why. She was constantly telling us that we were right. But she never concluded to the fact that she had a problem. The doctor on the other hand, who presented the issue in his own way, caused the shock that put her in the position to accept the problem and make a decision. He made her look in the mirror and see the root of this bad habit.

She had to choose. She would either keep on smoking and enjoying her daily life, putting her future at risk as the doctor warned her, or she would *accept* the problem she had, and get rid of this bad habit in order to have a future with her children. She would undergo a period of deprivation – which meant pain too – to lead her life as she had imagined it. The key point was that the doctor gave her a clear-cut purpose: the doctor made her see the person she would soon be.

He gave her a *reason* to quit smoking: her children.

This is where the difference between those who achieve great things and those who remain lost among the crowd lies. As mentioned in the last chapter, this is their "why." This is their goal. This is what motivates them to change. It is the moment they realize that their situation is not what they want, they put their ego to the side, realize their faults, look at the situation from an outsider's perspective and they come to accept it in order to change.

Some people prefer working hard all day long, even during the weekends, for a few years to achieve the financial independence they have imagined for themselves and then they choose the quality of life they want to have. Others prefer to have their job, and their schedule and be calm without many worries and responsibilities knowing, of course, that they will do the same thing until they retire. At the end of the day, everyone continues living on their terms.

The way I see it, both ways are acceptable. Everyone should do whatever they feel like doing.

I must admit that only a few people will sacrifice their present hoping that difficulties will turn into happiness in the future. Because simply, nobody can guarantee the future. We do not even know what will happen in the next second. There is no guarantee for anything. Without a guarantee, humans prefer to continue enjoying the present instead of trying their luck and losing their current joy.

It has also happened to me you know…

There was a pivotal point in my life where I started realizing that maybe, other people are not to blame for my situation. It was at that time that I started thinking of leaving Greece. I felt like I worked a lot but I could not see the outcome of that. I felt exhausted from the endless work hours but static at the same time. I felt that whatever I did would not lead me anywhere. Everything was in vain. As long as I was going nowhere, I started feeling that burn in my chest that maybe I did not belong where I was and that I had to immediately find my place. Otherwise, I would stagnate even more. Honestly, from a young age, I wanted to do great things. I was clearly a lost one.

Until one day, somewhere in 2015, when I looked at myself in the mirror and asked: "Hey man, is this what a successful person looks like? He wears All Stars, ripped jeans and hasn't had a haircut in a month? Does a successful person use the word "dude" more often than he breaths? Does a successful person honk at a traffic light? He doesn't have any patience? He doesn't have self-respect? Does he carelessly throw a can of Coca-Cola away? With what kind of people does he hang out? What does he put up with and what does he reject in his life? How many hours does he spend watching TV and how many books does he read in a month?."

I started out by studying the basic traits of successful individuals. I have to admit that I was not a big fan of this theory, but it honestly broadened my horizons to an extent I had never imagined. I started watching videos of famous leaders, what they said, how they talked, their posture, the way the looked at things, etc. I read one of T. Harv Eker's books that was about the way of thinking and the actions of all these extraordinary historical figures and discerned the basic characteristics of rich people. I was undergoing the phase of *"Understanding."* It took me, I admit, a long time to tell the difference between reality and fiction, and, in part, this was because all these examples were too distant to me. So I had a hard time relating to them and understanding what was possible and what was not. It was a bit hard to swallow.

This is why I felt the need to write this book. Because my example is extremely close to your situation. I am also my parents' son. I started working in construction and with patience and determination, I landed a position as a CEO in a company abroad. Nobody gave me anything. I fought tooth and nail with my demons to get here. My truth is much closer to you than it is the truth of most others. I hope you can relate.

As I was analyzing personalities from all over the world, I started observing myself constantly. I ignored what others did for me and I watched all my reactions. I used to listen to the words I said, I paid attention to my thoughts and observed my views and my habits. At the same time, I started doing self-criticism, drawing parallels to the ideal characters I was studying. My self-criticism was very harsh, otherwise, I would not have behaved myself.

As I was observing myself, I started observing people around me too. I started placing personalities and identities in boxes and I decoded their words and their reactions. I compared my real-life experiences to what I was reading and noted the differences that had to be highlighted or further explored. Unconsciously, I started letting go of egoistic crap like "This is who I am and I don't care" and I started objectively viewing the aspects which I wanted and had to – in my humble opinion – improve.

The deeper I was getting into this investigation, the more I understood that I had a long distance to cover and that my change was nonnegotiable if I wanted to do great things. I humbly accepted that my old identity was not enough to bring me to the point I wanted to get to. I supported it and fed it with my egoism for many years and it has led me to naught. It betrayed me. It sold me off. I was now at the stage of "acceptance" and was moving forward with great momentum.

I said, "Enough is enough! It's time to face the truth and see who I really am and what I do."

I haven't stopped since.

## ACCEPT YOURSELF (SO THEY SAY)

As you can see, I am not a big fan of the theory of "accept and love yourself." I am against those who adopt theories of stagnation. Things are simple. Do you have what you want? If yes, then accept yourself. If not, then you have no reason to remain unchanged. If you are poor, if you complain a lot, if you are a rapist or a hooligan, if you are too negative, if you smoke like a chimney, if you cheat on your partner, if you sell drugs, if you beat your wife, if you are a racist and a sexist, will you have to accept it? Why accept it when it will not bring you what you want?

When other books say to accept yourself, I say that this is nonsense. They are romantic novels and fairy tales that make you feel better in your routine. Agreed. This is how your parents have raised you, this is what you were taught in school, this is how you shaped your personality and how you have achieved what you have achieved up to now. This is what you have been doing until now. Good job. But remember this: "The enemy of the best is the good." If you believe that you are enough, you will never be able to become better and you will remain the same. You will remain unchanged and ordinary.

Accept who you are but when you are searching for success, you will have to accept that as long as you do not have it in your hands, you are not who you should be. You will have to adapt. If you have not secured your future and the future of your family, then you have not achieved what you have to, so accept that you are inadequate. In this way, you will change. If you are not at a point where you work because you want to and not out of necessity, it means you have not done everything you need to do, thus accepting that you are not who you ought to be and that you have to change. If you cannot choose the way you spend your time – not only the free time that is left over from your work and your duties – then you have not gained what you had to. So accept that you are not who you should be and you will have to change. Accept it.

Has anyone ever told you that you can become more than you already are? Do you know that you can be someone greater? Has anyone ever told you that you are being wasted and you should grab life by the horns before your hourglass runs out? Has anyone ever told you that the only thing you achieve by complaining and being negative is to cause disgust to yourself and the people around you? Has anyone ever told you that you are going nowhere?

I am pretty sure that the answer is "no." Nobody has told you that outright. Because they want you to be close to them. Because if you truly change, you will be different. You will be a better version of yourself and people around you will not recognize you anymore. You will become a better version, with greater potential. And those who remain unchanged will try to keep you close to them. This is the way those who love you protect you.

But they do not know that they are weighing you down, when in fact they ought to congratulate you on your perseverance and courage. Do not get mad at them. They do what they believe a good friend should do. It is their truth and their reality. They do their best, whether you see it or not. But know that they love you. You have to recognize that. But that does not mean that you have to accept their theory or *who you are*. Do not accept anything. Judge objectively, with determination. Decide for yourself if you have to change. Do not mistake a subjective truth for an objective one. There is no objective truth when it comes to such matters. Truth is whatever is better for you.

It is finally time to uncover the truth because it has remained hidden under your excuses for too long. Success demands you to be a leader and not be inadequate and small. It demands decisiveness, objectivity, daring and courage. I would utter another word but I am in danger of being censored. But I am sure you get the point.

There is a huge difference between self-acceptance and self-esteem. If you value yourself, then you must do what is better for you. If you value and respect yourself, as mentioned in the 1st Core Principle of the "Who I Am" philosophy, you will have to accept yourself for what you are and you will have to change. This is also the meaning of "complete acceptance" that you are called upon to recognize your weaknesses and your shortcomings and change them. If you fail to do that, then you automatically dispose of any chance of changing and evolving and thus, any chance of success and happiness. The key lies in change.

I have watched a video of a very well-known business coach who is generally very snarky and casual and he showed me how easy things are if explained outright. As shocking as it was, it inspired me like a few others.

One day, he was sitting in the back of a car and, at one point, the car stopped at a traffic light. He was talking to the camera doing his thing, until a girl, obviously a fan, knocked on the window and asked to talk to him. He rolled down his window to talk to her, as he always does in similar cases and the following conversation took place:

"Hi, Gary! Oh my God, I can't believe it's you!" And she got out her phone to take a selfie video, to catch the moment.

"Hello, how are you?"

"I'm good! Tell me three words that will inspire me whenever I feel down!"

"Three words?"

"Three words!"

"You will die!"

The girl was shocked!

For Christ's sake I was damn shocked also!

It is not bad to be harsh on yourself as long as you know that this will be beneficial for you. You do not need a Gary to remind you – once again – that our time is limited for you to become active. Make your self-criticism. In this way, you show that you value the time given to you and your abilities. Get angry at yourself and show him or her the next step. Realize that change will not come by itself. It will come when you decide it. But for this to happen, you will have to accept that change is nonnegotiable.

The catch in this whole thing is our ego. You might be an Analytical, a Lost, or whatever. You might want to create a whole empire. If you allow your ego to be in charge and you do not admit it, or at least find the flaws that hold you back, you have already lost the game. And if your ego is so fragile and sensitive that you cannot admit that change is of vital importance, then hug your ego and go to bed together. But take it for a drink first. Be a gentleman.

Because this is the reason why people do not want to change: their ego.

However, I am tired of seeing people who read quotes of success on the internet and when the time for action comes, they play dumb. That is hypocritical. If you read "never give up" then that means never give up, not whenever it suits you. This is harder than solving a Rubik's cube in ten seconds with your hands tied. Quotes are there to teach you a lesson. Not for you to post them on social media to get likes.

I am tired of seeing people who do not care about doing their job correctly and then, demand things from their manager. If they are out of work, they blame it on the government or the situation in their country. It is insulting. You are just lazy.

I am tired of seeing others honking at the traffic light or swearing while driving. It is a sign that their evolution stopped in the dinosaur age and they have remained cavemen. It is not the fault of the driver of the car in front that they did not start at the $0{,}0006^{th}$ fraction of a second. It is the fault of the driver who honks because it is their fault that they are late. The worst bit is that they often do it in front of their children. This is exactly what is meant by "bad examples being set."

I am tired of listening to people claiming that they know everything. They cannot know something if they do not experience it first. The most annoying people in the world are those who think they know it all but if you ask them about their experience, they play dumb.

I am tired of seeing people believing and following others who have a million followers but nothing to say. It is not important what the masses believe in. What is important is the truth and the value it has. This is how the average person ended up being shaped by all the "rubbish" posted by random people and the information shared by them can only cause division and disgust.

I am tired of seeing women being abused by their partners but staying with them. Ladies! Go back to your parents' house and leave the idiot alone. He does not need you and this is why he treats you like that. Be somewhere you deserve to be. Be with someone who takes care of you and loves you.

I am tired of watching people browsing the channels and watching quarrels that lower their IQ and get even deeper into the abyss of nothingness in the absolute nothing. The fear that the media promotes and sells with great ease causes inaction in people. It is better for someone to watch National Geographic and learn about how North Greenland jellyfish reproduce. It is more useful.

I am tired of seeing people taking everything so seriously and nagging about everything. They usually even tell themselves that they are right. With their complaining and constant nagging, they cause asphyxia and stomach ache to anyone who stands within a 3-mile radius.

I am tired of seeing people taking life for granted. Nothing is guaranteed. You might have something today that you will not have tomorrow. Since you do not take care about "tomorrow" when you focus on the joy that "now" brings you, when the hour of judgment is upon you, you will be more exposed than ever before. When your turn comes, remember Gary's words: "You will die."

Life is there for you to create things. Struggle for a better tomorrow for you and your family. Fight for what you want, adapt, but also stand out from the crowd. People have reached the lines of mediocrity because they do not accept change. They are egoists and stubborn and this is why they remain idle. As the rejection of reality is becoming more and more a common phenomenon for most people, a false reality becomes their truth. Since this is the case for the majority of people, because acceptance and action, as you will read further down, is a difficult task, those who stand out with their strong actions, courage and daring, are considered an outcast.

If you want to be a leader in your personal and professional life, then you must always stay true to the virtues of a leader, not whenever it suits you. And as stated in the 1st Core Principle of the "Who I Am" philosophy, you must have the ability to make the right decisions and act upon them. Otherwise, you have an expiration date.

You realize your current situation. You know who you are. You're not a baby. You are a grown-up person. You can understand if your current way of thinking can lead you where you want. Maybe the identities of the people I listed in the previous chapter helped you out. Maybe you found some points that reminded you of yourself. This is their purpose, after all: to help you understand if some of these characteristics are part of your personality.

The goal is not to create your psychological profile or make a personality test. The goal is for you to open your eyes and face the truth. Enough with the excuses and the whining. Either you treat yourself like a leader or you follow the path laid out for you by your current self.

## ANALYSTS

For example, do you consider yourself an Analyst? Does this identity remind you of anything in your past or your future? To what extent? To a large or to a small extent? If it does, do you understand the reason why you do it? Do you understand that you do it because you are afraid of any kind of failure and that you analyze every possible outcome? Do you understand that if you overanalyze, not only do you get lost in your thoughts, but at the same time you push yourself away from any possible positive outcome?

Do not deny it. It is true. On many occasions in your life, you could have done some thinking before taking action, without overanalyzing things, but instead, you got lost in all the possible outcomes of your action and you ended up with the most destructive one. In your attempt to protect yourself, you discarded any action that would make you move forward. It was probably the right thing to do at the time, but where did this take you? Did it relieve you?

Think about it. How many times has this happened?

In February of 2006, I traveled with a dear friend of mine to La Palma, an island in the Canarias. One night, we started talking about how we would open up a small local restaurant in Athens where people would also have the chance to listen to good live music. We started imagining how many of our friends would come, the feasts we would have, how fun it would be, and all these nice things. We got so excited that if we could, we would board the first plane to Greece to make this thought of ours a reality. It was like we had found the purpose of our life.

During our talk, we mentioned who would be in charge of the payments and who would go around the shop to talk to the customers. This is when our first disagreement came up, but we quickly resolved the issue and decided we would both do it on different days. Later, we mentioned where we would supply our tsipouro (a kind of Greek spirit) and how costly it would be since transportation is somewhat expensive. That means we would have to have high enough prices for us to make a profit. On the way, we talked about how many employees we would need to have, the taxes in Greece and where we would find a suitable location. As time went by, our enthusiasm faded away.

Until it fell apart. It was at this point that after 2.5 hours of analyzing every possible scenario, without having any idea about the actual situation, without any survey, and with no previous experience, we rejected this idea. We never even bothered to see if there would be any chance to find a way to actually do it. We did not even talk to someone who knew. We rejected it altogether.

We just went to sleep.

The end.

Have you ever found yourself in a similar situation? Do you think that this happens often in your life? Come on, admit it already!

You know, there are a lot of ideas that got lost in someone's thoughts. If you do have even the slightest tendency to analyze, admit that you are like this and that it is not helpful at all. Pick a situation, and think about it well, but instead of finding ways and reasons why it would not work, find people who have already done it and start from there. Find all the reasons why it would work. Over-analyzing might help you out sometimes but from my experience, more often than not, it will not.

He who wins always is he who acts. It is the person who thinks, comes up with a plan and acts according to it. Whatever big problem occurs will be resolved before you even start and every small thing will be resolved along the way. You will never be able to predict everything. You will deal with everything that will come up when the time is right. And be sure that if you want something very much, no problem will be able to stop you.

So, what do you say? Do you consider yourself an Analytical?

## THE BLIND

Maybe, on the other hand, you have traits from the Blind. You focus on the pretty life that others show on social media. At the same time, to fit in, you make sure to also show off yourself. You are obsessed with being recognized and accepted by others. You might as well call it sad.

One night me and my partner were sitting at a restaurant in Bahrain and we were having dinner. At a table near ours, exactly three meters away, there were four girls. Suddenly, the Happy Birthday song started playing on the speakers of the restaurant, and a few seconds later, a waiter came out of the kitchen walking slowly, holding a cake with some lit candles. The kitchen was at a distance of about 12–15 meters from the table, but I could tell immediately that it was meant for the girls since he was looking toward them. Everyone understood where he was going the moment he got out of the kitchen but few could say whose birthday it was.

You can make a bet out of this with a friend if you have a good eye, even if the waiter is 15 meters away from the table. I would have won this bet because I understood whose birthday it was almost immediately after I saw the cake. It is a pity that I did because it is kind of sad to understand something like that.

The birthday girl was the one who first got out her phone and started video-recording this moment, ignoring her friends and their surprise. The waiter with the cake was coming closer, her friends were singing and she was trying to "capture" the moment on her phone while recording… well, herself. She was recording herself while everyone was singing "Happy Birthday" to her and the candles were lit. She only cared about showing off on the internet by videotaping that she had friends. Well… maybe not for long, but still…

In fact, one of her friends started singing a bit more awkwardly than the others while looking at the birthday girl giving more attention to her phone trying to find the best angle than to the song of her friends. It was one of the saddest moments I have in my memory and this is why I am writing about it here. By describing this event, I might manage to change those who are Blind.

The girl preferred to record the moment and "post" it on social media instead of experiencing it and memorizing the emotions she felt when her friends surprised her. They showed that celebrating her birthday was a big deal to them and this was their way to express their love, with hugs, chocolate, singing and laughter. They did everything that can make a person full of emotions. They did everything that can make a moment special and unforgettable. This is why so many people claim that "Life is made up of moments." I would put it a bit differently:

*The value of a moment is defined
by the emotion it creates.*

When you sacrifice those moments with friends to record them, to have content to "post" on Instagram to get likes, then how many other things do you miss out on in life? How many sunsets? How many moments with your children and your partner? How many moments with a good friend? How many chances have passed by in front of your eyes while you draw your attention to how you "look"? How many beautiful moments have you ignored with your priority being to "capture" them, even if they were not authentic?

The next time you will find yourself having a cup of coffee or a drink with a friend, observe how much time you spend on social media and how engaged you are with what your friend is saying. Observe and notice to what extent can the conversation with your friend draw your attention away from Instagram or Facebook. If you are out with a good friend of yours and you ignore him or her, then know that you have a strong similarity to the Blind ones and this ought to be changed. Because simply you are missing out on more than you think.

## LOST

Of course, you might be a Lost as well. You might have a fire inside you without being able to explain it. Your soul might want to create so many things that go beyond the perception of your brain. You might want to do great things, but you do not know where to start. You might desire success but everyone around you make fun of you or ignore you. You might feel different but you fail to rise and prove it.

This type of person reminds me of Mohammed, a salesman who works in my company. When he first came, he was 25 years old, reserved, with his head low and with no driving force. Although he had a degree in Business Administration he did not look like someone who has the potential to progress in life. He seemed defeated before he even started fighting. Despite all that, I hired him because I like to give opportunities to those who want to work. And this young man, in April of 2021 showed me that he really wanted it.

During his training and his work, Mohammed used to look me in the eyes every time I talked. Whether it was regarding tips to improve his efficiency or my criticizing him, he listened to me and utilized my comments on the highest level. With no objections or excuses. So we had a meeting just the two of us to inform him about his progress and improvement in the company and to tell him that he had won my vote of confidence because he was the most disciplined employee I had ever had.

"Good job, Mohammed," I told him before he sat down on his chair.

"Why are you saying that, Mr. Spyros?"

"Because simply the first basic step you were called upon to take in order to succeed in my company was to be completely disciplined. And from your first day here, I have not heard a single word from you. You are always willing to do what I ask you to. I appreciate this a lot."

"Mr. Spyros, on my first days here, you told me that this is exactly what you did to get where you are today. I want to have the same knowledge and perception you have, so I am doing exactly the same thing."

He left me speechless. This young man who wanted to work for my company had already started to develop habits that others never would have accepted. They have failed because of their ego and their naivety.

Mohammed wanted to change though.

"Mohammed, do you have any goals in life? Do you have a plan, an aspiration, or a dream?"

He looked at me puzzled. There was a big chance that he had never heard this question from someone in his life up to this point.

"Mohammed? Are you with me? Do you have any goals in life or are you also a fan of the philosophy *day in, day out*?"

"I came here to earn money, Mr. Spyros."

"Of course, I know that. But is there an end goal? A finish line? A particular outcome that you would want your life to have?"

No answer. It was like talking to an empty can of Coke.

"I see," I told him. "Let me give you an example. Would you like, as long as your sales reach a satisfactory level, to become a manager? Is this something that would satisfy you?"

"Mr. Spyros, this isn't possible. I don't have the experience required."

"I know, Mohammed. Let me worry about that. But do you want this sometime in the future to happen?"

"I do. I have never thought about it but I would like that."

Mohammed was a Lost. He wanted something, but he did not know what it was that he wanted. From the moment he found a particular goal, he not only wanted it, but he also needed it. He found the courage to try and do more than he had ever done until then. Up to this day, he has read six books I have recommended to him, he continues to be the most disciplined salesman I have, and he holds the record for the most sales in the company.

I do not know if you are lost or not. If you feel like there are many things you want to do but you also feel like you cannot do them, then let me tell you that you are lost. You are not alone. What you have to do is to accept the fact that nothing will be given to you and that you have to earn what you want. The fact that you are a Lost does not mean that you are inadequate, it means that you need to find your way.

Your way lies everywhere. It lies in a good book about entrepreneurship, self-improvement, sales, leadership and psychology. Your way lies in attending seminars or conferences – there are thousands you can attend, whether online or with a physical presence. Your way lies in a person that you have found whose lifestyle you like. You might like the way they talk, the way in which they have succeeded, their wealth, their opinions, etc. Take notes from them. Write the most important characteristics down and use them.

Let's go a step further and accept which of these identities is closer to you. If you do it, it means automatically that you want to move forward but for some reason, you cannot. If you accept it, then write in your text the following:

*"I was lost but now, I found myself"*

6) Further down, write that you accept the flaws that you mentioned in the previous question with absolute awareness and objectivity and that you are determined to change. Simply accepting a situation is not enough. There has to be a written record of it. If there are no witnesses in an event, it is as if it has never taken place. Since nobody knows what you will be doing following the "Who I Am" philosophy, you have to write your actions down for them to be proven true.

*"I accept with full awareness, objectivity, humbleness and responsibility that I am (Description of whom you are, with your flaws, based on the previous answer you gave or the general conclusion)"*

At this point, the more you analyze the conclusion of the interviews you have done, the better. As I said earlier, do not go easy on typing. It can only be beneficial.

The fact that you accept your traits, makes your brain automatically switch to a mode of change. It means that you stop hoping that others will provide you with a better future and you start to create it. You stop holding on to a hope that is not real and you start laying the foundations. People never create a great present for themselves by hoping, without actually changing. The acceptance of change is vital and I commend you for that.

You probably find yourself at a place where you have understood which traits you must get rid of. The fact that you are writing them on your Core (that's right, I have just revealed that the purpose of all this writing was to create your Core – you will understand more later) on your phone is a very important step that most people do not take. Most people's attitude is, "Okay, I'll do it later," and they might read many books, like this one, that prompt you to act but do not take any action whatsoever.

I want to believe that you understand the gravity of the situation. It is you against yourself.

Realize though, that you can do better.

Realize it and let's move on.

# Chapter 6
# Who You Are

## Part 3 Decision

*It is in the moments of decisions that your destiny is shaped.*
*– Antony Robbins*

Robins says it clearly. The decisions you make, move forward or they hold you back. It has nothing to do with how your environment behaves. It is only about how *you* behave. Everything you do originates from a decision you have made. Every moment in our life is made up of a series of decisions. When you get up in the morning and you drink coffee, that is a decision you make. When you decide to wear a red tie instead of a yellow one or you drink your coffee with or without sugar, it is all based on your choice.

*We are* our choices. Nobody else is responsible for whatever is happening to us. If something, somehow, affects us, then it is up to us to choose the right way to handle it. The decisions we make come from the choices we make every single second.

Now you will have to make a decision too: you will either remain who you are or you will change. This might be the most important decision you will ever have to make.

I never wanted to leave Greece. When I happened to be in discussions about moving abroad, I proudly said that Greece is and will always be my home. Even if I faced difficulties in my life, nobody and nothing could make me leave the country. I was absolutely to the point that you would wonder whether I was wanted for drug trade and trafficking in the rest of the world and Greece gave me asylum. I was obsessed!

In May 2017, I was given the offer to continue my career in Dubai. My first thought when I heard the offer was "No." A resounding, clear and sober "no." A "no" bigger than the dept of Greece back in 2008, a "no" that made the one Metaxas had said to the Italians seem like a walk in the park on a sunny day. A non-negotiable "no."

I wanted to stay in Greece. My whole life was there: my family, my friends, the places I went out and the coffee shops I would relax in. That was where I wanted to stay. I was used to a specific way of life, with certain standards and I did not want to change a single thing. I have always loved Greece and I did not want to leave the country.

To sum up, I think that I made it very clear that I did not want to leave Greece.

My manager wanted me to go to Dubai because the work I would be doing over there would also be beneficial for him money-wise. He started finding sly ways to convince me by bringing beers to the office and asking me to chill on the balcony with him to drink and smoke a cigarette. That son of a bitch had a way of expressing his great desire to send me there. I adore him because he believed in me a lot. He still does. At the same time, he was constantly highlighting the financial benefits that I would have if I went to Dubai, the career that would await me, and how much I would be able to provide to the people around me if I made it. Because as he said, "What good can the 1.000$ that you are making here do to you? Nothing compared to what you want to achieve." That guy, Maik, was always a great salesman. And he sold me good.

My father did not even want to hear about it and my mother would hang her head down every time the issue came up. My friends would only talk about this topic when we were out, trying to help me make a decision. And I... well, the same, my answer was "No." I was a stubborn idiot. A 36-year-old man acting like a child. I was too afraid of losing what I already had. I was afraid of failure and of the idea of having to go back with my tail between my legs.

"Come on, what is it you have here in Greece that you don't want to lose?" said Giorgos who was sitting on the right side of the couch in Vasilis' apartment, a night that we hung out eating.

"His virginity," said Giannis, always provocative.

"I don't want to leave, what else should I say? I like Greece and I am not excited at all about the idea of moving abroad."

"Yeah, okay. But you don't have anything so important to do here. You won't leave anything serious behind. Just a job which pays you 1.000$. It will be exactly like that in a month and a year. What if things are different abroad?" said Giorgos while cornering me.

"I don't want to leave my country, man. Is this so crazy?"

"It is," said Giannis.

"Giorgos is right," said Vasilis. "Even if you stay here, you will not gain anything more than what you already do. What if you go over there and things are as your manager claims will be? Then a great future could be awaiting you."

"I agree," said Leonidas.

I do not exactly remember the course of the discussion, but the night went by like that. The next days were somehow silent. The thoughts in my head though were deafening. What will I see when I go there? What will I leave behind? I felt that if I left, I would cry at the airport. I felt like they would tear something out of my chest and I would not be able to bear it. I know, I might sound like I am overreacting, but this is how I felt. I felt that I would leave a huge part of myself behind. On the other hand, I was thinking that if I took the leap and had all this glory that my manager was "selling" me, then I would be able to create the life I had always wanted. I would have the chance to make good money and build the career that Greece had not allowed me to build until I was 36.

That was the key moment for me. While accepting my situation, as I mentioned in the previous chapter, I was automatically undergoing the stage of change too. In order for this to happen, I had to truly change. Not only in words, but also with deeds. Not only when I felt comfortable, but also when I was afraid. As my 16-year career in the construction industry and constant struggle had not yielded the desired results, then leaving home should probably be a part of my change. No matter how much it would hurt. I was determined to do great things in my life and leave my mark, no matter how many sacrifices I had to make.

On July 16$^{th}$, 2017, I announced to my manager that I would go to Dubai and his smile was as wide as ever. Within 4.5 years I climbed the ladder from a simple salesman to the CEO of a sales company. Do not even get me started on writing about the life we have lived with my friends and colleagues in Dubai because I will come across as provocative. Some things are not to be published.

"It is in your moments of decision that your destiny is shaped," said Antony Robbins and if you watch on YouTube the video "How Great I Am," you will get the meaning of this even more. If you search for the video with Greek subtitles, you will find a version I translated somewhere in 2014. I liked that quote so much that it made me decide to fly to other lands and other places. And not only did I not regret this decision, but I shrug at the idea of not having made it in the first place.

But do you know why I wanted to share this story? To make you understand that I was also afraid of change. I was also afraid of leaving and plucking out the habits that were so deeply rooted inside of me, but in the end, it was for the best. I learned new things, I experienced wonderful situations, I worked with people that pushed me beyond my limits, I got to know better *who I am* and I know that I am on a path where I am the only one who decides about my future. Do you want me to let you in on a secret? I lost absolutely nothing. On the contrary, all those things I thought I would lose have not even come close to bothering me. I was worried for no reason. As utopic as it sounds, this is the truth.

And you know what? I cannot imagine myself not going to Dubai. You see, I still remember the first day I got a cab to travel around the city. It was on September 3rd, 2017. I was shocked. I felt as if I had been locked in a cage for 36 years and I had just broken free. I had been to Italy, France, Spain and many other European countries, but this was different. The high-rise, made of glass, skyscrapers built one right next to the other on the major Sheikh Sayed Road highway and the luxurious cars passing by were enough to make me fall in love with the city. Whose mind was hidden behind all this greatness? What human took the trouble to build from scratch on the sand a world that would become a pole of attraction for millions of people from around the globe?

Is the sky the limit indeed?

The famous Burj Khalifa, an 830 meters high building which is the second tallest building in the world and seems as if it touches the sky, is a real miracle of architecture and engineering. The fountains in the Dubai Mall that seem to be dancing along to the songs playing in the open-air areas of the mall. Whose idea was that? Why this is not what all the fountains around the world are? Not to mention "The Palm" which is the first artificial island. It is palm-shaped and can be seen from the moon. If humans can build an island, is there anything they cannot do?

Your decision to change is the one that will shape your destiny too. Whether you choose to remain where you are, even if you admit that you need to change, is up to you. If you decide to completely ignore this book and consider it as just "another book" is also up to you. Whatever you decide is yours and yours alone.

The fact that you are probably around 25–30 makes you much luckier than someone who is in his 40s, like me. Not because you have more time to process it but because you have more to offer. If you are close to 40 or more, it means that you have to run even faster to cover the distance. It means that you can still achieve great things but you have to kick… (I will not write the words) it up a notch. You must act as if your whole life depended on the choice you would make. One way or another though, no matter your age, you will have to decide now.

Take matters into your own hands. Pull up your sleeves and sit comfortably and decide to change, as I told you. I will show you the way and you will do it. Enough with the theories and the lies. Together we will build your new self and your new habits to create the present and the future you want. I am talking about the future you want and not the one that you dream of. I am sick of these stupid lines!

"The future you dream of."

Stupid lines from stupid people who reside in their dreams. They are asleep and when they wake up, they realize what reality is like, they get disappointed, lose their faith, and distance themselves even more from their dream. Because the reality is so harsh that the dream seems more and more impossible. There you go. This is another reason why an "average" person remains "average." Because they simply dream of things. Because they expect everyone else to change in order for their present to change. That is the stupidest thing I have heard in my life. This is why the world does not change. Because people see others' faults and never their own.

Stop demanding from others to change and demand it from yourself. Take the decision now because otherwise, you will never take it! Slam your hand on the table and shout "Enough! I'm changing NOW and I'm taking matters into my own hands!" and really do so with great energy, passion and strength. Remember what is between your legs and demand from yourself to decide to finally take matters into your own hands! Order yourself! Demand it!

This is what it means to be a great leader!

Robins says in the same video I mentioned, *"Our deepest fear is not that we are inadequate. Our deepest fear is that we are powerful beyond measure. Your playing small does not serve the world. There is nothing enlightened about shrinking so that other people will not feel insecure around you. We were born to make manifest the glory of God that is within us. It's not just in some of us, it's in everyone. And as we let our own light shine, we unconsciously permit other people to do the same. As we are liberated from our own fear, our presence automatically liberates others."*

The "Who I Am" philosophy means nothing without change. Nobody is flawless in this world and nobody ever will be. This philosophy is for people who have the guts to decide to become the best version of themselves in order to reach the skies with their success. People who know that dreams exist only when we are asleep. As long as we live, we create and we build with all of our beings. This philosophy requires people to change every single minute that goes by.

In the following lines, you will start recognizing the aspects of your goal that matter and this will increase your faith that you can actually make it. Further down, we will build together the habits you need to have to become who you want to be and reach where you want to go. Only then will you be sure that every step you take will be taking you there. You will experience reality without utopic disturbances and you will be climbing up based on the actual reality and not that of a dream. You will be walking on the ground, not on the clouds. If you find yourself flying, it will be because you have grown wings and not because someone has thrown you out of the window of a skyscraper.

Your choice to continue was the right one. Your choice to change your world was the right one. Your choice to partake in this journey was the right one.

And you will be rewarded for this.

The next pages will be your alpha and your omega. They will be your starting and your finishing line. They will be the change you have always wanted but have never dared. They will be the future you have always wanted but have never believed in. The next pages are more important than anything else that you have done up to now.

I promise you.

# Chapter 6
# Who You Are

## Part 4 Action

There will be no talking in the chapter of Action. You will only find actions and results.

If you deserve to succeed and become the leader you need to be, it depends only on your results.

Keep in mind that the only thing that matters is the result of your actions. Nothing else. Everything else is just an excuse and a waste of time.

If you forget that, then you will make the same mistake that most people do.

So demand results of yourself.

Now!

# Chapter 7
# Designing Your New You – 1st Stage

# The Core

*Success is the result of the actions of a great leader.*

This is my definition of success. I have mentioned it before and I am mentioning it once again now. Because as you might have realized so far, your action has value only when it is backed up with results.

It is time to prove if you deserve the success you are after or if you are one of the Inadequates too.

**STEP 1**
**THE CORE**

As I revealed in the chapter of Acceptance, the process of answering questions and writing them on your phone is actually the process of planning your Core. In this way, you have your thoughts written down, so that they become clearer to you. This is also the first major task of the "Who Am I" philosophy since it is the only way for you to understand the exact meaning of your thoughts and what effect they have on you.

This is why the first step is to make sure that you have answered the questions that you found in the previous chapters. Reminder:

1) What was the most positive influence in my life as a kid, either from my family or my friends? Does it still affect me?

2) Who do I think is a great leader and why?

3) Do I have a goal or is it all in vain?

**TIPS**: If you do not have a goal, start by answering the following questions:

a. When was the last time you made time stop and stood still somewhere to wonder if your path is the one you want it to be? Are your relationship or your job as you want them to be?

b. What makes you feel complete as a human? What is your passion?

c. Who are the people in your life that you consider important and for what reason? Would you turn your goal into a reality for them or for anyone else? Imagine that person and describe him or her.

d. What would you be willing to do NOW for yourself, if you were not afraid and if the obstacles you face did not exist?

4) This is a tough one: Which of the traits or the identities I read about above is closest to me? Which of all these identities am I, more or less? What else is being missed from my equation? Who am I finally? Which are my basic traits? Good or bad. Here is a list:

**TIPS:**

a. Number them and start with "I recognize that I am…"

b. Call yourself.

5) Interview two friends of yours. Sit with them for a coffee (each one separately, of course) for at least one hour and ask them their opinion about you. Your good and your bad traits. Don't try to deny their sayings. On the contrary, listen really carefully, no matter what they are saying and write everything down.

Be careful! The people that you'll choose to listen to must be older than you, more experienced than you and have proven results. Don't confuse the right research with the simple one. Your friends will not help you at all if you are on the same level. Choose wisely. Not sentimentally.

## STEP 2
## DECLUTTERING

The second step you need to take is to take people who do not provide you with something important out of your life and focus on the ones who make you better and stronger. Start choosing your circle and make sure to make it smaller so that you can feel safe and not exposed. Start expanding your horizons, even more, joining new companies or groups of people who have something to teach you about how to move forward and how to evolve.

You will need to go a step further. For example, if you come across a situation where you have to pick up your phone to comfort a friend, avoid it. It will likely drag you down, psychologically, and the road up will be difficult for you. You do not need any more drama in your life. You are doing just fine on your own. Moreover, one of the most important reasons why people do not pursue success is because they hang out with toxic people who do not believe in it. Negativity, whining and nastiness are contagious. It happens before you even realize it.

If you think about it for a while, seriously and responsibly, I am sure that by reading between the lines, you will definitely find among the people around you one friend (or more) who does not smile, who always has an opinion on everything and who becomes critical at every opportunity.

You will realize it even more when you start avoiding going to parties with these same people and make other plans instead. Try that and see if you will miss them. It might sound like it is too much for you, but you would be surprised by how little you need some people. You will realize it when you step away for a while. Try that as an experiment and let's see what happens.

Through this process, I have no intention of making you snobbish or contemptuous. Do not forget that *humility* is one of the principles that determine a leader's integrity. The real goal here is to take care of yourself and at the same time, create space in your life for people who will make you feel fulfilled.

Let me remind you that in the chapter of Acceptance, I mentioned that sometime in 2015, I realized that no matter how much I worked, nothing changed in my daily life. I was a 34-year-old young man wearing All-Star shoes, with the attitude of a child, and my habits in no way reminded me of a person who wants to succeed. I did not like the fact that I was not developing, and I started observing myself through the groups I belonged to. This realization along with choosing which people I would keep in my life and which people I would let go, is one of the biggest challenges I have ever accepted in my life.

As selfish as it might sound, I never considered myself selfish, because I was simply taking care of myself. I focused on breaking free from people I used to spend time with, to get to know people who would help me discover my purpose and the journey that would lead me there. Readjusting the people around me was one of the most important steps on my way to change.

So, go to your Core and answer the question:

6) Who among the people in my outer circle inspires me and motivates me to go forward?

7) Who among the people in my inner circle makes me feel uneasy or uncomfortable, for some reason? Can I easily live my life without them?

## STEP 3
## GROWTH

The third step you need to take is to develop a new habit that few people have: read every day 10 pages of a book that will broaden your horizons and give you new ideas on your way to success. This can be done mainly at night before you go to sleep. In fact, it will also be more effective. Write down on your phone all the phrases worth remembering by numbering them. When you finish the book, spend a week going through your notes and choose the most important ones that deserve to enter into your Core.

You can find books related to the field of your interest. You can also read books related to sales, social media, leadership, psychology, finance and so on. Even if you do not know where to start since the options are endless, you can always look on the internet or send me an email and I will give you some ideas.

No, I have no intention of doing any sort of advertising, my sneaky friend.

If you want to take it a step further, do what I did during the process of my transformation. Along with two friends of mine, we attended a few sessions with a life coach to get an idea from an expert. The conditions were ideal, as we met once a week at a cafe in Athens for an hour and the coach broadened the horizons of our *ego*. In fact, in the two months that our sessions lasted, I learned more about myself than I had learned in the past 34 years. It is great to be exposed in this way as you realize that you still have so much to learn from the world and yourself, and this is something that few people realize. Little did I know, of course, that there would be moments when she would stab my heart with a dagger in her attempt to make me realize *who I am*. She did so, it hurt me, and she was smiling.

Finding a mentor will be beneficial. It will take you down paths you had never imagined existed inside of you. As you read earlier, a mentor can become your greatest weapon if you use it properly.

Personally, even if I have gotten to where I am, I still think that I have a long way to go. Even today, I make sure to read at least one book every two months, although even that does not sound enough to me right now. As I have already mentioned several times, books are the most important thing in my home because, in books, I find out truths that I never had the guts to admit and I discover aspects of people similar to me who can help me take another step forward.

8) Choose your next book and order yourself to read 10 pages before going to bed every night. Do not forget that it is equally important to take notes of the phrases you want to remember, the moment you read them.

## STEP 4
## RESEARCH

Your fourth step is to start observing the characteristics of other people and understand who they are. Observe and judge responsibly whether they are close to your temperament and your needs, or even if you act in the same way. Ask yourself, "Why do they have that smile? What does my smile look like and what is hidden behind it? Am I like that too?" "Hey, they go on for hours about themselves and when it is time to pay attention to someone else, they are on their phone. Am I doing this too? Am I so self-centered or am I different?" "Are they confident? Am I?" etc. You can also observe good examples like people who have better results than you in the company you work for. "How it's possible that they have better results than I do?", "What can I do differently so that I can have the same or better results than them?" etc.

Personally, this became a very interesting game for me when I started it. I went out with friends, relatives, and acquaintances, just to have the chance to notice new characteristics and general behaviors. For everyone. At the same time, I was rejecting the bad ones, fixed those that needed to be fixed, and moved on. I became a detail-oriented observer. I have changed a lot since then and I continue to do so.

During this process, on the same text, I started also writing down ideas, attitudes toward life and notes from the books I was reading. Everything was going straight to my Core. I was writing down phrases from a TV show, a movie, or something that I heard while sitting on a bus. I realized that the more I was writing, the more I was able to better understand whatever crossed my mind and eyes during the day. In this way, I could literally hear what my mind was saying.

And the funny thing is that till then I wasn't listening! Oh, my dear god! I wasn't listening at all.

So much information was missed. So many bad things that came to my mind destroying my mood and ruining anything that I wanted to build. A mindset full of crap and insecurities, buried in my subconscious mind. Like Tyler Durden (the amazing character from the movie "Fight Club") would probably say if he was me:

*"I was the ugly truth behind that beautiful positivity that with a blink of my eye, would break like a glass statue after falling from the 30th floor."*

I was that fragile. How could I ever be a successful man…?

That was the beginning of everything. The beginning of my understanding, of accepting myself and of the decisions I made. I used it to take it out on myself, with power and nerve, while I was trying to let go of anything that held me back. My Core was a stream of everyday stimuli that I did not allow myself to ignore. I thought that it was of great importance to write down every single thing I came across, as I would have the chance, later on, to analyze everything and decide what I wanted to keep. To this day, I have filled in four books of more than 200 pages each with thoughts and statements that I write down daily. It is a Bible.

9) The next time you get together with a friend, turn the process into research. Do not let them know though. In this process, authenticity is more crucial than anything else. Within the time given to you, discreetly write down your remarks in your Core, after you leave the premises, and set them as an example to imitate or to avoid depending on their nature and your subjective position on it.

## STEP 5
## REPETITION

The fifth step is to avoid making the mistake that everyone else makes: do not forget to repeat the steps you took in this chapter. As I have already mentioned, I have never stopped. I still choose my friends, I still study and develop myself, and I still observe reactions and compare them with my own. I admit I did not know how long it would take me to get where I wanted to be, but

I trusted the process and this system. I am not yet the person I want to be, but my so far development has brought me to the point I am today.

Do not forget that:

*It is not about why you didn't do something.*
*It is important that you didn't do it.*

This means that – I will write it once again because I like to repeat the very important parts of my philosophy – what matters is *the result* you bring. Nothing else. Everything else is an excuse and a waste of time.

I will complete the first stage of change by stressing that my development, like everyone else's, is a result of my action. Based on the 5th Core Principle of the "Who I Am" philosophy, my purpose was not simply to take action or to do something to change. *My purpose has always been to change*, regardless of how quickly I would act. My purpose has been to see the results of my actions, not just to act. The action itself is not enough to keep me motivated. It is not enough to sustain my faith and boost my confidence that I can do it. The only thing that strengthens my self-confidence is seeing the results of my actions.

If I wanted to constantly see the results which would give me strength on my journey of change, I had to set a new term that I came up with. You already read about it in the leadership chapter: "Aggressive Action." This was the key for me to see results. I am talking about continuous, unstoppable and expansive action. In this way, I have been strengthening my faith and self-confidence. It was the results of this action that would make me keep playing. It was not just the action itself.

*Nothing and no one has the power to boost your self-confidence*
*more than the results of your actions.*

In order to take my "aggressive action," I acted so much that people in my inner circle worried that I might have joined a cult. Even my own brother could not understand back then. When he saw that I changed my old habits and read a few pages from my book at night instead of going to sleep immediately as I used to, he was surprised. In my 30s, when I did not show up at our gatherings, my friends started complaining that I blew them off. My weekends were full of meetings with friends and acquaintances, so I did not watch all the matches of my favorite team as I used to. I had decided that I would change and that was exactly what I was doing. Not only me but also people around me could tell I took action.

The same goes for my transformation.

Can I tell you the truth now? Most people devalue or despise the concept of success because whenever they have tried to do something outside of their "comfort zone," they failed. At first, they fight, or at least they pretend they do. Then, as soon as the first difficulties come up, or if they do not see the results they expected, they start crying, pointing out various reasons why they cannot succeed. At the end of the day, they convince themselves that it was not what they wanted in the first place. Then, they decide that it is better to get back to their original path because they felt safe there. It reminds me of some 2-year-old brats who convince their parents to get them a toy (and most of the times a too expensive one), and when they finally get it, they use it for an hour and then they get bored of it and throw it away.

It is in moments like this when parents realize the true value of a condom.

My point is that your action must be effective. Since you have decided to change, then you should back up your decision with results too. Actions are not enough. The "Who I Am" philosophy is about results created by "aggressive action," not the other way around. Be careful. Action is a utopia and a subjective condition, as you read earlier. The result is the only thing that matters.

Let me make something clear to you. No matter how hard you try, sweat, or hurt, it does not matter if you do not get results. Nothing can compare to the pain you will experience while reshaping your internal DNA, that is your thoughts, your habits and your behaviors. When the time comes to let go of a deeply ingrained habit of yours, you will choose whether you are worthy of success or not. Only when you succeed will you be considered worthy and there will be some value in your action. Without that, you just waste your time.

Before moving on to the next chapter, answer the following question taking into consideration everything you wrote down in your Core:

10) Where do I see myself in a year?

(Spoiler alert… It has to do with your purpose…)

Take your time, think about it, write it down and move on only when you have the answer.

Because in the next chapter… you are in for great steps!

# Chapter 7
# Designing Your New You – 2nd Stage

# The Map

I will be honest with you. This part of the journey is the most exciting one for me. Because this is where the true transformation happens. The way you will handle things, your trust in everything you have read so far and in what this book represents, your attitude towards the real-life examples that prove my philosophy, your patience along with your discipline will all be the reason why you will succeed. I guarantee that, straight talk.

This is the "soul" of the "Who I Am" philosophy. This is also part of my soul. Let's start.

*Everything begins at the finish line*

When I heard these words coming out of my mouth at the end of 2017 while I was talking to my manager, I could not believe my own words. I took my notebook – yes, I used to have a notebook to write down my thoughts. That is when the Core text began – and wrote this down in huge letters. This quote made me realize that if you want to carry out a task, a sale, or a success in general, you first need to picture the final result you are after. This is a given. Everybody knows it (#not).

When I put that quote into words, everything became clearer. It was simple. It all begins from where you want to finish.

I have read all these books about how important it is to set goals, how to set them and how to achieve them. I have read that you need to write them down and number them. Another suggestion was to collect pictures that represent what

I want and put them on a Vision Board near my bed. The idea was to look at them so often that I could see myself having all that. However, I never really connected with all these processes. They never stuck in my head simply because they had not managed *to convince me that I could make it.*

I have also heard about the importance of positive statements. They never did anything to me. On the contrary, I found them too Insufficient to make me reshape my beliefs. I see myself as someone with a difficult and strict personality. So I did not find helpful that process either, no matter how hard I tried.

Later on, I understood that there was a reason for that. The reason was that I had a hard time convincing myself that I could achieve my goals. I had a hard time convincing myself that I, Spyros, who wears All-Star and a cheap hair gel, can become a successful man. That I could become someone who drives a luxurious car, manages companies, invests in Real Estate, and has put his life together being just 40 years old. Since I cannot convince myself, no one else will be able to do so. And for sure, I cannot be convinced by a so-called goal I wrote down on a piece of paper or a random statement without a clear beginning and end, with no coherence and duration.

## *Everything begins at the finish line*

However, everything changed the moment when I said that phrase. First of all, I realized that there were many people just like me. People who wanted something but could not get it and did not know the reason. I thought to myself, *" Instead of setting practical goals, why don't I focus on who I must be or who I want to be to achieve my goal while working on the goal as well? At the end of the day, it all starts with me."*

It just made so much sense. We have no control over our destiny. We do not know what will happen tomorrow. For God's sake! We do not even know what will happen in the next second. What we can control though is who we *will* be at every single moment. If I managed to train myself to become the person who would be able to convince me that I could get everything I wanted, then it would work. Since it all begins at the finish line, I should also use this theory with who I am.

Not with what I want.

So, what happened at the end of 2017? I'll tell you what.

It was when I first went to work in Dubai. Before I even boarded the plane, I had already decided that my goal was to become the best and to "lead the portfolio management team of Greece." Hilarious. It was not just difficult, it was impossible. It went beyond the limits of imagination and made "Mission Impossible" sound like a lullaby for children. Ethan Hunt would have rejected this mission before the self-destruction of the message and would have moved to a mountain far beyond any form of civilization!

When I got there and sat with my manager and told him what I wanted to achieve, he told me, "Spyros, if you want to lead a team, you will have to be ready when the time comes. If the time comes before you are who you need to be, you will fail."

I thought to myself, *So I need to lead an imaginary team before the team is created. It does not make much sense. And if the time does not come? What should I do then? Will I keep pretending and have trust in the Lord? What is this? A game? Is this a game? That's crap!*

"How is this possible? I do not have a team. How will I find out who I need to be when the time comes since I do not have a clue?" I replied looking honest and puzzled, but without saying out loud my thoughts.

"You have a team."

I lost it. I did not know how to feel or what to do. It was one of those moments when you do not understand if the other person is talking to you or an invisible hands-free.

"Are you talking to me? Do you mean me?"

"Is there anyone else on the team?"

"No."

"So?"

"So, are you telling me that I should lead a team in which I am the only member? So I am supposed to lead myself?"

"Yes, but why should you do that?"

"I think I got it. You are telling me that I should lead myself before anyone else joins the team so that when the time comes, they will know that I am worthy to be followed."

"Exactly. This is it. And now what? What are you supposed to do now?"

I shrugged my shoulders in wonder. It was one of the meetings with my manager that smashed my brain. He would not just give me the answers. He made me think and draw conclusions myself. Then, he explained the reason why we had reached that conclusion. I must say that it is time-consuming, but the best way to learn is to draw a conclusion on your own and have someone correct you if you are wrong. It is better than finding the answers to everything ready.

"Honestly, I have no idea what I should do."

"Come on now, you are smart. Think."

Pause. Wonder. *I am sure that he is using hands-free again,* I thought. *I just cannot see it. Maybe it is one of these tiny ones that disappear into the ear. This is it. He is not talking to me!*

"Spyros, who will be the manager of the first member of the team?"

"That would be me."

"Whose steps will the team members need to follow?"

"Mine."

"Who will give instructions?"

"Me again."

"Who will be in charge?"

"Me."

"Who will they have to listen to in order to succeed?"

"Me."

"Why?"

Here we go again. He started using the hands-free again. That "why" was not addressed to me. Does he want to wear me out? I was getting tired.

"What do you mean by *why*?"

"Why should they listen to you?"

"No offense, but what kind of question is this? They will listen to me because I will be their manager. They will have to listen to me. This is just what they will have to do. It is a matter of hierarchy," I said raising the tone of my voice as I was losing my temper.

"Why should they listen to you? And if they do listen to you, will that be because they want to or because you have asked them to do so? Will they get instructions from you because that will be an order or because they will want to? Will they listen to you because they *will have to* or because they *will know* that this is the way to succeed? Can you tell the difference, Spyros or not? Do you understand that it is different for someone to be listening to you because you demand it and different to be listening to you because they want to? The leaders who went down history and who had positive outcomes were not the ones who made people follow them. They were the ones whose traits inspired their followers. People should not just be with you. They should be excited to be with you. They should be excited both about your goal AND about the person they chose to follow. Leaders 'words should inspire and their results should prove that any goal is achievable. These traits made followers trust their leaders and follow them unconditionally. People must see the value of a leader in order to follow him or her. They must see their leadership skills, their manners, and everything else one must *be* to be considered a great leader. If they are not who they need to be in order to have followers, it means that they demand their "followers" to follow along. Do you know what I call those followers, Spyros? I call them slaves. People who follow someone because they "have to" are slaves. All the slaves, sooner or later, walk away from the so-called leaders, from those who demand people to follow them. So when the first member of your team comes, what kind of leader are you going to be?"

"The best one."

"Do you think so? Why is that?"

"Because I work hard."

"I don't give a shit about how hard you work," he said angrily. "How much do you earn?"

"I make good money."

"The money you make is not good enough taking into consideration what you represent. Go on. When the first member of your team arrives, what will they see? A person who makes *good money*? So they will believe that they too will start making *good money* and probably even less since you will be their manager. So your team will be formed from people who make *good money*. Is that right?"

"Yes, it is."

"But you were just telling me that you want your team to be the best. Is that right?"

"Yes, it is."

"If you want your team to be the best, the members of your team need to be making *great money*. Is that right?"

"Yes, it is."

"How will it be possible for them to make *great money* if their manager makes *good money*? How will any of the members of your team believe that they can make *great money* if not even you make great money? Why should they follow you, SPYROS?

"WHO ARE YOU, SPYROS AND WHY THE FUCK SHOULD THEY FOLLOW YOU?"

I was shocked! I stood there… frozen. I could hardly breathe and tears almost came to my eyes because of the tension of the moment. I stood there staring at him and I did not know if I should say I was offended or thank him. What he had said was a truth I needed to hear, as all these years I refused to see *who I was*. I did not have the traits that a successful person has and this is why my career in the Construction Industry was not so successful. I was not capable of great things, success, wealth and luxury. If I thought I was, it was only because I was a dreamer, romantic and as naive as I could possibly be.

The truth took me by surprise. I was relaxed and not prepared for that, and the truth hit me with all of her might. It hit me shouting, with intensity and strength. It turns out, it was the only way to face it.

"Spyros, what kind of reality do you picture for the moment that the first member of your team comes? What kind of person will you ask them to follow? What traits should your team members have? What clothes will they be wearing? How much will they be earning? What values should they have? Where should they stop? How much should they tolerate? How should they be dealing with obstacles that come up? How passionately should they work? How excited will they be about anything you say or any instruction you give? How cool should their manager be in order for them to know they can rely on him without second thoughts and achieve together everything they want?

"This is *who you* need to become if you want to be the best."

Now it was clear. If I wanted to become the best manager or the best leader, I had to become one right away. Not on the following day, not when the "right time" would come. I believe only a few can understand how badly I wanted it. After all these years working on construction sites, under the burning sun during hot days and in freezing weather during the cold ones, having spent all these hours stuck in traffic, becoming the best one seemed like a lifeboat to me. Being aware of the amount of money I could make, nothing and no one could stop me.

So, I decided to become whom I needed to be. I decided to become whom I was destined to be. After all these years, I had finally found the one thing that had the power to make me the person I wanted to be.

This is how the "Who I Am" philosophy was first conceived. If we want to get what we want, we first need to become the person we need to be in order to achieve our goal. This was the only way in which I would later convince myself that I could make it.

Before that, I was just pretending.

The night this idea stuck in my mind, I went back home, took my shoes off, made my way to the closet, took my suit, my shirt, my tie, and my watch off, and hung them carefully. I put on the sweatpants that I had left on my pillow in the morning, and I washed my hands. Right after that, without even turning the lights on, I sat on the sofa put some smooth Jazz on and lit a cigarette gazing at the view of the Dubai Marina. It was the first cigarette of the day. It's one of these cigarettes that helps you calm down and convinces you, "It will be OK, man."

One cigarette led to another. I was thinking about the conversation I had with my manager and that if I wanted to make things work, I should have in mind throughout the day whom I *wanted* to be. There should be no exceptions. I should not use as an excuse the work pressure, the long hours, or any other weakness. If I wanted to make it work, I should be more disciplined than the greatest army general. I thought that if I wanted to become a great manager and inspire the members of my team, I should have the right attitude, without exceptions, and I should do so before the time would come.

Having in mind what my manager had told me: "Become whom you want to be before you achieve what you want to achieve", I started writing down my first Map.

The first I did is to take the Core in my hands. The text that showed me my inner self and what was hidden behind my smile was ready to go to the next level! I needed to connect the dots and build a character that would definitely make my goal come true. The person to whom I wanted to become. Who I was, had proven unworthy to achieve what I wanted. I thought to myself, *Let's see what will happen if I keep my goal untouched and change myself.*

Challenge accepted! And I loved it!

I went over my notes again, decoded them, and let go of anything useless while giving more space to the thoughts I wanted to enhance. Every positive and negative thought I had written in my Core, was transferred to a brand-new script with a specific path and structure, aiming to change the chemistry of my brain. This was my Map. The way to become the person who would DEFINITELY achieve my goal!

Using my Core as a guide, I started planning whom I had to *be* when the time to become what I wanted to be would come. I wrote what behavior I wanted to have, what clothes I would like to wear, whom I wanted other people to see me as, and how much they would trust me. I even analyzed what I would like other people to say about me. I analyzed how highly I would like them to speak of me and what I wanted them to say to their friends and families about me. I even wrote down the ideal daily routine, including all the habits I should build if I wanted to be whom I needed to be.

Writing down on my Map, I noticed my thoughts, my moves, my words, and my reactions daily. Apart from myself, I also kept watching everyone else and I kept writing things on my Core. When I went home at night, I was transferring the notes I had written in my Core, to my Map, but in a better way. This way, days went by, and a new version of me, who would be able to make a difference, was being built. You got it right. Because of a text written on my phone.

While I was writing, which was on a daily basis, I changed all these small things I had to change to build the right version of myself. My transformation had begun. I started thinking, talking, walking, and fighting in a different way. I had more and more self-confidence and as days went by, I could not wait for that much-anticipated day. The day I would become a manager. As this day was approaching, I was getting anxious about whether I had become whom I had to become or something else. The more anxious I was getting, the more I was seeing myself changing at work or in my life in general. I had even changed the way I drank my coffee and the cafes I went to. A precious process that has never stopped since.

I wrote nonstop. I wrote at night before I went to bed, in the morning when I drank my coffee at the office, during my lunch break, and at night when I went back home. I split my notes into paragraphs. I used exclamation marks. I erased a few words and then, I wrote them differently. I wrote some words in bold to emphasize them. These words were so powerful that, every time I read them, I felt as if I shouted them. And I kept writing. I even wrote when I was at my office. I wrote everything I heard and thought would be helpful even on a piece of paper so that I could copy it into my Map later. I wrote down every single negative thought that crossed my mind but reversed. In this way, I wanted to make sure that it would never cross my mind again.

In my Map, I described my ideal me using the tense I would use if I had already been me. It was as if I lived in a parallel universe as if I took part in a virtual reality game. In this "ideal" life, I knew how much money I earned and what my personality was like. I described what I saw as if I had a camera. I pictured the way I entered my office, my clothes, my thoughts, and what everyone else thought about me. I described what I said and what other people said. I described my feelings, how I faced my fears, and how powerful and bold I was.

I added all of these to my Map in a way that my stubborn mind was convinced. Every single detail was important. Every single situation was added with such intensity that there was no way that it would not get into me. Every trait of mine and every thought found its place in the ideal version of "me" that I was creating in my mind. That was my goal: to create the ideal version of "me." The one I thought would be right for me and that would help me achieve my goals. That was the goal: to get where I wanted to be.

It took a while to write it. But while I was writing, I could hear my thoughts changing. I felt that I was letting go of my old habits. Habits that I had always wanted to quit, but I had never thought I would be able to. This is what I programmed myself to do. I could see my fears and insecurities slowly fading away. I woke up in a better mood and I walked into the office feeling cool and confident. I worked as if I had been working in this job forever. Because this is what I had *ordered* myself to do. All the negative thoughts I previously had, were now replaced by positive thoughts and proactive methods. I started to enjoy my work. Because this is what I had programmed myself to do.

When I finally became the manager of a team, as part of a pilot scheme to see if I could make it, the members of the team met a version of myself that was quite different from that guy who had arrived in Dubai a while ago. They met a leader who had all the necessary answers, who was not intimidated by challenges, and who could handle his team even in the most difficult situations. They found a version of me on whom they could count on and who they knew would take them to the top.

In my first month as a manager, I managed to help the first member of my team bring the best results in the whole office. I made him No1 among all these highly-experienced professionals. It was much more than luck. It was the result of hard work, devotion, and leadership.

My experiment had worked out. I took off my All-Stars and never looked back.

It did not take long to understand that what I wanted to achieve was of secondary importance. The priority has always been me. It turned out that I was not fair to myself. I was too small to carry the burden. Even though some people do not want to see it, this is exactly the reason why they are still small.

*You act based on who you really are,*
*not on who you wanna be.*

I wanted to become even better so my transformation did not stop there. Even when I already had my team, I kept changing. I saw every difficulty as a chance to develop. I found solutions to problems that if I faced before, I would step back and would see the situation in a quite different way. I was becoming the person I wanted to be. It was the result of daily effort, consistency, discipline, and objectivity.

Three months after that, I formed a team the members of which shared the same goal: to become the best, as a team and individually. In June of 2016, 6 months after I had taken over as a manager of my team, we were the best team in Europe, based on results of course.

I know one thing for sure. None of these would have happened if I had not done everything I could to become the person I had to be, long before I became that person. This is the secret. I wrote my first Map in October 2017 and I have not stopped since then. I have written more than seven Maps during my career so far. When I got promoted to a higher position, I wrote a new Map. And another one when I got promoted again. When I became the CEO of my own company in Bahrain, I wrote a new one. I created a new Map for each new chapter of my life. Each one of them had a different goal and different attitude towards things. Because even today, I get motivated by myself. I am the one who reminds me *who I am* and what I have to do. No matter how many books I read, how many personal development seminars I attend, and how many leadership and sales Masterclasses I will train other people in, if I did not have my texts, which have been my way to program myself, I would have succeeded nothing.

Nothing at all.

You are next...

## A GOOD STARTING POINT

In the following lines, I will share with you the four most important steps you need to know to create your Map. So far, you have created your Core, which helped you unwind from the mess you had in your mind. The answers you gave to all these questions can help you realize what is important in your life.

Your Map though is something different. Your Map is the beginning and the end of your transformation. It will help you develop the traits of the person you need to be to succeed, whatever that means to you. The Map we will create together will have everything you should have but did not know how to get. It will have everything that you should be, but you never realized that.

Let's start, shall we? We should already have taken action.

## STEP 1

You should keep in mind that you should find the process of creating or reading your Map fun. So the first thing you need to do is to find a name for your Map. A name that you like. A name that implies change, that refers to the new era that is about to start and to your new "you."

**1st Paragraph**: In the first paragraph, I want you to write the reason why you want to change. For instance, this could be something like:

*"The aim of this text is to turn into a habit to daily reinforce my mind with positive thoughts because I keep forgetting that and I get carried off. I have behaved as a child many times. I have behaved as an asshole as well. This text is the transformation of ......... (your name) of yesterday, to the ........(your name) of today."*

You should know that this is the first thing you need to write down because your mind must know beforehand the goal of this text. In this way, it is convinced that this is something important and thus, keeps reading and processing what it reads. So the more personal elements you add to the above statement, the better.

The next **3 paragraphs** should be about:

1. Accepting your nature and who you are now. To do that, you should use your research and the feedback you got when you interviewed your friends. Highlight that you take full responsibility for the person you are today. You are fully responsible for who you are.
2. Write about an incident that proves your nature. Your bad traits. Use a striking example from your life that makes you want to let go of this nature of yours. For example, if you are a jealous person and you know it, but you can't help it, write down an incident that proves the size of the damage you create every time you express it to your partner. An incident so extreme that made you sick of who you are.
3. Write how important you are and mention 3 incidents of your life that made you feel unique and proud. Mention 3 incidents that you wanted to share more than the rest and that made you feel proud and happy.

## STEP 2
## YOUR DAILY LIFE

*Everything begins at the finish line.*

I am sure that this quote rings a bell for you. Well, do not forget it. Never.

In the 4th chapter, the one about the purpose, you wrote what you want to achieve. I am almost sure that you have used only 2–3 words max at that point. Not bad for a start. But we need to take this one step further because this is how most people write down their goals and fail.

I will repeat for one last time that you need to be sure that the goal you have set is so great, that only the thought of it gives you shivers. Your goal should be so great that it will be the only thing you will be talking about with your friends. It should be so great that your partner will get sick of listening to all the details you will be sharing. Make sure that it is so valuable for you that it is the last thought that crosses your mind before you fall asleep and the first one when you wake up in the morning. It should be so powerful that you will be waking up before the alarm goes off in the morning, full of power, energy, passion, and determination to work in that direction. You should want it so bad that no obstacle will be able to stop you. No grumbling, no envy, no difficulty, and no compromise will be able to hold you back. Your goal should be so powerful that will make you put your foot down and scream in the face of everyone who questioned you.

Remember the 2nd Core Principle of the "Who I Am" philosophy: *"Leader is his Purpose."* The only thing that stands between successful and unsuccessful leaders is their *purpose* and their *belief* in it. However, we are not going to work on your purpose itself together. If you are a smart person, a potentially great leader, if you are someone who actually wants to create something and you are not reading this only because you have nothing better to do, you should have understood by now that you are not going anywhere without a purpose. I think we have made this clear.

The $2^{nd}$ step in your Map is to convince your mind that the goal you have set is achievable and it is not just something you have dreamed of. This will be done by *analyzing the everyday life of the life you have pictured*. I am sure that you will question the process at first, and you will wonder if you need to be that analytical. Trust me though, it works. As long as you put into practice the methods suggested by this philosophy, you will see the change soon. Not only your thoughts will be different, but your beliefs as well.

Because I will show you a way in which you will be able to "convince" yourself to believe in something instead of just "dictating" it.

## WHAT DO YOU MEAN?

"What do you mean?"

What do you mean by "What I mean"?

If you have ever set a goal in your life and you have not achieved it, it is because the method you used was trying to force your mind to believe in something which did not seem to be important. You have just forced it, as if you were a dictator, to believe that your goal was just what you wanted. You did not provide it with any explanation or well-supported points that would convince it you could actually make it. You did not inspire your mind. You did not explain why your goal is achievable. So your mind rejected this piece of information as it thought it was something useless, meaningless, and unattainable.

To put it simply, when a piece of information goes into our mind, the mind tends to reject it if it is not supported by rational proof or analysis or/and a powerful feeling. If you keep forcing it into your mind, your mind will pretend that it has saved the information, but it will throw it away the minute you turn your back. When you will remember your goal again in the future, your mind will say something "Yeah, yeah! All good, man! Don't worry, I got you!." It doesn't. It has forgotten your goal, just like you. No result whatsoever.

Imagine that when you are reading your goals, your mind will be objecting. Imagine a conversation like this:

"I want a 2000€ salary!"

"Why?" replies your mind.

"What do you mean by *why*? Because that's what I want."

"I know, but why? What have you done to deserve it? Who are *you* that makes you believe that you deserve it and you want me just to believe that you deserve it? Give me a well-informed opinion and I'll pass."

"Why do you even care? I want 2000€. In fact, I can also picture myself having it already. I even put it on my vision board so that I can see it every day."

"Sure, my boy, whatever you say. Do you want to give me one reason that explains why you deserve it?"

"I don't know what this is all about. I was told to set a goal and that's exactly what I'm doing. My goal is a 2000€ salary."

"OK… whatever, man…"

The next day…

"I want a 2000€ salary."

"Here we go again… Why?"

"What do you mean by *why*? Didn't we talk about it yesterday? Because that's what I want."

"I know, but why? What have you done to deserve it? Who are YOU to deserve it?"

"Why do you even care who I am? I want 2000€. In fact, I can also picture myself having it already. I am holding it and I am happy."

"I don't know what is that you are holding and makes you happy bro, but I know it isn't 2000€. Would you mind giving me a reason that explains why you deserve it?"

"Smart-ass! I was told to set a goal and that's exactly what Im doing and I will keep doing it. My goal is a 2000€ salary."

"Whatever… keep holding it and let's see what happens."

I know. It seems weird to present you your mind (or your unconscious–conscious mind) as a separate entity, but the above-mentioned example is quite realistic. Our mind integrates new information in a particular way. It is not enough to randomly say something a couple of times, because it will not believe you this way. How many times have you said "I'll go on a diet starting tomorrow" and you turn around to eat nine chocolates from the box? The reason for that is that your mind is not convinced that you can actually go on a diet.

This is the main reason why people do not achieve the goals they set. Because they simply cannot believe that their goals are achievable. Because they fail to turn their dreams into their ultimate purpose. People do not know how to convince their minds.

Blaise Pascal said, "It's not the 'it' that you want, it's the fantasy of 'it'. So, desire supports crazy fantasies." Pascal's point is that we can be truly happy only when we picture our future happiness. Even if we do not get it or we do not try to get it, we will keep having it in our minds as thinking about it will be enough to make us happy. This is why people like dreaming.

Using your Map, you will teach your mind to be unable to live without what it wants, just by convincing it that you are who you want. You will keep exposing it to your fantasy until your mind decides to turn it into a reality. Yes, you will brainwash your mind about what you want more than anything else by making it believe *who* you are. To succeed, your fantasy should be as detailed as possible, you should describe the ideal environment and you should use a tense that implies that *your goal of who you want to be, has already been achieved.*

Yes, your fantasy will become your reality.

In the following paragraphs, I want you to pretend that you have already achieved your goal and describe in detail a simple day of your life. I need you to provide as many details as possible. Imagine that someone is holding a camera. Recording. The accuracy with which you describe everything you see is the key to your Map. So that you do not get lost and to get an idea of what you need to do, try to answer the following:

1. What day is it?
2. How did you wake up in the morning? Where are you?
3. What do you see? What do you hear? What is the first thought that crosses your mind?
4. Are you alone?

5. What did you do when you got up? What clothes did you put on?
6. Did you drink coffee? In case you did, what kind of coffee?
7. In case you own a car, where is it? Is it in a garage? Is it on the street?
8. What's your car like? Which model is it? What color is it? How much did it cost? How do you feel about having this car?
9. What's the weather like?
10. What did your friends tell you the night before about your success? What did you do that was so great?
11. Where are you going to? To your office? To your company? Which destination would be ideal to make you realize that you have achieved your purpose?
12. What do you come across on your way there?
13. What can you see? What are you thinking about? What's the weather like?
14. Do you stop anywhere? If so, why is that? What do you see? Whom do you meet? What are you talking about?
15. Where are you heading next? Did you arrive at your destination? What kind of building is it? Where is it? Where are you going to park your car?
16. After you have parked your car, what do you need to bring along? What are you holding? How do you feel?
17. Are you using an elevator? What's the place you are like? Describe it a little bit so that you can get the feeling.
18. What do you do there? What have you come to be? What have you achieved after all this work?
19. What traits or habits of yours helped you get here? Was it your discipline? Your persistence? Your patience? Your faith? Your power? Your boldness? Your courage? What else?
20. In case money is part of your definition of success, how much money did you make last month? How much money did you make in the last six months?
21. Why did you make so much money? What did you do exactly and managed to get to this point?
22. Which new habits and kind of discipline that you lacked before led you to the point you are now?

23. Was there a significant incident that you think defined the result and your destiny in that place?
24. What do you see when you arrive at your destination and enter the office? What do you hear? What are you thinking of? How do you feel? How do you walk?
25. At the same time, how are other people looking at you? What do they see? What are they saying? How do they feel?
26. If you have your private space in there, what does it look like? Where are you sitting on? Who are you with?
27. Are there any pictures around? What pictures are they? What do they represent?
28. How do you feel now that you know you have achieved your goal?
29. What are your plans for tonight? Where are you going? With whom? Where will you go and what kind of drink will you have?

**TIP 1**: It is quite important to choose the right words to describe your feelings each time. Your emotional world will be the one that will change the facts. It is the reason why each piece of information will find its way into your subconscious and through repetition, it will become your new reality. This will be fully analyzed in the next chapter. Until then, try to use phrases such as "I feel proud," "I feel confident," "I feel admiration," "I remember to be," "I laugh when I remember…," and so on. It is of paramount importance to focus on the feeling created and to understand and explain what you feel.

**TIP 2**: Keep in mind Pascal's words. People would hold onto anything that makes them feel good. So make sure that you use phrases that make you laugh, smile, feel nostalgic, fight for something, and get you excited. For example, while I was writing my Map, there were many moments of humor that made the process a lot more fun. I made sure that my Map was the most exciting text I had ever read. This was one of the reasons that it kept me disciplined in the philosophy's system.

**TIP 3**: You will not become a writer. But you will need to write more things on your phone to complete that. Use your own words and at some point, we will check it together.

**TIP 4**: Your mind will never believe that you can make it unless there is a kind of objectivity. For instance, you cannot be an Analytical and refuse to admit it. You cannot be 42 years old and want to become the next Messi (or Ronaldo

CR7). Do not confuse the words "achievable" and "ideal." You can reach a very good level, but you will not get to the ideal.

**TIP 5**: Get rid of your negative traits. Give them the opposite meaning and let go of any trait that ruins your identity and probably, keeps you away from your goal. For example, when I first got to Dubai and I had to face one difficulty after another, I wrote on my first Map: *"I see myself laughing before every challenge. I see myself taking a stand and dealing with all the challenges. I see myself as someone who does not take ANYTHING AND ANYONE seriously, who smiles and gets what he wants, with strength and confidence."* This last sentence was when my last trace of fear disappeared.

**TIP 6:** Numerous small successes create glory. It is impossible to believe that you will have glory and money within the next 5–10 months, even if you are the most optimistic person in the world. This is why you will probably need to create a first Map aiming at doing your first step toward your success. From 2017 until today, in 2022 I have written seven Maps. I started off by setting my very first goal and once I achieved it, I moved to the next one. You will not get to success overnight. You must see your results and then move on.

Maybe now it is clear why you read four sub-sections about understanding, acceptance, decision, and action. By now, you should know what your identity is and what you need to change. I think that you understand that over-analytical people will not be successful entrepreneurs unless they find the strength to take action and believe that their next step is doable and achievable. You must take decisions quickly in this industry. You must be ten times more effective than average people and move fast. Entrepreneurship will not wait and anything that can be done today cannot be left for tomorrow. People who act like this fall behind.

I will repeat something you read in the chapter of Understanding and I hope that it will be more than clear to you. If you do not change your life attitude and your identity, you may never reach your destination, not even in 50 years. Deal with it. Your success depends on who you *are* and you will need to follow the philosophy rules. You will not get away with "cheating."

Do not forget the 5th Core Principle of the "Who I Am" philosophy: "A Leader is his results."

Design your Map now, just as a great leader would do to get to success. In moments like this, you will have the chance to prove – mainly to yourself – that you deserve to become a great leader. In fact, moments like this when no one is watching are even more crucial as your next actions will define you.

## STEP 3
## WHO YOU ARE

According to modern psychology, people who want to become successful must follow the steps of people who are already more successful to reach the same level. It makes total sense. This is exactly what almost all personal development coaches support in order to motivate their trainees to change. "Do what they do and you will become who they are." Of course, it is harder than it sounds, but I totally agree with this method. It is a quite rational approach.

However, as you have probably already understood from the last example, you cannot easily convince yourself to do something that you normally would not do. You will do things in your own way which, more often than not, will be wrong. It is not enough to copy successful people's actions. I have tried that and it was a complete failure. Maybe the same has happened to you.

This is where the following came from:

*You act based on who you really are,*
*not on who you wanna be*

If we want to find the answer to this development theory, we need to search deeper than the surface of the actions we need to copy on our way to success. It all comes down to the same thing: what defines us. Who we are. Our habits. The simple, small, and – for many people – insignificant habits. Based on that, if we want to succeed in something, we need to act and behave like people who have already succeeded in this field. Only by getting to that point of personal development and by redefining our beliefs, we will be able to carry out the "mission" that our model would.

However, we first need to learn to think in the same way our model does.

Of course, we must admit that each one of us is a unique entity and cannot be imitated fully. It is easy to copy some habits though. As long as we choose the right habits which will change us and will bring different results (meaning, of course, the desired ones), and we incorporate them successfully, then everything is doable.

There is a drawback though. How is it possible to know how successful people think, their habits, and what their personality is like in order to copy them? How is it possible for someone to form a great team in a multilevel marketing company if he or she is not aware of the main traits of the best network marketeer in the world? Whose habits should someone copy to increase sales in an insurance company or real estate? Whom do we need to become if we do not know what those who already have what we are after are like?

This was exactly the change I made while creating the "Who I Am" philosophy.

According to that philosophy, you will never know Elon Musk's traits, Grand Cardone's habits, or George Washington's strong beliefs. You will never find out Steve Jobs' morning routine, Jordan Belfort' techniques to motivate his team, and Ray Croc's thoughts when he made the most of someone else's product and distributed it worldwide. What you are supposed to do is to find YOURSELF an ideal model easy to analyze and copy. A model whose habits and behavior, as you see it, would guarantee the success you are after.

A model who would achieve your goal if he or she were you.

You are probably at a dead end right now. You are reading that if you want to bring the desired results and get to your definition of success, you will need to find a model and build the same habits with him or her. However, that would be a different model than the one you had probably in mind and that would make you believe that you can make it. It is not a dead end though. It is guidance that will lead to a certain point, defined by you. It will be your point X on your map.

Maybe it is time for an example. Let's go!

Let's say that you are in the sales industry. Let's say that you want to increase the traffic that your website gets and your popularity in general. To do that, you will need to make some videos and develop your skills as a speaker, both for interpersonal communication and public speaking. There are numerous workshops and groups that can help you.

Let's say that you want to communicate the following in your video:

*My name is [your name]. I am a senior vice president at [name your company] and my goal is to become one of the greatest in my firm within the next year. I will not do that by making mistakes. What I can offer will not make you rich but it will not make you poor either, that's for sure. Our cooperation will be your reference point for your future business. Are you comfortable with me now?*

Read that loud a couple of times. Don't hesitate. Just do it.

Now go and watch the "The Wolf of Wall Street" and watch how Leonardo Di Caprio says the same words. Do you think that you say that in the same way? Do you think that you would get the same results?

The answer of course would be "no," simply because movie characters are fictional and can do anything in front of the camera. They are the finest creations of the most brilliant minds. However, can you imagine what would happen if you did that in the same way Di Caprio did? If you leave aside *rational thoughts* for a while, if you get rid of any limitations, and allow yourself to be open to new things, you will be able to copy the traits of any fictional character who is close to the person you would like to be and who would achieve what you are after.

Who would you like to be, if you had the choice?

Is there anyone who would not like to be as charming as George Clooney? Is there anyone who would not like to have Brad Pitt's self-confidence and Matt Damon's lateral thinking? Is there a woman who would not like to be as sexy as Angelina Jolie was in Lara Croft, as glib as Robin Wright in the "House of Cards" or as decisive as Emma Stone when she played Cruella? I am sure that all of us have admired such characters even once.

If you watch carefully the traits of the model you look up to and if you handle them in the right way, they can become a great example to follow and after a while, they can become your reality. I call this point Model X, as in the treasure maps. The goal here is for you to have a reference point about the personality you want to have. If you build the habits that Model X has, then your actions will have the power that corresponds to such a personality.

This is where my belief that it is impossible to evolve without having a reference point applies. When we decide to evolve, we are supposed to develop our knowledge, our traits, and our habits. However, our mind does not know WHICH traits need to be developed and which traits we need to have. Everyone is into personal development, but the generality that exists out there is close to chaos.

Model X is your point on your own Map that will help you in your journey in the personal development of your choice. That would be a kind of personal development chosen by you and will be personal, and more specifically, spiritual growth. You are the one who gets to decide which character and which personality would be able to achieve your goal. There are no limits and there is no one who will say "no."

There is no such thing as "A better version of myself," or "I'll be better than yesterday." And that's because this way you compare yourself with yourself who both have the same traits, therefore the same point of view of growth. Right? It's like trying to cover a distance by moving away from yourself. How is that even possible?

If you skip that, I can guarantee that no matter how hard you will try to change, all your efforts will fall in vain. They will fall from the 21$^{st}$ floor, with no parachute or seat belt, and will end up with crushed bones. There is no doubt.

I once read an article about how we tend to be interested in people who have skills that we lack. For example, people who would like to be physically attractive can find a well-known person they admire, such as a character on a show or a series, who has traits that they would like to have too. They might copy techniques to speak, eyes expressions, ways to hold a pen, tonality, and body posture.

I am a huge fan of these kinds of films and I have found myself hundreds of times thinking 'What would … do if he were me?' As a kid, I used to be a big fan of Michael J. Fox in "Back to the Future" trilogy, which was my favorite. I admired him so much that I bought a skateboard, I rolled up my jeans just like he did and I started walking in the same way, trying to adopt his style and the way he spoke. This way, I actually found a girlfriend. Who's crazy now?

I never thought that this belief of mine would become my philosophy and purpose in my life.

It's funny how things work out sometimes…

According to this modern belief, and according to psychology, of course, there is no doubt that if we imitate successful people, our personalities will change in the desired way. This means that by copying the simple habits of a personality we admire, if we have a vision and goals, our personality can be enhanced and we can become a better version of ourselves. Be careful though. It is one thing to copy every single move of someone (which is not going to lead you anywhere), and another to adopt some aspects of his or her personality. It is quite easy to do the former. The latter though takes constant observation and understanding. You need to remind yourself again and again that you are changing.

You will better understand further down.

Even if you cannot think of an ideal model to copy, I can give you an idea. In case you have not noticed, I like to use examples from my own experience when I present my philosophy. In this way, it becomes easier to digest, it is down-to-earth, and I can prove my words.

This is what happened one day a few years ago…

When I first started to use the "Who I Am" philosophy to train people, one of my trainees and a member of the team I was managing, thought that it did not make much sense to choose a TV character. I clearly remember what he had said:

"Spyros, can't you JUST tell me what to do? You know that if you tell me, I will do it. You know me, I have discipline and respect. Just tell me what to do. Let's skip this Model X thing for a while and tell me what to do."

"I have told you hundreds of times what to do and you always do it. I do not doubt it. But you do not do it right. I can be training you forever, but still, you will not do it right because you lack the dynamic and the self-confidence that is required to fully accomplish it. It isn't your fault. But it will be my fault if I don't make sure that we change that."

I spent quite a while explaining my philosophy and he then chose his character. He chose Harvey Specter who played the lawyer in Suits. He thought that it was a good match and that his traits were powerful enough to make him succeed in our industry. From that day, he started creating his Map in the way I had shown him.

I checked his progress and his development almost every day and he made sure that his Map was constantly enriched with even more powerful traits, as I had taught him to have fun with the process itself. At the same time, I shared some tricks with him and showed him how to recall the character he had chosen more often throughout the day. In this way, he got even more into his character.

One day, two months after he had started putting into practice the "Who I Am" philosophy, he had an issue with a client who demanded that he was available at any time, in case something would come up. There had been a couple of times that this client had called my partner, but he could not answer the phone at that moment. The client would make it a big deal, he insulted my partner's professionalism and demanded to speak to someone "in charge." It was insane. He was just a 70-year-old manbaby who was probably breastfeeding until he was

16 and the umbilical cord was not cut until he got married. There are many manbabies in the world. This is what we call "abandonment issues."

My guy was afraid that he might lose his job because of that, so he tried to call him back and explain why he had not replied earlier. He was terrified by some threatening emails and he panicked. I tried to explain to him that he could not be manipulated by a random guy and that if he made the mistake to apologize for something – and especially when he had not done anything wrong – there would be no way out. If he obeyed, it would be as if he were a slave.

I am allergic to slavery. I am allergic to the sound of the word "boss." If you still use this word, let me tell you that the abolition of slavery started in 1792 in Denmark. It was then expanded to Britain and the US. These words cannot be used nowadays. You can use words such as "my supervisor" or "my manager." If you still use the word boss, subconsciously you are a slave and you hate your boss.

My partner would not listen to me. He could not think of anything else than calling back his client to apologize. It was one of these moments in my career that I just wanted to slap him to make him calm down and get back to his senses. He was really out of control. The thing with me is that I am against violence. I had to bring out the big guns though. It was now or never.

I took him aside and I shouted so loud that everyone was staring:

"What are you doing?" I asked.
"I am calling him back. He has called five times in two minutes."
"WHAT THE FUCK ARE YOU DOING?" I screamed. My veins were popping out as if they would explode and my face was red.
"What should I do Spyros?" he asked and looked at me with a sad gaze.
"Is this what you wanted to be? A victim? The kid to be slapped? The *bullied by everyone* guy of the class? A defenseless, insignificant creature exposed to the power of random people? Do you want to allow an old man who is used to manipulating everyone to embarrass you? Do you want to bow down to him and be one of his items? Would you bend over just to get the soap for him in prison? Do you want to allow him to pull the puppet's strings and make you dance?"
"No," he replied looking down and I could tell he was almost in tears.
"AREN'T YOU ASHAMED OF YOURSELF? Don't you feel bad that since day one, you have been claiming that you want to become someone important? This is humiliating not only for you but also for everyone who has believed in

you and your skills. This is humiliating for your family back in Athens who speak so highly of you to family and friends and who are proud of their son who lives abroad and is the pride of the family. You are someone who stood out from the crowd, took his life into his own hands, and wants to make the most out of it. You should be ashamed! I should send you back to Athens and let your parents know that they were wrong and that you have disappointed them. Shame on you!"

"What should I do?"

"I'm not gonna tell you what you should do. I will only ask you this: *What would Harvey do?*"

No answer…

He just turned around and disappeared.

The problem was solved within 1 minute and 20 seconds. A short call was enough. I do not know what my guy told his client or how he spoke. But I do know one thing: when he hung up the phone, he came out of the room he had gone for some privacy, he came towards me and he said:

"What is your secret and you always manage to *program* me like that?"

I thought to myself…

*Only when you push someone to the edge,*
*you realize what he's made of*

"What do you mean? I didn't do anything," I said. "I just reminded you who you want to be and it seems that you have already started changing radically."

"Spyros, I swear to God, since I started talking to him, he didn't say a single word. That bastard didn't have the guts to say anything."

"I'm sure about that. Do you know why? Because even though you thought that my philosophy was *different and out of the box*, you realized that in fact, it might be the right solution for you after wandering for 20 years, and you chose an inspiring character. This is huge and this is exactly why I'm sure. I knew that if you wanted to convince your client, he needed you to know who you are. He needed you to be self-confident, with no doubt, without taking a single step backward, and with no insecurity. He needed you to be powerful and strict. To do that, you needed to be the person you needed to be. Regardless of what I might have told you to say, you were so panicked that you would have made it worse. Now tell me, what did you say to him?"

He never answered. From that moment though, he realized that our work on his Map was of vital importance. The Map allowed him to see who he wanted to be and what *particular* traits he needed to have. He was turning into the ideal version of himself. A person who would make any challenge look like a playground and who would jump over obstacles easier and easier.

I was really proud of him.

Through the process, he found a character that seemed to be ideal and set a reference point. The Model X in his Map.

When he started studying and processing his character, he could see that the gap between the character and himself was huge. They had different traits, different prestige, different attitudes, and different self-confidence. This is exactly why he had thought that this was quite different from any other leadership philosophy he had come across so far. The more he studied his model and the more he processed the character in the way I had suggested daily, the more he bridged the gap. Every day, every word and every effort took him one step closer to the ideal self he had in mind.

If he had not used the way suggested by the "Who I Am" philosophy, he would not have a point reference and the inconsistent repetition would make my philosophy just "another theory which will be forgotten after finishing this book." I do not want it to be the case as it has worked on myself, and on many others, and it has got me where I am today.

I'll repeat… It is impossible to change if you have no reference point because you end up having yourself as a reference. Without Model X, you measure any change based on how far it takes you from who you were the day before. So the only thing that matters to you is to be different from the person you were yesterday? Is that all? So it is enough for you to be at a different point from the one you were at yesterday? Is that what you truly want? So if you want to go on vacation, it does not matter where you are going, it is enough to leave home?

I cannot think of anything more irrational than that. It does not make sense that you want to change and you are happy as long as you are not the same person you were yesterday. The problem here is that if you have yourself as a reference point, the human brain is unable to tell the difference between development and stagnancy. You are walking away but you are not heading anywhere else. You have no one to compare yourself to. It is an unrealistic situation. Because you think that you are moving but you are not. You always need to compare yourself to someone else so as to be able to tell the difference between who you were and whom you have become and to measure the distance you have covered between you and your goal.

Enough is enough! It is simple and it is common sense.

It goes without saying that my partner was aware of the fact that he would never become Harvey Specter. I knew that too. We are not kids. However, he managed to bridge the gap and get as close as possible to the character, by implementing as many traits as he could. By having him as a reference point, he kept getting closer and he kept changing.

This is the aim of the 3rd step of change: to choose who you want to be.

What do you think? Who is that person whose name will find its place in "What would … do if he/she were me"? Whose traits would help you fully accomplish your goal?

Choose a character who you think would make it in whatever you define as success. It needs to be clear to you what is that you admire about him/her and what are his/her best traits. Define:

1. What he wears.
2. The way he talks.
3. The way he answers questions.
4. The way he walks.
5. The way he sits.
6. The way he smiles.
7. The way they perceive situations.
8. Is he used to win or to lose?
9. Does he usually quit or he fights for what he wants?
10. Is he strict or communicative?
11. Is he tough or soft?
12. Is he strict or easy-going?
13. What other traits does he have? Is he self-confident? Is he sociable?
14. Is he selfish? Is he stubborn? Is he vigorous? Is he passionate?
15. Is he firm? Strong? Determined?
16. Does he walk at a fast or a slow pace?
17. Is he afraid of something or not?

18. Is he worried or not?
19. Has he said any quotes that motivate you?
20. What do his eyes tell you?

Of course, if your Model X is a female character, just replace the "he" with the "she."

Based on your answers, add as much as possible into the $2^{nd}$ step of your Map. For example, when you walk into the office, what do you look like? What are you wearing? How do other people look at you? What do you perceive? How many enemies and how many friends do you have?

This "boost" in the 2nd step is the **most important** part of your Map. I urge you to do it carefully, repeatedly, without rushing, and without limits. The last thing you want is to set limits to your own growth. I urge you to be consistent here because this is the beginning of "the best version of yourself," as many colleagues of mine say.

As I have already mentioned, most people choose a TV character for the $3^{rd}$ Step. This is because these characters are familiar, highly respected, and too good to be true. They are fictional creatures inspired by creative writers and directors and they tend to be perfect. It is also quite easy to spot the main traits of these characters and study them further if needed. You only have to watch the movie once again.

Be careful though. In the "Who I Am" philosophy masterclasses, I have come across instances where people indeed chose characters, but these characters had nothing to do with what the particular trainee needed to change. All of them understood the value and the power of this philosophy, but some did not choose the character correctly, so they did not make any progress in the way they thought or reacted. Because it was fake.

Keep in mind that when choosing a character, you need to take into consideration how this character would *react* if he/she were you in the industry or area, in general, you want to succeed. You should care about what traits they have and the way they move around. In what way would they look at what you look at and in what way would they speak to the people you speak to? You should care about everything that makes them who they are.

In the sales field, where I belong also, many people have chosen James Bond, and others have chosen John Shelby, the evil character in Peaky Blinders. Other people choose a life coach or a leadership coach whom they happened to follow.

It is no surprise that some people try to imitate Antony Robbins, Simon Sinek, or Jordan Peterson. You must choose to take into consideration the nature of the person you want to be and you need to make a responsible decision.

Even if you do not know which character to identify with, you can always search. Stop reading, take your phone, go on YouTube, and search. Take your time. For example, if you want to be a master in sales, Specter or Cardone would be really good models. If you want to become a great singer, study the attitude of a successful artist such as Bono from U2 or Dave Grohl, the voice of Foo Fighters. They are different characters and different personalities. If you want to become a good football player, copy Ronaldo's or Messi's habits. If you want to become a politician, there is no better way to do so than watching politicians' talks, focusing not on what they say, but on the way they say it.

If you are anything like me and listening to politicians makes you feel bored, you can watch House of Cards instead and watch the character played by Kevin Spacey. Leave murders aside, please. By the way, in case you want to become a serial killer, the best thing you can do is to get yourself checked by a doctor. If you have already done that and the doctor failed to figure you out, I think that the right character for you is Hannibal Lecter. At least you will do everything in style, you will be polite and romantic, and the food will always taste good. Your success is guaranteed and yammy!

You might as well reconsider your initial choice and choose a different character. If this is the case with you, then the right moment to change your Map is now. Not later. Now.

The Map you have just developed by writing down the traits and the attitude of a person you admire – real or fictional – is the most important step you will take in this book. This is the goal of the "Who I Am" philosophy: to be a game-changer when it comes to your beliefs on who you must *be* based on what you want. This is the only way to convince your mind that your goal is achievable. This is the only way to make it clear to your mind that *you* have changed and that your success is *now* guaranteed.

And you deserve it!

# STEP 4
# CLOSURE

As you have probably understood the 3 first steps of the Map are the most important ones. No further analysis is needed. However, there are a few extra points that you need to be aware of so that everything is stored in your subconscious faster and more effectively.

**TIP 1:** Make sure that your Map has a flow and energy. Make it passionate, emotional, and hot. You heard me right. Hot! If you are realistic, you will get bored and throw it away. Play with it. You should fancy reading it. It should motivate you day in, and day out to be something you want to spend time on.

**TIP 2**: Do not forget that on the Map, you are not who you are. You are who you want to be. This means that you should always use expressions and traits that not you, but your model would use. The goal here is to change your perspective on things and the way you react in various situations.

**TIP 3:** Use only past tenses while writing. For instance, if you create your Map in December 2022 and you believe that you might have reached your goal by December 2023, imagine that it is June 2024 and you are writing about something that took place in December 2023. In this way, you will write everything as if it has already happened. Imagine that you are recalling memories.

Sounds weird? It is not.

The theory behind this is exactly what happens with all those videos that are stored on your phone. The camera has real power. This camera allows you to watch videos from your journey. You can see who you used to be and what you used to do. As long as this video exists, no one can question its content. So while watching this video, your mind considers that this content is a confirmed memory. It has happened. Imagine watching a video of your son's first birthday party. You have evidence from that day. Since your mind is watching a video, it automatically considers its content as authentic. This is real so your mind tends to believe it.

It is not easy to reject such a memory and believe that it has never happened. Do not forget that it is easier for your mind to believe something it has seen than something it has not seen.

This is an important step because it defines the level at which anything is absorbed by your subconscious mind. It defines the level at which your mind will be convinced and turn something new into its reality.

**TIP 4**: Do not stop until you are completely satisfied with what you have written, even if it takes days. Even if you need to delete something and replace it with something else. You might as well have to search online to get a few ideas.

**TIP 5**: Make the process fun. Use expressions and situations that make you feel good. You should have fun only by reading the Map. Imagine you are hanging out with your friends or that you are at a party. What kind of jokes do you find funny? What makes you smile? What makes you feel excited? It is crucial to make your Map attractive, otherwise, it will end up being another boring task that needs to be completed.

**TIP 6: (This one goes only to fully determined and open-minded people)**: At the end of your Map, in the last paragraph, imagine you are being interviewed and answer the following question:

What is your next step? How excited are you about it?

Yeah, yeah, I know what you are thinking. "Let's get there first, Spyros, and we'll plan our next step afterward." I hear you. Do it now though. You must understand that the aim of the Map is not to help you get into the habit of writing. No one said that you must become a writer in order to succeed and no one can guarantee that you will live happily ever after if you write for hours.

The aim of the Map is *to convince your mind that your goal is achievable*. To do that, you must be able to provide it with the next step *as well*. If your mind realizes that you already know what the next step is, it will automatically consider the previous goal as achieved – regardless of whether it is true or not. It is the most effective way to change the flow of your mind. The thing is that the way you will program your mind and what you will choose to provide it with is your own choice. I am here to show you the way.

All you have to do is to put it into practice.

And trust me. Everything you ever wished or dreamed to have, will come. Your Map will be the most important partner throughout your journey.

*When you feel lost, build your map.*

# Chapter 8
# Let's Change, It's Time Already

Do you know what is the most challenging thing for a sane writer? To consider himself *capable* of sharing effectively his knowledge. It does not matter what people are going to think. It does not matter if he will be judged or questioned. The important thing is for the writers to have the integrity and the objectivity to see themselves if they are indeed capable of that. What is the right way to do it? Based on their past experiences, of course. Remember the quote you read in Chapter 5:

> *Acceptable knowledge is only the one that derives from strategies already put into practice.*

This is exactly why I did not believe my teachers. They taught me other people's theories that they had never put into practice themselves. To me, that is nonsense. It is as if you are "selling" a product that is not yours and that you have never used. It is as if you make promises that you will fail to keep. This is why I am careful about the people I choose to listen to and the people I get advice from, regardless of the topic or the situation. This is the only reason why you are currently reading my stories about my life and my career.

I am not a multimillionaire (yet). I am just the man who lives next door. I am that guy you used to run into in your building and talked about football because you had heard him cheering while watching a game with his friends. I drink iced espresso with a little sugar and a few ice cubes. When I go out with my friends or with my partner, we usually drink tsipouro and eat well-cooked traditional dishes.

But I am also one of those people who reached a tipping point, realized that his country had nothing to offer, and decided to do something about it. I am the down-to-earth modern reality. I cut the umbilical cord that used to keep me back in Greece and opened myself to the choices the rest of the world had to offer. The more I realized that the higher I desired to get. I am one of those people who has suffered as much as most people have. I have gone through Clashing Rocks and I have walked on mud and dirt, but I managed to come out on the other side still sharp. I am so close to your reality, that my example might as well become yours if you want it.

I am not a superhero. I am my choices.

This book is my truth. It is my own story, without any exaggeration or unrealistic points. You can learn something useful from it, without having to follow Elon Musk's or Jeff Bezos' stories which seem to be too far from your reality. It is my story about how I managed to start as a salesperson and become the CEO of a company abroad in 4.5 years, putting into practice methods used by great leaders, but also the methods presented in this book.

The method I developed to give life and substance to the "Who I Am" philosophy got me where I am today. This is what I do daily, as I trust it and there is still a lot of ground to cover. I would advise you to trust it as well because nowadays, it is difficult to believe that we *can* do anything. Believe me. Even if it seems weird to you, this philosophy has been put into practice successfully. It is the best way to hack your mind. It is the best kind of meditation. You just need to have consistency, discipline, and most importantly, desire.

It is a personal bet for me to share the knowledge that has got me here. I see it as a mission to help as many people as possible to break free from their reality and to become the best version of themselves. I honestly believe that people are hypnotized by their everyday life and their routine. They keep running on the wheel, but they do not believe they can actually break free. Some families have loans to hold them behind, some people live in countries with limited offers, there is controlled information on media, and in general, there is disorientation from anything that might help us break free and evolve. All the politicians are the same and there is not a single beam of light.

Instead of building palaces as we are supposed to, we got to a point where we end up digging in shit to find the soil and we feel grateful for that.

I call this "irony."

## **DESIRE**

I did have the desire though. This is where it all started. I had the desire to stand out of the crowd, to create that little something extra, to accept the challenges, to destroy my image, to fall, to get up, to keep going. This is where my journey of change started and this is where your own journey will start too. Without desire, everything you are reading in this book will be a waste of time.

I cannot give you that. You must find it on your own. If you don't, you will remain the same person. You will continue living the same life, in the same country, with the same stimuli, and the same prospects.

My desire though did not last for a long time. I soon realized that our mind is like a maze. We have so many thoughts that it is difficult to organize them. This might be the most challenging obstacle you will have to deal with.

From one moment to the next, you might be thinking about what you will have for dinner before you get distracted by a car advertisement. The advertisement catches your attention because it reminds you that you need to change the oil in your car but you will not have time to do that tomorrow, as you will be in a meeting until late. You will have to call your mechanic and ask if he can come and get the car from your office. It is past 11:00 though and it would be rude to call him that late, so you have to text him. You get your phone, only to see that there is a crack on the screen, which means that tomorrow, after getting your car from the mechanic, you will have to go to the mobile phone repair shop to fix the screen. Where are you supposed to park your car there though? The last time you tried to park over there, you got into a fight with that asshole who did not stop honking and yelling that you should get the hell out of there because your car blocked the street. His child was not older than 7 years, sitting in the front seat, without a seat belt, watching his father behaving as a jerk. It was such a wrong message to send to a child. You cannot help but think that the guy would be such a bad role model for the poor kid.

Anyway, have you decided what you will have for dinner?

It is difficult to control our thoughts as our mind is racing. Even if we try to organize them, it will be difficult or even impossible. **Writing** is the easiest way to give direction to the flow of our thoughts.

When I was **writing** and then reading my Core, I could clearly see every single thought that crossed my mind at the time. I could see all my fears, my anxiety, and all my doubts. Reading my Core, I could recognize smaller or bigger flaws in my mind, and my desire to fix them was getting greater and greater as I could see that they would not take me anywhere.

In order to fix them, I used my self-respect which is my Core value as you already know. I did that by writing down my desires too. Instead of getting lost in endless thoughts, I managed to separate the rubbish from the flowers in my head. I managed to keep my desires out of the maze, so I would never have to let them go. That was one of the reasons I created my Core and then, my Map.

So if you want to make your mind think in the way you want, writing is the only option for you. It is the only way to unravel the puzzle in your head and organize your thoughts. Your mind cannot make it on its own. It needs your support. Writing is the best way to do that.

If you want your desires to stand out, come to light, and then put them into practice, you must complete these two texts first: your Core and your Map.

This way, you'll never forget your true desires. You'll never lose your way.

## DISCIPLINE

What needs to happen next is quite simple, but at the same time, it is the hardest part of the process of change.

First of all, you need to know that some people call this way of identity change *"behavioral psychology."* However, Jorge Bucay, an Argentinian Psychotherapist and Writer, suggests that external aid is needed if we want this kind of change to work. This means that apart from trying to change yourself, you constantly need to have someone reminding you of that. Otherwise, behavioral psychology is impossible. It is a utopia.

This is where most people go wrong. Change cannot happen from one moment to the next. You must be disciplined and patient, and give it time. This is why there are so many resources about identity change, but the vast majority of the people who have tried it claim that it is not enough. Because their patience was equivalent to their *need* to achieve their goal: from too little to zero. Know that: If we were not disciplined and patient, and if did not give things time, we would still be living in cages, eating raw meat, and we would congratulate our chief on his leadership in one word: "ugh"!

There is no such thing as fast change or fast success. To create anything, you will have to give it time. So if you are one of those people who want to get as ripped as Stallone after going to the gym three times, you might want to reconsider that.

Once, there was a trainee named Sameem in the "Who I Am" philosophy. Sameem started implementing my philosophy and chose Bobby Axelrod's character in Billions. He was a fanatical trader and the character played by Damian Lewis had been Sameem's model since the show was first released in 2016. Sameem got excited about my philosophy, but his excitement lasted only a week. Every time I asked to see his Map, he would always find excuses about why he had not found the time to complete it.

What would anyone expect to happen next? Not only did he not change, but also, he said that the reason why he did not give it more time was that he had not seen any change within that short period.

"Can I ask you something?"
"Of course, Mr. Spyros."
"You asked me to help you develop and achieve more in your life, didn't you?"
"I did."
"Did you do what I asked you?"
"But I've already told you that I didn't have time."
"OK, so did you do what I asked you?"
"I didn't."
"How old are you?"
"25."
"This means that for the past 25 years, you have built habits and have adopted beliefs that have made you who you are. Is that right?"
"It is, Mr. Spyros."
"But still, you expected to change all these habits you've had for 25 years in a week? That's hypocritical."

I am sure he is still standing astonished at the same point. Oh, I forgot to mention that he quit because he wanted to concentrate on his studies. A few days later my secretary told me "But…he is not a student."

Do not be like Sameem. He is a good guy and I am still in touch with him, but do not be like Sameem. Just… don't…

Since this book is not just a theory, I want you to do the following:

Set two notifications every day as reminders to yourself to read your Map. Five minutes should be enough. Remind yourself to take a break from whatever you are doing and sit down to read it.

Instead of scrolling down on Instagram, set some time aside to do that. At first, you will not see any change, but if you stay disciplined, a few days later you will see the results.

I used to read my Map during one of my breaks at work and then once again before going to bed at night. In fact, at night I often wanted to add or delete something to get the Map even closer to my goal, since my Core was always full of new notes. It was my daily routine. I wanted to make it and this is how I have managed to keep up this habit until today.

## EMOTION

When I first started writing my Core and my Map, I must admit that discipline was the most challenging part for me. My goal was to keep my excitement – and the excitement of anyone who puts into practice the "Who I Am" philosophy – going, and to continue even if there are no obvious results.

The solution I came up with was to add here and there humorous touches that would elevate my emotions. They were supposed to make me have fun as if I had a drink with my friends. In other parts, I added powerful phrases that made me shiver. Just like in some movies where the generals, riding their horses, motivate the warriors before getting into the fight. Just like William Wallace in Braveheart. This is exactly the feeling I wanted to have.

*"Nothing in the world can stop me! When obstacles or rejections come up, I laugh and move on because I don't care about what people say. I am an extraordinary type of person, for whom bravery, nerve, and trust in himself are the strongest driving force! It is what makes me unique! THERE IS NO ONE OR ANYTHING THAT CAN STOP ME! BRING IT ON, BITCH!"*

Shall we go deeper into the importance of using emotions?
We should as it has to be perfectly clear.

Are you familiar with the phrase "It's not what you say, it's the way you say it"? I have heard this since I was very young. As I was growing up and putting it into practice once in a while, I realized that a phrase can be interpreted in multiple ways depending on the way it is expressed. More often than not, the interpretations given are completely different one from another.

Our mind perceives information differently if it comes with some kind of emotion. The information itself might be straightforward, but the emotion of the person speaking might modify its meaning:

"Good morning," he said casually and trudged to the kitchen.
"Good morning," he said sadly and stopped for a second before walking to the kitchen.
"Good morning," he shouted happily with sparkling eyes and walked with a quick step to the kitchen.

It is one phrase, but three different emotions and three different meanings. Each case would have a different impact on you than the rest. Which one do you think you would choose?

The vast majority of people would go for the third case as a powerful feeling such as "shouting happily" would have a greater impact on you than "looking casually." We can tell from that simple example that people tend to accept more easily powerful emotions (joy, sadness) and reject, or better, ignore neutral ones.

The more powerful the emotion is, the bigger impact it will have on your subconscious, and the more easily it might become a new reality.

The following diagram, which I put a lot of effort into making myself, can tell you a lot.

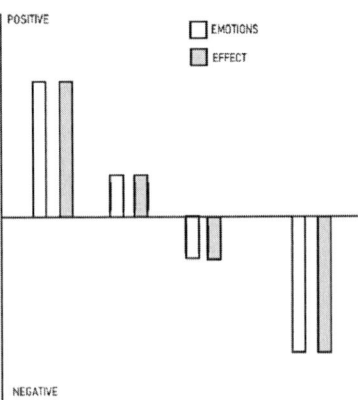

This is why we find action movies exciting, why some people cry when they watch romantic movies, and why some of us get up off the couch when we watch horror movies. This is the method used in film and advertisement productions, as well as on the news on TV. Using this method, you can sell anything to anyone. I will analyze it further in my next book which will be about sales. For now, keep in mind that the power of emotion that comes with any kind of information is extremely more powerful than the information itself.

This is why it is not what you say, it is the way you say it.

This is why I insist that you use powerful emotions in your Map, because it is the only way to get across the information quickly, and to keep you disciplined in the mood of change. In fact, I must admit once again that if it were not for the powerful emotions, I would have stopped creating my Map on the second day and that would be a pity.

The Map can bring change for real but only to those who will develop the habit of reading it and working on it at least twice a day.

I made sure that I enjoyed the process by constantly using phrases that made me laugh and feel strong and invulnerable. At the same time, I pushed myself to focus on change without seeing it as another boring task I had to do. I did not have anyone to motivate me to continue as suggested by Jorge Bucay, so I became that person for myself using powerful emotions.

Another trainee of mine used another emotion that had this great impact on him that laughter has on me: pride. While creating his Map, he wanted to feel proud of himself. He wanted to feel that everyone depended on him, that he was the center of attention, of trust, etc. All that made him feel proud for standing out from the crowd and for being at the center of discussions. It was his driving force. This is why I used to call him a Superstar!

Some people might say, "Well, Spyros, what you've just described is not pride. I would call it self-centeredness." Well… the way I see it let it be anything. No one has the right to judge others. When that guy first came to the company and I began training him, he had 150€ in his pocket and a broken arm. He currently has two companies in Dubai and makes much more money than he used to. I think the important thing here is not the word we will use to describe him. Follow my instructions and keep in mind that your Map is something personal. You create it yourself, you work on it yourself, and you enjoy the results yourself. As simple as that.

## CONSTANT INVESTIGATION AND READJUSTMENT

Once the Core and the Map become part of your daily life, you will get a new perspective of the world. You will start watching your actions more closely and you will get to the point where you will be analyzing them and comparing them with the ones you have written down. What a great process! At such moments, make sure to grab your phone and write in your Core. These random thoughts that cross your mind for a few seconds and then go away must be written down and processed. More often than not, this process is pure gold.

Besides, this is the purpose of the Core, to help you keep the important things.

Then, after sorting out the thoughts that deserve a place on your Map, you will have to find the right place for them. The place in which they will make more sense, give you more satisfaction, and help you maintain your flow of speech. While looking for the right place, you will have to read the text. While reading it, it will be stored in your subconscious. Once you find the right place, you might have to find a new place for the piece of information you substituted. In case it was worth it and it still deserves a place in your text, you might have to move it above or further down. This means that you will have to read your Map once again to find the right place for it.

In this way, with constant investigation and readjustment, you create the repetitions (twice a day) that are needed anyway. These repetitions can help you get the desired results and see the changes in your behavior and way of thinking sooner than you thought.

By seeing these changes, your self-confidence will be enhanced and you will know that you are doing something right. So your mind will be motivated to keep going. This will further motivate your body, your body will motivate your mind, and so on. Long story short, constant repetition brings more results and faster, and more and faster results bring further change.

The only thing that can go wrong here is for you to be expecting to see the results soon. On the contrary, what you have to do is to embrace the process and put it into practice with modesty and discipline. Sooner or later, you will see the results. Trust me.

This is the way to re-program yourself and change.

As time goes by, you will realize that some of the things you used to write are not valid anymore. You will be reading about weaknesses you used to have which have been replaced by strengths, about doubts which have grown to be confidence, and about emotions that you can now recognize and control. This will give you the strength to keep moving forward. Your psychology will be at so high levels that you will know that you can manage anything, even to become the No1.

The simplest example I can share with you is that when I started writing my Map, I was afraid to deal with some "angry" clients. That's right, I never liked arguments. One month later, after being fully committed to my Map, I did not even notice that I was not afraid anymore. One month later, I even thought it was silly to be afraid of arguments since I wanted to become No1. As I am sure you can understand, it would be impossible.

To sum up, your Map will keep reminding you whom you will become tomorrow and you will be turning into the person you have always wanted to be. Trust me, you will not be the same person anymore.

Nor your results will be the same anymore.

## THE PRICE YOU WILL PAY

What I have not told you yet is that over time, while being in the process of change, you will realize that you do not have time or space for information and people who mean nothing to you. When you will start seeing the first signs of your development, you will realize that some people around you remain unchanged. Do not find that intimidating. When a car runs at a higher speed than another one, the latter falls behind.

However, your true friends will still be there, throughout your journey of change and development. Keep in mind that only those who push you move forward deserve to be around you. These are people who want you to get what is best for you, not for themselves. Even if they do not totally get you from time to time, it does not matter. As long as you both keep developing, you will stay together forever.

I have personally kept around me only people who develop daily and make me have fun. Fewer, but better.

Everyone else has left and I do not miss them.

This is the price you will have to pay.

# Chapter 9
# Change Is Inevitable

So here we are in the last chapter. Congratulations. If you have found it difficult, then I am sure you have made a step forward, because this means that you put your ego aside and appreciated my effort to broaden your horizons. I am really glad that you are still here and I am pretty sure that you have what it takes to achieve great things.

However, the truth is that many people will read this book, but only a few will actually do what is needed in order to change. This is the harsh reality as the process of change makes us fight against the power that our old habits and way of thinking have. Even if someone shows us the way to do it, we will probably deny it. Even if this way is proven to work, as is the case with the "Who I Am" philosophy.

As I am sure you have figured out, what lies behind that is that no one likes change because he is afraid of it. We are all afraid of it. Change brings out fears that we did not even know existed. It creates chaos in our souls and the only way to deal with it is to run away. Even denial is a way to run away. Do not forget that.

We love stability and predictable things. We like to have control over things because we like balance. We want to keep living the way we have lived so far, without limitations and without having anyone telling us who we should be, even if we know that we are doing something wrong. That is exactly who we are: victims of our own beliefs.

This is why the vast majority of people do not get what they want, because they choose to find excuses and underestimate the value of success, over trying to "fix" what is wrong. Even if "what is wrong" is CLEARLY the reason why they keep failing, they will not admit it. They will consider that it has nothing to do with them or with the goal itself. It is someone else's fault. It is always someone else's fault.

This is why people make some efforts in the beginning, but then they cry blaming everyone else but themselves for their failure, and in the end, they convince themselves that they were never after happiness. In this way, they make any possibility that implies that they were responsible for th393eir failure disappear. The same goes for any kind of improvement. It is more convenient to be in denial and refuse to see the truth than to admit that we have failed, or simply that we need to change.

As I mentioned in a previous chapter and as I have said to an old colleague of mine in the past:

> *Your ego can be your greatest ally or your worst enemy.*
> *Nurtured in the right way, it can help you build an empire.*

Do not stick to your beliefs. There are two sides to every point of view: yours and the objective one. You might be right, but you might be wrong too. I cannot go into further details, but if you read once again the Identities presented in the previous chapter, you will understand what I mean.

Always keep in mind that your ego shows a mirror reflection that has never existed. It makes you believe that you deserve more than you already have. The truth lies somewhere in between. You should start seeing things from a scope of view different than yours.

The only way that you can actually achieve this is to want something a lot. The only way you can let go of any kind of ego is to have a clear goal that you want to achieve and (maybe, if you have the guts) to let someone guide you. A mentor is the best possible choice. You cannot do everything by yourself. If you want to succeed, do whatever it takes, without hesitation or any limitation, and know that you can do everything. You can even tame the beast that is inside you. This is the only way to see the truth.

You see, the ego is the part of you that is the hardest to change as it is the one that "thinks" it is right. As long as you believe that you are better than someone else or that you do everything right, you refuse to accept reality regardless of the evidence you might have. In such situations, you live in a twisted reality that you have created yourself and by supporting this, you feed your ego. Your ego keeps asking for more. The bigger it becomes, the more powerful it gets.

It reminds me of The Gremlins, a 1984 movie with some adorable, cute animals that turn into goblins that terrify people and destroy everything. This is exactly how the ego works. Do not pet it, do not protect it, and do not feed it. It can only bring destruction unless you put it in a cage to control it.

I think that people of lower social classes resist changing the most because probably, they have never had the chance to get educated in the right way as other people have. Their resources have been limited, such as access to knowledge, values, education, and to rational development in general. As a result, it might be more difficult for them to realize their capacities. No matter how many times someone might tell them that they "can" make it, they might still reject anything that would get them out of their comfort zone. Because simply, they do not think that they deserve it. They live in a world that has made them believe that good enough is great and sometimes, worth rewarding.

It might sound weird, but it is true, this is sad. People who have not broadened their horizons are more likely to have a strong ego. They are easy prey.

What I want you to get out of this last part of the book is that no one will be satisfied if you think and act having low standards. Allowing your ego to be the one in charge is also a form of weakness that is guaranteed cannot help you move forward. If you have no control over your emotions, you will always find yourself at much lower levels than you could be based on your skills.

You can reject everything you have read in this book. You can also accept it but do nothing about it. You can accept it and work until you become the person you want to be. Even the decision itself is the result of the person you *are*. Who you are or whom you will become depends on whether you will decide to get rid of any kind of selfishness and face the truth. This is also a form of leadership and as you might remember, in the 1st Core Principle of the philosophy, I wrote that true leaders admit their mistakes. This is one of the principles that will help you and will further develop your integrity as a person. It is in situations like this, when no one is watching, that the leader is being formed inside you. You are the one who gets to decide if you will reach your goal or if you will stay on the bench.

This is exactly where most people belong, to be honest.

However, Rome was not built in a day. The same goes for you too. If you want to see direct and significant results "aggressive" action is needed, as well as firm discipline, and patience.

## "AGGRESSIVE" ACTION

This is something that must be completely clear and that has also been mentioned in the chapter about leadership:

*Even the smallest action is more important than the greatest theory.*

In other words, regardless of how much work you put into your Map and even if the character of your choice is perfect for you, you will not succeed in anything if you do not take "aggressive" action too.

While working on developing your mind, you should also be acting *faster and m*ore than anyone else you know toward the achievement of your goal. Your action should have the power to discourage anyone who might even think to doubt you. You should become an example to follow. Your actions should be so powerful that you do not have the time to eat or even go to the bathroom. Your actions should give you the nickname "The Next Best Thing!"

This is the only way to get the results you want. This is the only way to keep going nonstop, tirelessly, and without limitations. The goal of your "Aggressive" Action is to constantly see results. You should be able to see the fruit of your work and feel that burning feeling of self-confidence in your chest. Without results, your actions will be meaningless and boring.

I used to have an assistant who worked non-stop, all day long. The only thing was that she was not able to complete the tasks she had to do. For example, if I asked for three quotations from three different equipment suppliers, she would wait until each supplier decided to actually send it. This meant that a week later I did not have a single quotation on my side, which was disappointing.

It used to take to my next assistant only one day to receive all the quotations I would ask for. Why was that? Simply because when she requested them, she used to highlight the exact date the suppliers should send it. If she did not receive it on time, she kept calling them until they sent it. I had explained to her over and over again that almost always people would not get back to her on time, since most people are used to doing everything at their own pace.

I also explained in detail that if she allowed others to have control over her productivity, she would definitely allow someone else to have control over other fields of her life. I helped her, through hard work and patience, to build the habit of getting what she wanted and to demand it without fear. She is still grateful about that and as for me, well ... I had all the quotations on my side in one day.

*Actions are subjective.*
*Your results are your true judge.*

As you have already read and as I like to repeat, the results you will see yourself are the ones that will shape your progress and your faith in the outcome. This is the best ally on your way up. This is the best way to support your mind at moments when it struggles to keep its trust and its passion alive. No video, no speaker, no book, and no friend will maintain your self-confidence more effectively than your own results.

*Nothing and no one has the power to boost your self-confidence more than the results of your actions.*

While almost everything – people, speakers, philosophies, books – is about how much you do and how fast you act, you should make a difference and focus on the result. There is no such thing as "enough action" when you focus on the completion of a task. There are no limits. The more and the faster you act, the more and the faster you will see the results. What you are supposed to do is to keep working to close one chapter after another. You should take so much action that your competitors will ask for your opinion. You should make so many phone calls or arrange so many appointments that you will need a secretary to help you out. You should be talking to so many people daily that if you threw a party for all of them, you should book an airport runway to have enough space.

Once, someone said, "Success is never owned, it is rented, and the rent is due every day." It is true. Success is just another habit. It is an attitude that unless it becomes a way of life, you will ALWAYS be able to live without.

*Success is the result of the actions of a great leader.*

## ROME WAS NOT BUILT IN A DAY

Tell me, do you know what discipline means? Allow me to tell you, just to be clear. *"Discipline is to act as you are supposed to, regardless of how you feel"* would be a rough definition.

Soldiers are the perfect example of discipline. If you think about it, all the soldiers follow the orders of their superiors to carry out a mission. Even if soldiers disagree, they must follow the orders if the superiors have the experience and the knowledge to carry out the mission in question.

Even if a soldier has not slept well, he will get up at reveille and will be ready for the morning report. Even if his girlfriend has broken up with him the night before, he will do the guard duty as requested. Even if he is not into sports, he will run around the military camp. It does not matter what the soldier believes. The only thing that matters is that he does everything he is asked to do, whenever he is asked to. No reactions, no postponements, no resistance whatsoever.

If a soldier is not disciplined, the chances of him getting killed in a fight are extremely high. It is a guaranteed failure.

This is the case with you as well. If you want to make this effort work, you should do what you have to do even if you do not feel like doing it at times. You should not have any hesitations or doubts. You should only trust your plan and be disciplined… Regardless of whether you will make the most out of it or if there are other theories for "success" out there, the "Who I Am" philosophy is a process that works. It has been tested in difficult situations and has been proven to be effective.

*Change without discipline is a delusion.*

That's right, my friend. It is a delusion. If you are not disciplined, you will not manage to change anything. You must understand that repetition is there to remind yourself of your goal and of the person you want to become. You should always have in mind where you are going and why. Until now you probably used to forget, but this will never happen to you again regardless of what your everyday life looks like.

It is simple.

## **PATIENCE IS A VIRTUE**

I like what Mark Twain once said, "Continuous improvement is better than delayed perfection."

We live in an age where everything is changing at lightning speed. You take a picture, you post it and you get ten likes in less than a minute. Back in the day, you needed at least two days to print a photo in a copy shop. Today, it takes you a couple of minutes to heat up leftovers from yesterday in the microwave. It used to take an hour to heat it up in the oven. Nowadays, you have access to thousands of movies at the press of a button while in the past, if you could not make do with low-grade films you had to go to the video store and rent a movie. If it was not available, you had to either wait till the other renter is "done" with it, or compromise with another one.

Of course, the fact that we have shortened the distances is not bad. We have minimized the required time and have increased our productivity. I am also a die-hard cinephile. If I had to go to a video store every time, I wanted to watch a movie, I would have to rent an apartment on the floor above the store. It would be cheaper for me.

This is not the case for your mind though. In order to change its composition, that is the way it perceives situations, it needs TIME. It requires constant repetition of the processes and – as we have said that is the case with discipline – time is required before you see the results, lots of time!

I do not know if you got it, but it takes time, a lot of time.

How much? Well, I do not know. It depends on what you want to change, how you present it to yourself, and how dedicated you are to the process. For this very reason, as I have previously mentioned, as I was processing my Map I was laughing a lot. I made sure it would be a text that I would enjoy reading and every emotional outburst would motivate me to read a little bit further and to build a bit more. I wanted to find pleasure in this process. Without noticing the days passing by, I realized that I had already, without knowing it, begun to adapt my habits and started avoiding actions that I would have never been able to avoid before. My Map became the best movie I had ever seen. Because I saw myself in the way I wanted to be seen.

This is how I fought with the might of my impatience.

Many people have started out with the ambition to conquer the world. What they did not know was how to carry on while not being able to see the immediate results. Since they could not see any results, they believed they were doing something wrong even though the system or the theory their actions were based on was proven to be correct. As time passed by, the doubts in their minds grew until they strayed away from their goal.

This is the point where the vast majority of those who seek success fail: the lack of patience.

*People fail because they quit before they succeed.*

Do not try to find the logic behind the process of programming. You would first have to read half a bookshelves' worth of books to understand how the human brain works and then I could tell you. But there is no time for that. The way you have to follow to change your internal DNA, to change who you are, is proven to be correct. And that is why as long as you remain on your Map, you will be on the right track. Even if the days go by and you cannot see the sun rising, it does not mean that you are going the wrong way. It only means that you are not there yet.

Read your Map every day for 15 minutes during your lunch break and just before going to sleep. That should be enough. Even reading and processing it a bit is enough. If you are more determined than the majority of the people who will read this book and who will be content with just that, dedicate another 15 minutes of your day. Instead of browsing social media while waiting for the bus, do something for yourself. These extra 15 minutes are extremely valuable.

## THE PROGRAMMING OF THE MEDIA

I have never stopped writing. Even today, I open my Map to remind myself of the things that I ought to remember. I do that because reality tends to distance us from our foundation and our goal. It fills our brain with all this random information that 9 times out of 10 is of no substance and significance.

If you think about it, the quantity and speed in which you receive information every passing minute is very powerful programming. Whether you watch the news that TV is spewing out, you partake in online discussions, you browse on your phone or you watch all these advertisements flashing before you, every bit of information is presented in a way to program you in the way it wants to whenever it wants. Every time you waste your time on these things, you "sell" yourself to a reality that others have chosen. If you think about it, the overwhelming percentage of information that you consume is about reasons to stay inactive.

Yes, they sell you fear.

It is hypocritical not to realize that by reading and reproducing the trash that the media pump out, you achieve nothing. You are simply a pawn that they move and the more you react from your couch, the more the influence they have over you grows. You "fight" for a reality that will never come while you are glued on the spot. You are like a barking dog but they have pressed the mute button.

You have to understand that by pouring gallons of poison on your face, they cut off any hope that you could have had until yesterday. You allow yourself to be reprogrammed by garbage as long as you do not change the channel. The best future and the hope that you had as a child gets lost in a sky of insecurities and fears. As long as you talk about all that, you program your mind and constantly remind yourself that you *cannot*.

Wake up. You do not protect yourself from failure, you just find excuses. You find excuses so that you do not proceed. You feel comfortable in the lies and you reject every form or chance of success because you are afraid of failure. You think that because it has happened to someone else, it will happen to everyone. Your preoccupation with "public affairs," the "shouldn't I know what's going on next door?" urge you to remain scared and idle. You hide and you feel safe. But you are still at point 0.

This is why I choose what I put in my head on a daily basis. This is why I have the TV turned off. I still inform myself, of course, I am not questioning reality nor am I disinterested in public affairs. But I have set limits. My limits are at the point where the recycling of information starts. When something I read on a site comes up every time I talk to someone, I reject it. Because I know from my experience that the programming of the brain occurs through constant repetition. Not simply by information.

In the same way, I choose to program my brain as I want to. This is what made me *who I am* and what will shape me into who I want to be. It is the smartest thing I have ever seen and done. The fact that I caused a "brain-wash" to myself constituted the foundation of my career and the "Who I am" philosophy. I allowed access to my brain only to what I wanted, in the way I wanted, and whenever I wanted.

It became an obsessive idea. When I started seeing the results, I valued the process even more. The more I was coming closer and closer to who I wanted to be, the more I was processing it.

Only like this, is change inevitable.

## NIKOS THE POLITICIAN

A typical example of this kind of person and the influence that the media have over him is Nikos, an old colleague of mine. Nikos was always the "example to avoid" for me and I thank him from the bottom of my heart that we met. I worked two years with him and they were more than enough.

He worked as a sales engineer in a company in Greece. Every morning, he entered the building and he gave off the impression that he was five years older than the previous day, always with a crooked face, always complaining, and always tired. Mondays, in particular, were the worst. Even on the sunniest of days, when he entered the building, the sky would blacken. I did not get it back then. After a while, though I did. *He did not hate Mondays. He hated his job.* And probably his life altogether.

I must admit that he was a nice guy. But he had one flaw: he knew everything, politics, sports, governments, and all other kinds of crap. I had seen him quarreling with our boss more than once about what the government did. who was responsible for that, and other such high tales. They talked about who was at fault and who pulled the strings that Greece reached this point as a society with a 600€ monthly salary and so on. Our boss would find the opportunity to joke with him a bit – he did not care much about all this, but he found the opportunity to poke fun at Nikos, which led to fighting and shouting.

One day, I remember our boss sitting on the stairs opposite our offices and as Nikos was barking at himself, like a dog chasing its tail, he asked me:

"What do you believe about all that?" Petros asked me with a light smile. (Nick was still barking)

"I don't give a shit about all that," I replied. "I'm going to tidy up the storage room because it's a mess."

"That's why I like you. Go my boy and leave all this shit outside."

"Yes, keep saying such things to him," Nikos barked loud out of nowhere. "Let's build a society that doesn't care about anything and accepts oppression without doing anything about it. Leave him in the dark about what might come and don't tell him that he is in a worse position than someone who has an uncle in the parliament and makes two or three times more than him. Because the people you voted for will not allow me to get up from this chair and find a better job to shape my future."

*That and because you are 130kgs* I thought.

"Is it their fault that you have remained in the same company with the same salary for so many years?" Petros answered with some irony.

"Yeah! Because due to taxation and the conditions in this country, who dares to raise their voice? Who dares to go to the parliament and beat them all up to teach them a lesson?"

I got tired just listening to them. It would be better to glue a pair of earphones on my ears and listen to someone chewing screws. You know, the big ones!

I know that many people will disagree with my philosophy. But I will say one more thing: Nikos might be right. He could never see that though because he had his eyes shut and firmly refused to open them. Nikos and anyone else like him, choose to be right over going forward. He prefers to reinforce his ego rather than accept that his outlook keeps him idle. He might be seeing that, but his ego and all this bullshit have blinded him. They have turned him into a mouse that spins its wheel and squeaks! He squeaks because the wheel needs to be oiled and outside the cage is a reality that others want to impose on him to make him stop running, but he says NO! He has seen through their trick! HE WILL KEEP TURNING THE WHEEL! Just for them to learn a lesson!

Well, he managed to change nothing. With his constant and daily preoccupation with the "government's underground targets," he allowed the years to pass by and lose moments and chances that went by him like a wild river. He remained idle. In the same position and probably with the same salary up to this day. He never realized it.

Sad, isn't it?

I will repeat that my goal here is not to judge. I do not plan on becoming the next president or changing the world. My goal is to make you see things from a different perspective. I hope that you find the courage to see it as your obligation to think about it, in the least. If in the end, you reject my approach, then so be it.

One thing is for sure: each one of us is unique. We have our own talents and potential. If we set them free, regardless of the problems that do not affect us, and look straight ahead, they will allow us to shine and build our future the way we have imagined it. Whatever makes us proud should be the reason that we get out of bed in the morning. As long as we waste time on things that do not push us forward, we are being consumed. And as long as we are being consumed, we shrink.

Neither I nor you are inadequate. You are a unit that can lead and affect millions of people. You can lead others to reach their personal success and make them shine. You can make them follow you and consult you at every chance. You can be a source of inspiration and have your story written on the front page of newspapers and affect other people's lives. You can build whatever you want. Even today. If you think it is too late, just look at Mick Jagger. He will outlive us all and the madman will still be dancing!

Respect.

You brainwash yourself with your daily habits which make you doubt the extraordinary abilities you have, and you choose to remain small and lose touch with who you really are. You relate with a twisted reality that urges you to distance yourself from an ideal world because you believe that it is impossible to reach it. You bury your ambitions because you think that you are inadequate and that the difficulties are too many to overcome.

Every incident that is being recycled in the media automatically becomes the "objective truth" because of how often it is shown. Many people fall into this trap because it is easy to be tricked as they do not let fresh air in. The same goes for the tribal cannibal villages. As long as the chief of the tribe adamantly supports a "different" kind of diet, this diet becomes a way of life for everyone. According to this artificial objectivity created by the tribe, there is no tastier snack than a human foot.

I know, I know, "That's completely different." But it is true. As long as you partake in conversations that are not about going forward, then automatically you are left behind. And this is a fact.

After an event has become an objective truth, then the party starts. This is where the fears and, by default, the excuses appear. People refuse to take responsibility for their actions and twist reality to excuse their idleness.

It is exhausting to meet people on the street or at work who do not have a goal. They do not have a reason to get out of their fucking bed. They live in a state of shittiness, complaints, and misery. They look forward to the weekend because they do not have anything else to do. They despise Mondays because they hate their job. They have no hope, no goal, and no horizon. There is no tomorrow and nothing to look forward to.

Even if you give them a chance to change something, they prefer to remain stationary because it is comfortable. They ignore the consequences of this action though. They ignore that time flies faster than our thoughts do. They ignore that they achieve nothing but going back to their cage. They lock the door and keep walking at a slow and torturous pace. They fail to see the absence of variety and imagination within their daily lives.

When they see someone who has dreams and aspirations, jealousy takes over. They know that their misery does not allow them to find themselves in the position of those who want a lot. It is the kind of jealousy that makes someone wants to vomit. It is the kind of jealousy that makes you cut off people from your life completely. "The lucky guy," they say. "If he is so good, then why doesn't he give us something?" How funny and miserable is that? Why should anyone give you anything?

People have no need or wish to evolve. They do not need to fight for what they want, build what they are after, or face the challenges that come up. The only thing they need is to feed their ego by claiming that they are right, remain small, and remain locked in their cage while watching TV and complaining about the number of advertisements that come through their screen.

It is funny and even absurd that people seek answers that suit them instead of using the answers that those that have made greater strides generously give them. Few will follow the advice and guidance of the "Who I am" philosophy because simply they will not believe that it is the answer that they have always been seeking. They are looking for that one phrase instead, that specific action that will unlock them and make them millionaires or successful in general. Even if I were a billionaire, few would act on my advice, because most people would give my words the meaning they want or they think they are after.

It is exhausting to see people demanding from others to change instead of demanding it from themselves. It is hypocritical to deem yourself ideal and worthy of success when you have not even looked at your flaws. By ignoring something so important, people deny themselves any possibility of evolving. By not demanding from yourself to change, you automatically become like a tree, an old tree, without branches, in the middle of nowhere.

People are constantly making promises but when the time to act comes they play dumb. They do not act. They are only good in home-spun philosophies and meaningless words. They say they will be somewhere at 8:00 but they arrive at 9:00. They say they will go to the gym, but they eat junk food instead. They say they want to work but on the first day, they are absent. They say they love someone but at the same time, they cheat on them. They talk about equality but they hit their wife. They talk about education, but they hit their child. Excuses, lies, and hypocrisy.

It is exhausting.

People do not change simply because they do not want to change. They do not want to change. The end! Only those who are addicted to action and success change. Those who want to stand out from the masses that are hypnotized by social media. Those who are not satisfied with mediocrity. Those who do not need to post fifteen times a week in order to increase their followers. Those who make a difference are those who have results. Everyone else is subject to misery, endlessly waiting in lines for social insurance and in traffic.

You are afraid! You are afraid of going forward so that you do not lose what you already have. You are afraid of leaving the wheel because it is the only thing that you have that keeps you alive. You are afraid of what your friends, your family, and others will say about you. You always choose based on what they think is good because you do not trust your wants.

Let me tell you about my friend, Giannis, who has a wife and a child, and decided to quit his depressive and underpaid job at the age of 37 for a job with better working conditions and a better salary. I will tell you one thing: not only did he find an excellent job that was much closer to his house, with a 50% increase in salary, but after working there for four years, he was at the point of rejecting offers from Microsoft. Today, he holds one of the highest positions in the company and he is healthier and more financially independent than ever before.

I will introduce him to you. When you see him, ask him, "Do you imagine never having left your previous job...?" and let's see what answer he gives you.

Do you think that you have problems? You don't. If you want to understand problems, read the book *Man's Search For Meaning* by Victor E. Frankl to finally understand that you do not have difficulties. On the contrary, your life is a fairy tale. You are a Cinderella that tripped over a twig and had an owie.

*No limit can stop the urge of a man with a purpose.*

We all have our problems. We have all owed money to someone at one point in our life. We have all let go of chances. We have all cried over a breakup, and we all fought with a friend to the point that we would not see each other for years. We have all been mistreated by our boss and honked at the traffic light. We were all born from a mother, we have all drunk milk from her breast. The sun rises for all of us from the east and escapes to the west. There is no difference between us. The only different thing is the choices that we make every passing minute and how much we allow situations we face to affect us.

Eleanor Roosevelt said it clearly, *"No one can make you inferior without your consent."* Nobody can step on you if you do not allow them to.

In the end, no destruction remained only ash. Somebody was burned and someone simply passed by and swiped the ashes so that there is more room. Chance can only be born out of ash.

We have reached a point where we are smart when it comes to judging others but stupid when it comes to judging ourselves. We waste our spit by giving the fault to those who do not directly influence our lives and when it comes to talking about our faults, our mouth is dry. Our index finger is longer than our thumb and when it is time to pay, we play dumb. People remain idle and complain, they are half-hearted and jealous. Because this is who we are.

We do not see that our time on this earth is limited. We always figure things out just before the end. We should get it when the time is right and when we still have the chance to catch up. Because we live in a utopia of security. In a utopia of "God is giving" or "it's okay, if I don't do it today, I will do it tomorrow." Suddenly your time is up and you wonder how stupid you have been that you did not act differently when you had the chance. In the end, neither the size of your ego is important nor anything else.

You know the phrase, *"The way you do anything is the way you do everything"*? I believe a lot in that and I also believe that the universe is constructed in a way that it throws at you the same situation again and again so that you may realize your incorrect outlook and see that something has to finally change.

*Passions turn into lessons only for those*
*who have the guts to read between the lines.*
*Anything else is mediocre.*

The universe has never conspired for you to succeed. This is just a fairy tale you used to be told to have hope and stop crying. Being an adult though means facing the truth, and not repeating the same mistakes. Success is not easy, so do not try to make it look easy.

Look at yourself in the mirror. Watch what your reflection looks like, but be sincere, honest, and modest. Our world needs people who have the objectivity to see what should be different and actually change it, people who look ahead and have a vision. Our world needs people who do not focus more on social media than on their development. Our world needs uniqueness from leaders, and from people just like you.

It is not fair to see your time going by without being happy. Time is not endless. It is not fair to accept situations that do not work for you and just accept it. Instead of accepting everything that you cannot change, choose to change everything that you cannot accept. No relationship, no job, and no person should hold you back from creating great things.

If you believe that you cannot change your situation, allow me to tell you that this is the damnest thing that came out of your mind. You can change everything, as long as you are not afraid. It is all up to you. You can even change the way you think. You can even change the color of the sky or go to the moon. You can do anything you want. It is just one decision away. It is a decision that you should make with responsibility, based on your priorities and taking everything into consideration. You should do it soon. In fact, you should do it right now.

Because time flies, my friend. It flies so fast that you do not even notice. It flies so fast that at some point, you will look back and there will be no tomorrow left and no chance. By the time you realize it, it will be too late. Do not postpone it. Look around and make the decisions that will change the course of your own story. A lot of people have made an important decision and regardless of the price they had to pay, they have moved on. They got over it and their future turned out to be great. They lived the life they had always wanted.

You will get to a point when you will not be able to walk or you will be bedridden and the end will be close. You will then be nostalgic and you might cry thinking how stupid you were back when you were strong and full of energy, back when you smiled, you made new friends, you went out with friends, you loved and you had sex. When the whole world lay at your feet and you rejected it instead of embracing it. You used to judge it, to spit it, to despise it. You used to find an excuse for every single cowardice of yours. You used to prioritize all the reasons why you could not do something over the ones why you could.

When this time comes, you will wish that you had a few extra hours in the years back then to choose differently. You will wish you had broken up with that partner you had and that you had not wasted all these years in a meaningless relationship. You will wish you had quit your job and pursued the career you had always wanted. You will wish you had not wasted your money on items that brought nothing but fleeting pleasures. You will wish you had played less PlayStation, watched less TV, had eaten healthier. You will wish that you had gone running outside and had exercised more. You will wish you had been a bit bolder, knowing that pain is temporary. You will wish you had created everything you imagined and had destroyed anything worthless.

But you take everything for granted. You believe that you will live forever and that things will turn out in the way you want in any case. You think that you will never get old and that you will be able to walk or run forever. You believe that you will be able to think, to wonder, to draw or to sing, to travel or to swim forever.

You are funny.

When I saw my grandmother who had raised me, my brother and my cousin suffering from dementia, I thought about everything she had gone through and I was devastated. I used to think that she was still relatively young when her husband passed away from cancer and that she helped her two daughters to raise her three grandchildren, me, my brother, and my cousin Teresa.

What was the last thought she had before her mind stopped? How happy she must have been when she saw her granddaughter getting married or when she saw me and my brother excelling at work? Did she have any other desire or was she happy with what she had? I would really like to know if she had received enough love from my grandfather who died young or if she would have wanted a partner for the rest of her life. But I will never know because, even though she was at a relatively advanced age, she left us too soon.

Oh, grandma...

During your last few hours in this world, you will understand. You will understand everything you were too afraid to do. You will be blaming yourself for allowing others to have control over your thoughts and your life. You will then understand that it has always been your fault.

During those hours, there will be only one question stuck in your mind: "God, how foolish have I been?"

Why do we always need to go down before we get a lesson? Why do we follow leaders who fail to lead effectively? Why do we love people even if we know they are not the right ones? Why do we stay with them? Why don't we let them go? Why do we seek perfection in others but not in ourselves? Why do we expect to see a change to feel good but we do not change ourselves? Why do we keep asking but never give? Is there a limit to the ego of the people who destroy everything they touch and then demand others to fix it? What kind of people do our parents create and what kind of kids do we raise? When will the world be ready to accept us when we keep seeing the hump of others but never our own? How many theories and philosophies do we need to hear before we change? How many causes and how many triggers are needed?

What are we waiting for to live?

Will we start living once we die?

Buddha said that our biggest problem is that we think we have time. If you think about it though, you have already lived half of your life and you have wasted it. If you think about it...

*It is later than you think.*

If you want to do something, do it. If you say you will be on time, be there 10 minutes earlier. If you want to start going to the gym, do it now. If you say you want to escape, jump the fence that is separating your jail and your freedom now. If you want to break up with your partner, do that too. If you want to invest, just invest. If you want to become a basketball player, work more than anyone else and become the best. If you desire world peace, become a politician. If you want to stop global warming, join any organization that works on it.

Stop using excuses and defeatism and grab life by the horns. There is no such thing as "accept what you cannot change." What I am saying is "Change what you cannot accept." This is what I call "attitude". It is not just a spontaneous decision.

Stop sleepwalking, wake up and live! Those who do nothing but daydream, do not develop. There is no greater gift than life itself. We were given life and we should make the most out of it. We should dare even if we lose. We should fall and then get back up. We should tear things down and then build them again. We should break up with people and then create new bonds.

Life is so fragile that can be destroyed by a breeze. Accept the challenge, put your ego aside, realize that it is action time and that the time for change has come, and make the most out of the chance your parents gave you. Change. Pursuit actively your chance to become whom you want to be. In the end, the value of your ego will be smaller than your penis. No matter what you do, it will abandon you on a lovely sunny morning when you least expect it.

Stop seeking acceptance. Stop agreeing with people on things that are not their business or on things about which they have no experience or no knowledge. You do not need anyone because none of them will follow you. Everything you will lose or everything you will win will be just yours. No one will be around when you will get to the top, except for a handful of people who believed in you from the very beginning. No one else is important, just you, your beliefs, your ethics, and your goal.

Stop caring about what happened yesterday and focus on what is going on now, at this moment. Focus on what you are reading and on your emotions. If something did not work in the past, it does not mean that will never work. It means that you can try as many times as you want until you make it. Leave behind anything that keeps you chained to the past and to your mistakes and let yourself sink in the fascination of creation. Allow your mistakes to become your Core and learn from them as they become a part of your Map.

Laugh at any obstacle that will come up. Deal with any difficulty as if it were the biggest challenge and slap anyone who will try to stop you. Get everything you have not already got and dare to do all these things you have been too afraid to do. Commit yourself to becoming the best version of yourself -the one that is hidden inside you and cannot wait to get out there and shine!

Dare to be proud of yourself at any time, with any decision that you make, if it helps you develop and go further than you have ever been. Keep intact your eagerness to succeed and change and bury in the ground all this criticism you hear daily. Cherish every moment and create. Build. Be different, be unique, and be brilliant.

Make the most out of the philosophy I have shared with you. Since it has brought me to where I am and is still guiding me, it can do the same for you. I will help you. Just ask it, and I will. Stop procrastinating, find what you need to do from the beginning, and do it. You have nothing to lose. You have already lost a lot and there is no more time to waste. Do not wait until the end comes, because it will come before you know it when you least expect it. Wake up!

Humans are the only creatures who can destroy and create at the same time. It is up to us. I myself, you, and everyone else has the power to construct a machine, to stop slavery, end world hunger, and bring world peace. We can hug, kiss, and have sex. We can run, swim, and cheer if our team scores. We can choose happiness, success, duration, taste, and carefreeness.

At the same time, we are absolutely nothing without us. We are another drop in the ocean that evaporates in the first sunlight. We are a small cloud in the vast sky that disappears with the first breeze. We are an hourglass with sand that will not stop falling for a moment so that we can stay a little longer on this earth.

Stop looking for the meaning of life.

You are yourself the meaning of your life.

You are your beginning.

And you are your finish line.

This is who you are.